IMPORTANT TEXTBOOK RENTAL RESPONSIBILITIES

Each student is responsible for any and all damages done to his/her assigned textbooks. Damages include pencil or ink markings, torn covers, bent corners, deliberately torn pages, water, gum, food damage, hi-lighting, etc. Each student will be fined according to the severity of the damage. Fines range from $1 to the full price for any text that cannot be reissued. It is also the responsibility of each student to carefully check his/her textbooks for any previous damage which missed being repaired. Any textbooks found to be damaged must be returned to the Bookstore by the FIFTH DAY of the semester, or the assigned student will be accountable. For an added class, the student has one week from the date the textbook was issued

EDITION 4

BASIC DEBATE

LESLIE PHILLIPS
Lexington High School, Lexington, Massachusetts

WILLIAM S. HICKS
Brebeuf Jesuit Preparatory School, Indianapolis, Indiana

DOUGLAS R. SPRINGER
New Trier Township High School, Winnetka, Illinois

National Textbook Company
a division of NTC/CONTEMPORARY PUBLISHING GROUP
Lincolnwood, Illinois USA

ACKNOWLEDGMENTS

This new edition would not be possible without the work of the authors of the previous editions of *Basic Debate*: Lynn Goodnight, Maridell Fryar, and David Thomas. Special appreciation is expressed to those authors.

Grateful acknowledgment is extended to the following reviewers who assisted with this Fourth Edition: Lanny Naegelin, Speech/Theater Arts Program Coordinator, North East Independent School District, San Antonio, Texas; Dale McCall, debate instructor, Wellington High School, West Palm Beach, Florida; and Barbara Miller, Debate Coordinator, Charlotte-Mecklenburg Schools, North Carolina. We gratefully acknowledge the National Forensic League, the American Forensic Association, and the National Catholic Forensic League for their contributions.

Special thanks are due to the students of the Brebeuf Jesuit Preparatory School, Indianapolis, Indiana, whose photographs are included in this edition.

Photo Credits

Jeff Ellis, pages 138, 234.
William S. Hicks, Brebeuf Jesuit Preparatory School, Indianapolis, Indiana, all other photographs.

Library of Congress Cataloging-in-Publication Data

Phillips, Leslie.
    Basic debate / Leslie Phillips, William S. Hicks, Douglas R. Springer.
  — 4th ed.
     p.   cm.
    Rev. ed. of: Basic debate / Maridell Fryar. 3rd ed. c1989.
    Includes index.
    ISBN 0-8442-5981-0
    1. Debates and debating. I. Hicks, William S. II. Springer, Douglas R. III. Fryar, Maridell.
Basic debate. IV. Title.
PN3181.F75   1996
  808.53—dc20   96-2731
ISBN: 0-8442-5981-0   CIP

Published by National Textbook Company,
a division of NTC/Contemporary Publishing Group, Inc.,
4255 West Touhy Avenue,
Lincolnwood (Chicago), Illinois 60712-1975 U.S.A.

00 01 02 03 04 MV 12 11 10 9 8 7 6

CONTENTS

PART THREE

STUDENT CONGRESS: LEGISLATIVE DEBATE   191

CHAPTER 11

The Nature and Purpose of Student Congress   193

CHAPTER 12

Student Congress Procedures   201

PART ONE

BASIC FORENSIC SKILLS

BEGINNING PROBLEM SOLVING

Before exploring either debate or student congress, you need to become acquainted with some of the basic skills of argumentation along with forensics, the activity of giving speeches. The first part of this text introduces the skills of analysis, research, and reasoning. These form the basis for any work you will do in competitive forensic activities. As you study the chapters in this part, pay very close attention to the explanations and guidelines offered. The skills you acquire will equip you to move with ease through many academic pursuits.

DEBATE IN A DEMOCRATIC SOCIETY

OBJECTIVES AND KEY TERMS

After studying Chapter 1, you should be able to

1. Explain what debate is,
2. Identify situations in which debate experience would be of value,
3. Identify skills that are either learned or enhanced through debate, and
4. Identify the principles on which debate is based.

After reading this chapter, you should understand the following terms:

    arguments

    criticism

    debate in a democracy

You live in a society that gives you the right and the responsibility to make choices about how to conduct your life. You are called on to make decisions and value judgments. Every day you have to decide whether to spend your time at work or at play, by yourself or with others, or planning for the future or thinking about the past. If you use your time wisely, you can create opportunities and make decisions that will lead to success. If you squander your time, you will limit your options and make unproductive decisions.

THE NATURE OF DEBATE

Learning how to debate can help you develop decision-making ability. Debate is the process of generating argumentative clash. There are many different debate formats. Different forums have distinct formats and procedures. Common to all debating, however, is the intellectual exchange of ideas. Debate involves reasoned argument put forward in the service of statements of belief or propositions of policy.

To debate well, you must be able both to compose precise, stimulating, and well-supported arguments and to critique arguments offered by an opponent. Some people are able to do this easily. Others, either because they are shy or inexperienced, have trouble composing and critiquing. However, all people have a right to express their own opinion and to ask others to provide support for the opinions that they state. To the extent that people can talk to one another intelligently, they can come to productive agreements.

What You Will Learn

In this book, you will learn some new skills. For example, you will learn how to make arguments. This is an important skill for several reasons. First, learning to make arguments requires you to take statements and studies, facts and options, and shape them into a convincing case. In one sense, these formal requirements for finding reasons to support an idea help sharpen your own thinking. Rather than making judgments solely based on likes and dislikes, you will be able to reduce your own biases and reach a more objective judgment about what is really good for you. Second, learning how to make cases increases your ability to influence others. People usually want to do the right thing. To show them what to do, you must provide the right reasons. Argumentation teaches you how to put together strong, clear, forceful positions that lead to good decisions. Without such a skill, you might have good ideas but no way to communicate them.

In this book, you will also learn how to criticize arguments, Sometimes an argument sounds good, but it is really misleading or incorrect. Argumentation teaches you how to examine arguments systematically and see if the proof is sound and if the methods of reasoning are valid. Criticism is not be confused with mere negative thinking. It is not enough just to reject arguments because you believe they are wrong. Criticism is a powerful corrective. It permits you to isolate what is wrong with an argument, to say why, and to provide a better alternative. In this way, argumentation expands your ability to influence people or at least to clear out bad ideas and make room for better ones.

The Value of Debate

If argument did no more than sharpen your judgment and aid you in influencing your friends, it would be a worthwhile pursuit. But there is much more to the study of forensics than personal improvement. Thus far in life, you have been working and playing in a limited domain. You know your family, your friends, and people you encounter at school. As you approach your eighteenth birthday, your life will take on another dimension: that of an active citizen in a democracy.

The language of democracy is the language of debate. In a democracy, people are given the power to decide for themselves the values of government. A great many issues must be decided, and values often conflict. Should money be spent for more schools or should taxes be lowered? Should one support the Democratic or the Republican party? Should the United States increase funding for AIDS research or direct scientific efforts elsewhere? No one has final answers to these questions. There are risks to any choice. Only argument can serve to determine which is the least risky alternative.

You have a responsibility to be a good citizen, and debate can provide you with the communication skills necessary to fulfill that responsibility. Those who are untrained in debate and critical argument may not understand the need for public discussion or even how to evaluate cases that political leaders make for and against changes in public policy. Easily swayed, uncritical listeners may support bad policies and demagogues.

Good argumentation, on the other hand, can provide you with an improved ability to make critical choices. This book is designed to enable you to become familiar with policy debate and argumentative analysis.

THE FUNCTIONS OF DEBATE

Debate in a democratic society has many functions.

1. Debate helps people decide the meaning of the past. Arguments in history class, as well as those in the public forum, are sometimes directed to the implications of an historical event or document. The Constitution and its intended protections and constraints, for example, have been the subject of controversy for some time. By examining the Constitution, students can come to understand how this historical document shapes present institutions and orders society. By finding the meaning of the past, students can better determine the values that are shared in common.

2. Debate helps people decide the values of the present. In a democracy, there are many competing groups, each with a different history and a different view of the present. Debate brings into focus public obligations and duties. Difficult questions arise concerning conflicts between human rights and freedoms. The best way to resolve these is to develop a consensus through argument, to focus and what *ought* to be done to preserve and advance a just and moral society.

3. Debate permits people to evaluate alternative futures. The status quo never stands still. Problems continue to arise. How should resources be allocated? How should technology be developed? What programs are necessary to secure defense? All these questions can be answered by arguments that in some cases defend existing policies and in other cases provide alternatives.

Academic debate provides training for good citizenship. While the term *argument* might be equated with squabbling or mean-spirited disagreement, this is not what is meant here. Debate trains people in such a way as to maximize the chance that any critical discussion they participate in will be an honest exchange of views leading to an intellectually respectable decision. Toward that end, students should realize that this book is based on an ethic of communication.

In debate, you should always work within a sound intellectual framework. Debate is based on the following principles:

1. The debater should respect the intellectual integrity of argument. Debate requires the search for the best arguments based on the most informed opinion in fields related to the resolution.

2. Debate is based on the fair exchange of opinion. Debate is not an intellectual game that aims at getting in the last word. It can only work when students are committed to advancing and defending ideas.

3. Debate should be conducted with respect for others. Debate that aims only at a display of intellectual dominance is a pointless activity. Rather, debate upholds the dignity of individuals insofar as it affirms their right to be listened to and critiqued.

4. Debate should be the product of honest research and valid evidence. There is no room for distortion or fabrication in forensics.

5. Debate should be treated as a learning experience. The process of debate should be directed not only toward training strong advocates and good speakers but also toward developing open minds and good listening habits. By helping students learn the significance of good and timely arguments, debate should enhance, not impede communication.

SUMMARY

Debate is more than an academic exercise. The skills and values you will acquire in debate can be applied in nearly every occupation as well as in your relationships with other people. Look on your course in debate as an opportunity.

QUESTIONS FOR DISCUSSION

1. Debate can be of benefit in everyday life. What elements of debate make this true?

2. What is the value of learning to make arguments?

3. If you learn how to criticize arguments, how will you be able to better defend your own position?

4. Describe the functions of debate in a democratic society.

5. How will debate help you to develop an analytical mind?

6. In debate, it is important to have an open mind when you prepare arguments. How does this help you in preparing your positions or in attacking an opposing position?

ACTIVITIES

1. Keeping in mind your career plans for the future, explain how debate will help you to succeed.

2. Attend the next city council, school board, or PTA meeting. As issues are discussed, identify instances in which speakers are not able to analyze critically the arguments or previous speakers. Also identify instances in which positions were bogged down because the participants did not listen critically to their peers.

3. Using the issues outlined in Activity 2, analyze the position and outline a counterposition (or, rewrite a support of the position).

4. Choose an issue currently before the legislature (state or national). Outline the pros and cons of the issue. Try to equalize the number of pros and cons. How has each of these issues been handled in the legislative process?

THE SKILLS OF ANALYSIS

OBJECTIVES AND KEY TERMS

After studying Chapter 2, you should be able to

1. Present an in-depth analysis of a debate problem area,
2. Formulate a properly worded proposition that will meet the characteristics of a proposition, and
3. Explain the differences among propositions of fact, value, and policy.

After reading this chapter, you should understand the following terms:

analysis
problem area
problem statement
proposition
proposition of fact
proposition of policy
proposition of value
resolution

Forensic events, such as debate and *student congress*—a forensic event in which students engage in parliamentary debate while conducting a mock Congressional session—are modeled after decision-making situations in the "real world," such as the legislature or a court of law. The problems considered in forensic events are similar to those confronted by "real world" advocates. However, the overriding principle of problem solving remains true. Even in these serious, complex problem areas, the best possible solutions can be found if the best methods of decision making are applied. Before you can effectively take sides on an issue or even develop a personal opinion, you must be able to analyze a problem and its solutions.

DEFINING ANALYSIS

Analysis is the process of separating a whole into its essential parts. It is the opposite of *synthesis*, which means to combine separate elements into a complete whole. Analysis is an active thought process. Generally speaking, you already analyze many different objects or concepts, using many different methods to break them down into essential elements. In chemistry, you analyze compounds to identify their separate chemical elements. In bookkeeping, you analyze the records of a business to determine debits and credits. In an English class, you analyze a piece of literature, observing its essential features of plot, character, and style.

Analysis can be complicated when you look at the many possible ways to divide concepts into parts. But the purpose of this chapter is to point out the essential elements of analysis used in forensics. Consider three distinct levels that require analytical thinking: the problem area, the problem statement, and the audience.

Analyzing the Problem Area

A *problem area* is a general area of concern to a community. Usually under the problem area umbrella are many particular problems. A clean environment may be a problem area. Clean air and water and good land use are specific problems to be discussed within the area. How can a problem area be analyzed? At a minimum, all the pertinent facts about the problem area must be discovered. Use the following questions to discover those facts:

1. What is the goal or ideal thwarted by the problem?
2. How far off is that goal?
3. What are the identifiable reasons for being short of the goal?
4. What possible solutions can overcome these reasons?
5. Which of the possible solutions appears best in comparison with others?

The answers to these questions will show you two important things. First, they will indicate where your knowledge of the problem area is strong and where it is weak. These findings will then guide your research and further investigation. Second, the answers will pinpoint some of the issues that you must consider in your own presentation of opinion.

Analyzing the Problem Statement

A *problem statement* narrows a general discussion area. Instead of examining all aspects of pollution, you might wish to know why one specific aspect persists or what the merits of a single solution are. The statement of the problem must be analyzed. It has been said, and rightly so, that it is useless to seek agreement on any course of action until agreement has first been reached on the meaning of the terms used. In other words, the beginning point for analysis is a definition of the terms by which the problem is stated. Each forensic event places the problem in a different form, but each states a problem for consideration. Debate asks students to advocate a resolution, such as "Resolved: That the federal government should exclusively control the development and distribution of energy resources in the United States." Student congress presents a bill or resolution to be debated by the group. The place for you to begin your analysis in each of these situations is with the meaning of the terms of the statement.

The logical first step is to consult dictionaries, textbooks, and encyclopedias. You should be particularly aware of specialized dictionaries that include technical terms. Such publications as *Black's Law Dictionary* and *The American Dictionary of Psychology*, for example, should be consulted if the topic, bill, or resolution falls into the specialized areas that such books cover. You should also explore the prevailing connotations for terms and try to use definitions within the social, political, economic, and historical contexts of the statement. Further, you should determine how the key terms are interpreted by the experts in the field.

When you are involved in the analysis of definitions, you should also be aware of the presence of value terms. Words such as *fair, free, new, significant, best, comprehensive,* and *control* are vague because the realities to which they refer are not absolute. They are relative to a standard of measurement that is not uniform to everyone everywhere. Before agreement can be reached on a question of policy, there must be an agreement on the terms by which the policy is to be justified. If your task, for example, is to justify a "comprehensive program to significantly increase the energy independence of the United States," you must fully understand what constitutes *comprehensive* and what is a *significant increase.* Thus, your analytical task is to arrive at the best possible understanding of what these terms mean within the frame of reference represented by the total statement of the problem area.

Analyzing the Audience

Once the problem area is analyzed, you must adapt your ideas to the intended audience. It is not enough merely to accumulate and organize a stockpile of information. To achieve your purpose, you must know which pieces of information to select and present to your intended audience. In this stage of analysis, you attempt to determine which issues will best speak to the particular audience you will address. In student congress, you use features of both discussion and debate in a legislative framework. Ultimately, the group will vote on proposed bills and resolutions. Audience analysis should lead you to select information that wins group support for your position. In debate, you may use special forms of issue presentation to influence an expert judge. Specific methods of analysis apply to each of these events.

There is no single method of analysis in forensics. Some methods are used for investigating a problem area, and other methods are used for planning a strategy for presenting a case to a legislative assembly or a debate judge. Regardless of the setting for decision making, whether student congress or debate, the common denominator is the use of the English language. In all these events, you think, speak, reason, persuade, and argue with words and sentences. The beginning point is the *forensic analysis*—the breaking down of the proposition under consideration. Thus, some understanding of the statement of that proposition is valuable.

STATING THE PROBLEM

What is a proposition? The root of the word is *propose*, to offer for consideration. A *proposition* is a statement offered for consideration, specifically a statement made to others for the purpose of gaining acceptance after due consideration. A proposition may require explanation, discussion, or proof. Some propositions are uncontroversial; these are rarely debated. Others may be too vague to spark disagreement. When a proposition presents a clear and important choice, it is often the subject of debate.

The function of the proposition is to provide focus for discussion and debate. Specifically, it is the means by which the problem under consideration is explicitly verbalized. It will present or assert a claim for eventual acceptance.

Problem Selection

Where do the problem areas for forensic events originate? Each year, a national debate topic is selected; the topic is then debated for an entire academic year. The National Federation of State High School Associations conducts the topic selection, a careful, time-consuming, and thorough process. An annual meeting of representatives from every state is preceded by research and questionnaires. Then, at the annual meeting, suggested debate topics are discussed and critiqued, and a limited number of possible problem areas is chosen. Subsequently, a series of mail ballots is sent to forensics teachers for registering their preferences. The results of the ballot count are then announced by the National Federation.

High school topics for the past several years clearly show the variety and scope of problems yielded by the selection process:

Resolved: That a comprehensive program of penal reform should be adopted throughout the United States.

Resolved: That the federal government should guarantee comprehensive medical care for all citizens in the United States.

Resolved: That the United States should significantly curtail its arms sales to other countries.

Resolved: That the federal government should provide employment for all employable U.S. citizens living in poverty.

Resolved: That the federal government should establish a comprehensive national policy to protect the quality of water in the United States.

Resolved: That the U.S. government should substantially strengthen its immigration policy toward other countries.

Resolved: That the U.S. government should substantially change its foreign policy toward the People's Republic of China.

Once the resolution has been selected, the process of analysis focuses on that resolution. To make a meaningful analysis, you should understand the characteristics of the proposition.

Problem Characteristics

Propositions must meet five criteria. First, the problem area should be *significant* in scope, affecting people throughout the country or even around the world. For example, the problem of how to provide for national defense is significant because it affects all Americans. Other examples are poverty in the United States, world hunger, organized crime, welfare, inflation, access to medical care, civil rights, and energy shortages. All these problem areas are significant in scope. By contrast, purely local or state-level problems are not chosen nationally for forensic events because they lack the scope to involve students in forensics nationwide.

Second, a problem must be within the realm of government *jurisdiction*. It is not enough merely to describe a problem, even though it might be significant. It must be possible for a proposed solution to be enacted into law by the government. This characteristic of problems for forensic consideration does not mean that other types of problems are unimportant, only that governmental action must be feasible. For example, we might agree that the lack of religious faith is a serious problem throughout the nation. But it would not be fitting to suggest some new law requiring increased devotion to our religious heritage. Forensic events generally deal with problems for which a concrete solution is possible.

This implies problem areas, such as international relations or domestic health and welfare, where there is public interest in government policies and their alternatives.

Timeliness is the third standard that a proposition should meet. Since the success of forensic events hinges on generating student interest and involvement, a problem area must be current. A by-product of timeliness is widespread coverage by the media, government publications, and scholarly journals. A premium is placed on using up-to-date evidence in any forensic event.

Although the problem area must be timely, it cannot be transitory. *Durability* is essential. The National Federation selects forensic problems carefully so that the problem will not pass quickly from the national interest or be suddenly resolved by an unanticipated governmental action. National debate questions are selected so as to ensure that they will continue to be problems for the duration of the debate year.

Related to the standard of durability is *debatability*. The problem area must be arguable on both sides. On the whole, the problem should favor neither the affirmative nor the negative. The problem area should be carefully considered before the choice is made to be certain that arguments and issues of merit are inherently contained in either position. If the topic is not debatable, one side has a built-in advantage over the other.

Forensics directs your attention to a significant public problem. The forensic experience permits you to study the problem in depth and debate proposed solutions. Thus, the educational nature of forensic events is established because, through forensics, you become informed about significant and timely problems you might otherwise ignore.

The continuing process of analysis leads from consideration of the meaning of the terms in the proposition to consideration of the characteristics of a good proposition. Now you need to develop an awareness of the types of propositions that can be argued.

UNDERSTANDING THE TYPES OF PROPOSITIONS

There are three types of propositions in forensics, each calling for its own unique levels of support, explanation, development, and proof. Propositions may be classified into three categories—propositions of *fact*, propositions of *value*, and propositions of *policy*.

The simplest of propositions is the proposition of fact. It involves definition and classification in order to establish the truth or falseness of a claim. More complex is the proposition of value, which calls for the application of criteria to determine the worth or value of a particular thing. At the highest level of complexity is the proposition of policy, which demands that after certain facts and values are established, considering such things as expediency and practicality leads people to propose a certain defensible plan of action.

To illustrate the progressive nature of propositions, consider the following case taken from the criminal courts. The charge is that A was wounded by a bullet fired from the gun of B (fact). Additionally, however, it is claimed that B's attack was totally unprovoked, unjustified, and premeditated (value). Consequently, capital punishment is advocated (policy). At each level of complexity, new types of issues emerge, and each successive proposition builds on the preceding one. As a consequence, if you would analyze accurately, you must understand the unique characteristics and the interdependency of each type of proposition.

Propositions of Fact

A *factual proposition* is an objective statement that something exists. Moreover, the statement can be verified by someone other than the person making the statement. A factual proposition may be about an object or event that can be experienced directly by the senses of sight, hearing, touch, smell, and taste. An abstract statement may also be considered a factual proposition as long as it can be objectively and accurately justified. "Spinach is a green, leafy vegetable" is a factual statement about a tangible object. It can be verified through the senses by someone other than the person making the statement. Even so, it is also classified as a factual proposition because probable truth can be measured scientifically.

Compared with value judgments or policy propositions, propositions of fact are considered the least controversial. Notice, we do not say they are uncontroversial. Disagreements can and do arise over factual propositions. Every trial in a court of law involves at least one factual proposition. That the defendant committed (or did not commit) the criminal act with which he or she is charged is a factual proposition. However, factual propositions are less controversial than other types of propositions because they may be verified objectively by reference to other facts—to what is or what has occurred. They are not obviously in the realm of attitudes and opinions, as are value judgments.

Forensic events require you to be familiar with several different types of factual propositions. An *observation*, or statement of what you observe, and a *description*, or statement of the characteristics of what you observe, are factual propositions. For instance, "That is a car in the driveway (observation). It is my father's red '95 Chevy Lumina (description). " These are objective, verifiable statements that a thing exists. It is a car. It exhibits specific characteristics.

Statements of fact may be about the past as well as the present. A newspaper report and a story from history thus qualify as factual propositions. The person asserting the fact need not be the same person who witnessed it. The statement must be objective and subject to independent verification. Establishing whether a fact exists (or existed) does not always hinge on the person who makes the assertion, as long as the statement can be verified.

Factual propositions are sometimes more complex. Conclusions drawn from reasoning about a set of facts are also considered factual propositions. However, the process of verifying such conclusions is also more complex, more hypothetical, and more obviously debatable. Such propositions are called *inferences* (conclusions based on possible relationships between known facts). For instance, it is a fact that cigarette smokers have a much higher incidence of lung cancer than nonsmokers. Based on this observation, we may infer that cigarette smoking causes lung cancer. Here is a situation where the facts are not clear. The tobacco industry maintains that the evidence linking smoking with cancer is not strong enough to prove that one causes the other. Instead, other factors, such as environmental pollution, may be the responsible causative agent. Perhaps, for some unknown reason, persons who are predisposed to cancer are also more likely to be motivated to smoke. We can still treat the proposition "Cigarette smoking causes lung cancer" as a factual proposition, even though it is an inference based on reasoning from the known facts. Naturally, inferences of this sort are more debatable than direct observations, such as "55 million adults smoke cigarettes."

Propositions of fact that might be called "future" in type are predictive in nature. Like the inference, the *prediction* is a statement of how one thinks present facts are related so that one can expect certain results in the future. The concern here is not unscientific predictions like Jeane Dixon's astrological forecasts or the school yearbook's comments on the future career possibilities of graduating seniors. Rather, what is meant are the predictable forecasts and trends based on present observable facts, such as "At the present divorce rate, by the year 2000 more than half of U.S. children will grow up in broken homes" and "The United States will rely on foreign sources of petroleum for more than 50 percent of its needs within the next three years." As with inferences, the accuracy of predictions hinges on the quality of factual data and the quality of reasoning used in drawing relationships between known facts.

You have seen that a factual proposition is an objective statement about the existence of something, capable of independent verification by others. Among the important types of factual statements are observations, descriptions, history, reports, inferences, and predictive generalizations.

Although national organizations avoid selecting propositions of fact for debate, obviously it is essential for you to be able to prove the facts or refute the claims of your opponents using these factual propositions. In addition, factual statements are useful in the academic application of forensics in other fields. Social studies and English classes as well as psychology, philosophy, and science classes frequently make use of propositions of fact. Clubs and organizations may also consider them more frequently than they do other types of propositions. Furthermore, propositions of fact are debated by attorneys in both criminal and civil trials. Obviously, the basic issues involved in propositions of fact need to be defined.

The issues inherent in propositions of fact are relatively few. One needs to determine (1) what occurred, (2) what data are required to establish the alleged fact, and (3) what data are available for use. Consideration of these issues will result in the accurate analysis of propositions of fact.

Examples of propositions of fact are the following:

Federal intervention in state policies is unconstitutional.

Shakespeare was not the real author of the literature that bears his name.

America was first discovered by the Norse.

Television viewing contributes to the mounting crime rate.

Propositions of Value

Propositions of value express judgments about the qualities of a person, place, thing, idea, or event. Therefore, when you make a statement about values, you move from the realm of senses and inferences into the realm of opinions and attitudes. When you say, "Spinach is a green, leafy vegetable," you make a factual statement. But when you say, "Spinach is *yucky*," you give your opinion of its qualities; you have made a value judgment.

In forensics, understanding value judgements is very important. Although knowing the facts about a problem area is vital to discussing it or debating about it, only our value judgments can serve as a guide to what should be done about the facts.

There are several different types of values. Before turning to those types, a crucial distinction between facts and values as propositions should be made. Facts are either true or false, and their truth or falseness can be verified. Values can never be considered as literally true or literally false. You can verify that someone holds a value, but not whether the value is the one he or she ought to hold. To say that "spinach is yucky" is to say something about your attitude toward spinach, not about spinach itself. To someone else, spinach may be "yummy." Whereas values are not literally true or false, they are nevertheless important because people believe them, and people allow them to color their thinking about everything else.

Artistic values, also called *aesthetic values*, express pleasure with a person or an object. Among artistic values, you attach great importance to beauty, symmetry, good taste—and their opposites. You hold the value judgment that civilized people create various works of art, literature, and music and that such creations are good. The standards applied to works of art express taste, whether the objects please or displease. This is true even when you are not conscious of your standards. You may say, "I like that song" or "That picture is pretty." To make such statements indicates that you have critical standards of some sort. It is also important to note here that value judgments say as much about the person holding the opinion as the thing being judged. Value judgments vary from one person to another and from community to community. Someone else may find your favorite poem dull, sentimental, or otherwise displeasing.

Artistic values are often brought into play in forensic events, if only indirectly. In a debate on energy shortages, for instance, the facts may prove it more economical to build all automobiles using one mold for body style and one shade of black for paint. Yet most Americans share the value of having artistic choices even at higher cost. The value proposition "We should build cars in the most economical way" would probably not win many votes if it resulted in denying all possible choices to consumers except a black Toyota.

Moral and *ethical values* form the basis for judgments of right and wrong, just and unjust, good and bad. Of course, our religious heritage teaches us such values, and we live our daily lives more or less according to a learned set of beliefs and convictions. Yet, it is a mistake to pigeonhole all moral and ethical value judgments into sectarian religious doctrines. Many values underlying laws and policies reflect civil values. For instance, laws related to family life and child protection, crimes against persons, and the human welfare triangle of jobs-housing-education derive largely, if not entirely, from moral and ethical value judgments cutting across the boundaries between specific religious groups.

Related to general moral and ethical values are *political values*, which express judgments as to what is *expedient*, that is, what should or should not be done for the common good. Political values include democracy, rights, justice, and many others. The U.S. political system attempts to maintain a historical balance between the values of individual liberty and equal protection under the law. The core value of liberty requires that we believe that the best government is the least government, that government interference and regulation must be checked. The core value of equality dictates that we believe that government should protect the basic rights of citizens to the vote, police protection, education, decent housing and nutrition, medical care, and employment. Often, if one of these core values is advanced, there is a corresponding encroachment on the other. We can expect lively debate over any proposed government action along these lines of political values. In some areas, government involvement is viewed by everyone as essential. Government regulation of the power utilities and its provision of fire departments, public schools, and national defense are examples. In other areas, the relationship between government and the people is subject to much debate.

So far, what have you learned about value propositions? They are statements about judgments. They concern a thing's qualities, rather than the thing itself. Judgments are important because they express opinions and attitudes about the underlying meanings of facts and events, whether we like or dislike them, whether they are good or bad, whether or not they should lead to action, and what type of action they should lead to. Value judgments may be of an artistic, moral, ethical, or political nature.

Examples of propositions of value are the following:

Environmental protection is more important than economic stability.

When they are in conflict, freedom of speech is more desirable than national security.

The use of tax money to support athletics is wasteful.

By now it should be clear that value judgments are highly relevant to your participation in forensic events. When you decide that a problem is significant or harmful, you are making a value judgment. To say that a plan has results that could be called advantageous or disadvantageous is to make a value judgment. Ultimately, to decide to act on a policy change and to specify the types of government actions that should or should not be adopted is to make value judgments. Every persuasive appeal in forensics—student congress or debate—inevitably calls forth the values held by those listening to you. Your success in forensics will be enhanced by a clear understanding of the nature of value propositions, how they guide the creation of arguments, and how your listeners will arrange your value appeals along their own sets of judgmental priorities.

This final point is crucial to understanding the role of value judgments. While there are many important values, there is no set priority or rank ordering of values. When relevant values conflict, priority must be determined. Often this is done through public hearings and legislative as well as public debate.

Propositions of Policy

The origin of the term *policy* is the Greek word *polis*, or city, the same root word leading to related modern English words, such as *metropolis, police* and *politics*. Broadly speaking, a policy is a course of action or a set of rules, regulations, or laws designed to guide present and future government and private sector decisions. In a corporation, for example, company policies govern employer–employee relations. A school district may set up policies governing how the school buildings may be used by outside groups. The body of local, state, and federal legislators passes policies that administrative branches of government enforce.

A *proposition of policy* is a statement of a course of action to be considered for adoption. The spheres of policy formulation include all those problem areas deemed appropriate for government action. In the classic statement of Aristotle,

> Of the subjects upon which all men deliberate, and upon which deliberative orators speak, the chief ones, we may say, are five in number, to wit: (1) ways and means; and (2) war and peace; next, (3) national defense; and (4) imports and exports; finally, (5) legislation.

Theoretically, every question requiring government deliberation falls within one or another of these general categories. Indeed, it is difficult to think of many items being considered today that are not pertinent to at least one category or another. All issues related to spending and taxing (fiscal, budget, or revenue bills) are matters of ways and means. The nation's foreign policy, regarding diplomacy, economic relations, and military matters, seems to be included in Aristotle's reference to war and peace, defense, and trade policy. Finally, all issues of domestic problems, such as welfare, law and order, commerce, and the rest, come within the province of legislation.

The status quo is composed, in part, of government policies that have accumulated over time. Rules, regulations, and laws begin with the basic documents established within a given jurisdiction (the United States Constitution, the constitutions of the various state governments, city charters, and others). They continue through the body of laws and statutes passed under the authority of those basic documents to govern citizens. There is some overlap between jurisdictions, such as between federal laws and state laws; but generally the existing policies are allocated to different levels of government corresponding to the authority of each level. Usually the level of government and the nature of a problem fit each other. For instance, local government has primary responsibilities for the public schools, local law enforcement, fire protection, and other matters because it is close to the people served. Conversely, the federal government assumes responsibility for matters of national concern, such as defense and military policies, interstate commerce, and regulation of broadcasting frequencies. It is easy to see why this division of responsibilities occurs. It would be inappropriate, even impossible, for the city of Midland, Texas, to make a treaty with Great Britain. Likewise, the federal government does not concern itself with parking violators in Midland's City Hall parking lot. Nevertheless, in all matters of public concern, policies are established and maintained by some appropriate authority possessing jurisdiction.

Where do policies come from? At this point in history, rules, regulations, and laws stand on the books, ready for easy reference. If you were to ask, "What is the policy of the U.S. Army toward deserters?" you could find the answer by turning to the relevant section of the *Uniform Code of Military Justice*. If you were to ask, "May girls wear short shorts to the senior English class?" you would probably learn the answer from the school's dress code. And you would also discover that these policies, like all rules, regulations, and laws, are binding on your decisions and actions as long as you remain under the jurisdiction of the authority in charge of the policy.

Yet to recognize this characteristic of policies—that they exist and are binding—does not truly explain the answer to the question of where policies come from. Even though policies now exist, they did not *always* exist. At some point in the past, policies had to be created in response to problems as they arose. At some point in the past, there was no answer to the questions "What is the policy to guide decisions about toxic industrial waste?" or "What is the policy to guide decisions about sexual harassment in the workplace?"

Moreover, there will be situations arising in the future for which no policy now exists, and new policies will be needed to guide decisions. In fact, existing policies are in continuous need of review and revision to adapt to changing conditions.

With this explanation of the nature of policy and policy formation, you are now ready to learn some important characteristics of propositions of policy. Keep in mind that a *proposition* is a statement requiring consideration. First, a proposition of policy reflects a rule to guide action or decision. As such, it differs from both factual propositions and value judgments. A policy is not subject to verification by observation of events or objects, like a factual statement; rather, it is validated by agreement among all the people subject to the policy and enforced by law. Neither is a policy a matter of subjective assessment of artistic, moral, or abstract political qualities; rather, a policy is an objective rule to guide decision or action regardless of any subjective evaluation of it.

Second, because policies are created and maintained ultimately by the agreement of the people they affect, they are considered to be subject to change through orderly processes. Policies are negotiable. On the other hand, a factual statement is either true or false. A fact cannot be amended by majority vote. Likewise, value judgments are not negotiable, although they may change as our attitudes and opinions change. We do not ordinarily think of a value judgment as a policy guiding decision and action among all people within a community. In this sense, you say you cannot legislate morality. On the other hand, you *can* legislate a policy.

Broadly speaking, any statement of a policy is a proposition of policy. However, in forensics the attention usually focuses on propositions of policy requiring consideration, that is, propositions for which you seek acceptance. There are three general categories of propositions of policy.

First, you may propose a new policy to guide decisions and actions where no policy exists. This is the starting point for all policies. To illustrate this type of policy proposition, imagine this hypothetical situation. Suppose great strides were made in the area of space travel by the wealthy industrial nations. What policies should guide decisions as to the allocation of space routes, ownership of resources discovered on previously unexplored planets, and safety and security regulations in space? The nations involved would naturally be required to work out a set of rules, regulations, and laws binding on all and to formulate a set of policies applicable to these problems. In the past, the development of nuclear weapons and of nuclear energy for peaceful uses generated a need for a whole new set of policies where none previously existed.

Second, you may propose amendments to alter policies that exist but for some reason are no longer satisfactory. The conditions that existed originally may have changed in significant ways, outmoding once-established policies. A good example of an amended policy is the reduction of the speed limit on interstate highways from 70 to 55 miles per hour, in order to reduce the nation's fuel consumption during the 1973 oil crisis. Other examples are the return to a higher speed limit on the rural highways of some states in 1987, and the 1995 amendment to speed limits on interstate highways, in which each state legislates its own limit.

Third, you may propose to abolish an existing policy altogether. Once, all high school students were required to study Latin. Now, only a few college graduate programs maintain this policy. At some point, the authorities in charge of educational institutions decided to abandon the policy of requiring the study of a language other than English.

The proposition of policy is highly relevant to forensics. In student congress, contestants are expected to make policy proposals for consideration by the entire legislative body. Whenever such a proposal is made, it is called a *motion*, which is a precise statement of the proposed policy to be considered for possible approval. Once moved, a proposition may be debated, amended, and disposed of by acceptance, rejection, or other means according to the rules of parliamentary procedure.

In policy debate, the opposing teams are concerned with a proposition of policy. As in student congress, the statement is precisely worded. However, in debate the proposition is called a *resolution*, rather than a motion or a question. Unlike student congress, debate does not permit the resolution to be amended. Also, at the conclusion of the debate, the debaters are not expected to agree among themselves as to the disposition of the resolution. Instead, they put their arguments for and against the resolution to an impartial judge who is responsible for making a final decision to accept or reject the resolution based on the merits of the case as presented in the debate.

SUMMARY

Analysis, understanding the different aspects of the problem under consideration, is the beginning point for any forensic event. In the specific parts of this book that deal with debate and student congress, you will examine how these analytical skills can be applied. For now, keep in mind that the characteristics of the problem area and the nature of the proposition give you specific directions in which to discover the basic issues in problem solving.

QUESTIONS FOR DISCUSSION

1. Debate begins with the *analysis* of a problem area and its solutions. Define the process of analysis.

2. What is the difference between a *problem area* and a *problem statement*?

3. When wording a proposition for debate, what characteristics should you consider?

4. Propositions may be classified into three categories: propositions of fact, value, and policy. How are they different from each other?

5. There are three general categories for propositions of policy. What are these and how are they different from one another?

ACTIVITIES

1. Using the resolution: "Resolved: That the federal government should exclusively control the development and distribution of energy resources in the United States," outline the meaning of the terms of the statement. Are there any value terms in the resolution?

2. Propositions ought to meet five criteria. Examine the following propositions. Does each meet those criteria? Rewrite in correct form those that do not.

   Resolved: That the federal government should increase social welfare programs in the current budget.

   Resolved: That enrollment in secondary schools is declining.

   Resolved: That the federal government should redesign the tax structure to tax citizens equally and use a significant portion of the tax dollars to improve the educational system.

   Resolved: That municipalities should establish comprehensive security guidelines for airports to make them safe.

   Resolved: That city governments should establish a comprehensive program to improve educational standards in the schools.

   Resolved: That the federal government should establish a comprehensive program to provide medical care for all Americans.

   Resolved: That all U.S. citizens have a right to clean drinking water.

3. The following are examples of poorly worded propositions. Rewrite these propositions, wording them correctly.

Propositions of Fact

Resolved: That action should be taken to balance the budget of the federal government.

Resolved: That the housing market is no longer attractive to young married couples.

Propositions of Value

Resolved: That every citizen should be guaranteed an annual income.

Resolved: That English study develops skills in grammar and punctuation.

Propositions of Policy

Resolved: That the jury system in the United States should not be significantly changed.

Resolved: That the federal government should establish a comprehensive national policy to protect the quality of water and guarantee a future supply of energy.

4. Formulate a proposition of fact, one of value, and one of policy on each of the following topics: arms sales, terrorism, global warming, excellence in education, age discrimination, aviation safety, and immigration.

THE SKILLS OF RESEARCH

OBJECTIVES AND KEY TERMS

After studying Chapter 3, you should be able to

1. Conduct a successful library survey on a particular debate resolution,
2. Make a list of resources in your community to be used for a particular resolution,
3. Explore computerized indexes in your research,
4. Explain and operate under the guidelines for ethics in research, and
5. Make a list of key terms to use when you research a debate resolution.

After reading this chapter, you should understand the following terms:

brief

evidence

indexes (or guides)

online/card catalog

primary source

secondary source

slug

vertical file

The analysis that is fundamental to successful participation in forensic events is both an outgrowth of knowledge and the foundation for continuing research. Much of that knowledge will be general, but more of it will be the direct result of extensive reading, listening, and discussion. Once the process of analysis is advanced enough for you to be ready to accumulate specific information on which to build debate cases or write student congress *briefs* (sheets of paper containing arguments on the same issue), you must be prepared to use the skills of research.

NATURE AND PURPOSE OF RESEARCH

Although most people have used the word *research* many times, its actual meaning frequently escapes them. It means what it literally says: to search again. How often do you pick up a book early in your search for evidence, look through it, and set it aside permanently? As your own knowledge increases or your grasp of the problem broadens, you may reconsider sources. Beginning to research a broad area is a hard job because so much information is available. But with energy and persistence, the topic gradually will become clear.

The purpose of research is to gather information and *evidence*—support for an argument—and to classify this data so that it is easily retrievable for use in competition. There are three reasons for this data-based approach to forensics. First, there is the ethical or moral obligation of anyone who attempts to influence others. To speak without adequate information is to violate the traditional ethics of public speaking. Second, there is a pragmatic consideration. If you lack thorough knowledge and adequate evidence, you have little chance to make your view prevail. Finally, there is the psychological advantage that comes when you are secure in your knowledge that you have the greatest possible accumulation of information on a problem area. The debater who is in constant fear of not having done enough research on a case and the student congressperson who hesitates to speak when the opportunity occurs because he or she cannot evidence a position are both at a disadvantage.

Competition in debate and student congress places a premium on printed sources of evidence. In student congress, however, there is room for the introduction of personal knowledge and experience as well as information garnered from interviews and correspondence. These sources may furnish a speaker with a background that enables him or her to interpret the printed sources and gather evidence from them. The competitor in forensics must, regardless of the event, be committed to research.

FINDING EVIDENCE

Library Survey

The first research step is a library survey. Find out what is available in your local library. The basic tool to consult in any library is the on-line (computerized) or traditional *card catalog*. This lists all the books in the library by author, title, and subject. You should look under any of the possible subject headings suggested by the problem statement with which you are working. For example, if you are researching the debate topic, "Resolved: That the United States government should adopt a policy to increase political stability in Latin America," the first subject you would refer to in the catalog would be *Latin America*. Following that, you would refer to specific countries, such as Honduras, Nicaragua, Guatemala, Costa Rica, Chile, and Argentina. Then you might move to subjects such as terrorism, illegal drugs, and humanitarian aid. In addition, the library's catalog might have other areas cross-referenced. Exhaust the most obvious ones first, but remember that there is a time lag in most libraries between acquisition date and final input or filing in the catalog for a book. Develop good relations with your librarians, let them know ahead of time what your debate topic is, and ask to be told of newly acquired books on the topic. Most librarians will respond enthusiastically.

Following a careful look at the on-line or card catalog, examine other general reference sources. Most libraries have *vertical files*. These are collections of pamphlets and clippings that relate to topics of current interest. You may have to ask the librarian about this collection. In addition, consult such *guides* and *indexes* as the *Readers' Guide to Periodical Literature* and *Ulrich's* periodicals directory. These works contain alphabetical listings (by author, title, and general subject) or magazine articles that have appeared in a particular group of periodicals. The *Congressional Information Service Index*, published by the U.S. Government Printing Office and also available on-line, lists government documents by title and subject. In addition, there is a regularly published index to the *Congressional Record* and *United States Government Publications: Monthly Catalog*. Special indexes, such as *The Education Index*, can be useful if your debate topic fits the special subject. Most libraries carry the indexes listed above in their reference departments, even though they do not have all the publications indexed in them. Keep a record of the promising articles listed, even if they are not available in the particular library you are using. You may have opportunities to work in other libraries, and there is no need to waste valuable research time recopying indexes at each stop. Also, keep in mind that any index will be organized under many different broad subject headings. Use your imagination. Explore all the possible ways the information you seek might be listed.

Using Computers in Library Research

Although there is a wide variety of library on-line (computerized) catalogs and computerized indexes, most fall under one of two categories. The first includes systems that index items you would find in a traditional card catalog, with publications listed according to author, title, and subject. To find listings under a particular heading, you merely enter that heading into the computer system by using the keyboard at a terminal. For instance, say that you want to find out which of Mark Twain's books are available in your local library. You first indicate that this is an author search (perhaps by typing the letter *a* and entering it). Then, you might type "TWAIN, MARK" and enter it. These steps vary from system to system. The computer then gives you a variety of information about each listing. It provides all the information you would find in the traditional card catalog, such as the call number of the book, its publication information, and perhaps a short summary of its contents. In addition, though, the computer probably will indicate the status of the book—whether it has been checked out and other libraries where the book might be found. This latter information can be very helpful in facilitating research: You don't have to waste a trip to the shelf to discover that a book has been checked out, and you know immediately whether the book can be found at other libraries.

The computerized catalog can also help facilitate subject searches. Using a traditional card catalog to find information on broad topics can be quite inefficient. You can find listings only under very narrow, precise headings, and looking under broad headings can be time-consuming. If you were researching Germany, for example, a card catalog would only allow you to examine subheadings (such as economy, history, geography, and demographics) one at a time. With a computerized system, you could enter the broad topic of Germany into the terminal, and it would display all the subheadings at once. You would then know immediately how the library has subdivided all the material on Germany, and you would be able to get all the listings under a particular subheading quickly. This technique of entering broad topics to examine subheadings can also improve the breadth of your research, since the subheadings themselves can spark ideas for new cross-references to check out.

The second category of computerized indexes carries periodical listings. These systems index periodical articles you might find in bound indexes such as the *Readers' Guide to Periodical Literature* and the *Social Sciences Index*. The operation of these systems is similar to that of the computerized catalog. You enter a particular heading, and the listings for it are then displayed on the screen. Most of these systems, like the bound indexes, are limited to subject searches.

There are two advantages to computerized periodical indexes, such as Readers' Guide Abstracts, ProQuest, and NewsBank. The first is that a computerized system permits the search of many years at one time. With bound indexes, if you want to find all articles written on the B-2 Stealth Bomber in the past five years, you must go through five or more bound editions of a particular index. A computerized system allows you to search five years at once. This can be particularly useful when you are doing newspaper searches. The NewsBank index, for example, has compiled listings from fifty of the biggest newspapers in the United States (including papers such as *The Washington Post, Christian Science Monitor,* and *Los Angeles Times*). Using this index saves you the trouble of looking through fifty different indexes.

The second advantage to computerized indexes is that the system may be attached to a printer. This means that after you call up the headings you are looking for, the listings can be printed out as hard copy. You can save a great deal of time by not having to write down all the listings you find.

Of course, computers can introduce you to research databases far beyond what your school or public library contains. Increasingly, libraries are offering their users access to the wide array of material available via the Internet, the global computer network. All manner of specialized indexes—more than most individual libraries could ever dream of owning—are available at the touch of a keyboard. So are abstracts, or even full texts, of hundreds of thousands of documents and articles on specialized subjects.

Key On-Line Resources for the Debater

The World Wide Web is easily accessible and very useful for many kinds of debate research. Search engines, which contain the URL's (Universal Research Locators) for millions of web pages, are a perfect place to start. For example, http://altavista.digital.com is a helpful search engine for almost any kind of research and can provide multiple links to resources on your topic.

The "official" debate page, http://www.debate.net, has information about all kinds of debate activities, and links for pages on the high school and college topics as well as various papers on debate theory.

E-mail listservs are also a good resource. The cx-l@debate.net (the high school debate list), ndt-l@uga.cc.ugz.edu, and ceda-l@cornell.edu are all helpful e-mail listservs that help you find out what is going on in the area of debate. If you or your team are interested in asking questions and engaging in discussions on the World Wide Web, consider subscribing.

To subscribe to the ndt-1, send a message to listserv@uga.cc.uga.edu, with the message "subscribe ndt-1 <u>your name</u>." To subscribe to the ceda-1, send a message to listserv@Cornell.edu, with the message "subscribe ceda-1 <u>your name</u>." Of course, this information is subject to change, as is true of any new technology.

Finally, usenet groups provide access to a variety of different discussions about almost any imaginable topic. If you have a question you want answered, or an idea on which you want feedback, usenet groups are useful. The advantage to using usenet groups is that you will deal with people in the professions in which you are interested—which can be better for factual questions that might not prompt a response from the debate listservs.

Current Sources

The alert and aware forensic researcher makes it a point to survey regularly the current issues of such noteworthy publications as

Christian Science Monitor, New York Times, The Wall Street Journal, Congressional Digest, Congressional Record, Current History, Foreign Policy Bulletin, Nation's Business, New Republic, U.S. Department of State Bulletin, and *Vital Speeches*. This is not an exhaustive list, but a representative one. The thing to remember is that you can and should attempt to locate the latest evidence, even before it gets indexed.

Special Sources

There are a number of special resources of which forensic competitors should be aware. Many of these provide additional ways for debate students to enhance their experience of *primary research*, which is research directly from books, magazines, newspapers, or documents. As such, there resources have particular value. The following privately published materials are among those currently available: *Social Issues Resources Series* and *Current History*, which are collections of articles, updated annually. A third resource is *The Forensic Quarterly*, published by The National Federation of State High School Associations, which has its headquarters in Kansas City, Missouri. Much of the material published in this publication is written especially for this quarterly and is not available anywhere else. All of it is *primary material*, or a *primary source*, meaning any publication containing firsthand information. A *secondary source*, on the other hand, is a source that has reprinted previously published material. Debate handbooks, or evidence books, are examples of such secondary material.

Another resource is the *Congressional Research Service*. Each year this research volume is published with excerpts of statements, speeches, and debates on the current high school debate topic. The extensive bibliography in this work can shorten some of the time spent in the library. (Available from your congressional representative.)

The *Congressional Quarterly* is a source that includes weekly reports on federal legislation and a sampling of expert opinion. Another source is the *National Journal*. This source follows national legislation and has good summary articles on major policy disputes.

The list of materials listed here is not exhaustive, but it illustrates that forensic competitors anywhere can get primary resource materials and experience the joy of seeking and finding answers to the questions formulated in the analytical process.

Private Interest Groups

A small investment of money and a relatively large block of time can garner excellent results from another type of primary resource. The money required is for stationery and stamps; the time is for writing letters to private interest groups for material. The best way to discover the identity of such groups is to pose three questions to yourself: (1) Who might be interested in the problem area? (2) Who would gain from the adoption of the resolution? (3) Who would lose from the adoption of the resolution?

When you have answered these questions, you will have identified a number of groups of people who represent special interest groups, which are usually more than happy to supply material. You will, of course, begin with the understanding that the conclusions and interpretations in the material you receive will not necessarily be objective. This does not mean, however, that the facts and statistics such material might contain are not valid.

At times, discovering the existence of such groups is a matter of creative deduction. Some of them are obvious. When health care is the problem area, your first inquiry might go to the American Medical Association. However, less obviously, the Social Security Administration, the Congressional Research Service, the Pharmaceutical Manufacturers Association, the World Health Organization, and the Department of Transportation may also have valuable information. These and several other unlikely sources were found by reading and noticing references to studies or projects. A careful look for citations in handbooks and bibliographies can reveal groups to which you can write for additional information.

One team, when debating the question of penal reform, discovered that no comprehensive nationwide statistics had ever been compiled about jails because of the strictly local jurisdiction over jails. The team members found, however, that statewide studies existed. They then wrote to the appropriate agency in each state, asking for selected studies and any additional materials related to the penal reform topic. They received an overwhelming response, about 85 percent, and materials that enabled them to become experts on the subject.

If the identities of these private interest groups are not obvious, you can consult the *World Almanac*, which lists more than 25,000 organizations; or the *Encyclopedia of Associations*. The information available from private interest groups may hold the key to specific topic areas that could lead to a case construction that might have eluded you otherwise. You must be aware, however, that such publications naturally reflect the biases of the group they represent.

Secondary Sources

Thus far, the discussion has focused on discovering primary resources. However, some secondary resources are also important. The forensic community has many different points of view concerning this secondary material. No one denies the value of original research, seeking out relevant books and articles and evaluating the positions and opinions in their original context. However, the information explosion had made the debater's task a difficult one and has led many debaters to employ secondary resources. Several observations can be made concerning this practice.

Although there is nothing inherently wrong with handbooks, relying heavily on them for evidence is not wise for two reasons: First, part of the value of debate is the acquisition of research skills. You forfeit that value if you depend entirely on handbook evidence. The second problem is far more pragmatic. Most forensic leagues have strict rules regarding the accuracy of evidence cited in a debate. These rules uniformly place the responsibility for accurate evidence on the person *reading* the evidence in a round. Consequently, even when you use a reputable handbook, you should check sources. If a flaw is found in a piece of evidence you read in a round, the claim that it came from such-and-such handbook will not excuse the error. Checking the evidence you find in handbooks will also give you the opportunity to locate additional resources.

A debate handbook works best when used as an introduction to a topic. Good handbooks include short introductory essays on the issues in the resolution and current controversies in debate theory and practice. In addition, they often contain extensive bibliographies, which can assist debaters in their subsequent research. Using the handbooks, many debaters will get a feel for the cases that might be developed by other schools, and the evidence and initial analysis the handbooks provide may spark some ideas that otherwise would have taken weeks of research to produce. However, since handbook evidence is gathered several months before the season begins, a debater will need to update his or her evidence continually.

Presenting and Organizing Evidence

Evidence accumulated for debate should be presented in a standard form. Every piece of evidence in your file should contain

1. A topic heading (commonly called a *tag* or *slug*)
2. The citation: author's name, title of article and magazine or book, place and date published, and page number(s). If the evidence came from an on-line information service, you should indicate that as well.
3. The author's qualifications.
4. The evidence quotation itself. This must be accurate and verbatim. If you intend to omit part of the quotation to save time, copy the entire quotation and then underline or highlight the part to be read. In this way, you can always prove that your ellipsis did not violate the author's intention.

A typical piece of evidence might look like one of the following examples:

Topic: China

CHINA Ø LISTEN TO ARMS CONTROL

(—) Efforts to stop China's proliferation have not worked Kamal '92 (Nazir, Research fellow at Institute of SE Asia, *Contemp SE Asia*, Sept. p. 125)

> < In its declaratory policy, China has consistently reiterated that it held a "serious, responsible and prudent" attitude towards arms sales.[98] An equally consistent feature of China's declaratory policy on ballistic missile export has been its periodic affirmation that it does not intend to sell missiles of medium or greater range—barring the exceptional case of CSS-2 sales to Saudi Arabia in 1987–88. The exception was justified as having contributed to the establishment of diplomatic relations between China and Saudi Arabia.[99]
>
> U.S. concerns about China's intended sale of M-9 missiles to Syria were first expressed directly to Chinese leaders in December 1989 when senior U.S. officials visited Beijing

as part of a wider effort to normalize Sino-American relations. China adopted an ambiguous posture, maintaining that it held a serious attitude towards the sale of medium-range missiles, which would not be transferred to the Middle East. The reference to "medium-range" missiles quite clearly meant that the sale of CSS-2s would not be repeated, while the question of M-9 sales was left open, suggesting that China did not wish to accept restrictions on the transfer of such missiles. Chinese reassurances initially placated the United States regarding the sale of M-9 missiles, but subsequent disappointment brought home the discrepancy in Chinese and American definitions of "medium-range." >

Topic: Elderly

_____ELDERLY USE FUTURE'S RESOURCES

R. Scott Fosler (dir govt studies, Comm of Econ Development, Washington DC), 1990, in _Demographic Change and the American Future_, p. 8 [Wade Gentz]

Because the number of elderly will rise slowly until 2010, the additional number of Social Security recipients (as distinguished from the level of benefits they receive) is not likely to be a major cost pressure for the next two decades. The more immediate source of increases lies in the rising cost of health and long-term care, especially for the rapidly growing number of people 85 and over who have by far the greatest need for medical and long-term care. This group numbered 2.7 million in 1985, and is projected to nearly double to 4.9 million in 2000, and to reach 6.6 million by 2010.

_____CURBING RESOURCE USE ALLOWS PROSPEROUS FUTURE

William Bueler (Chinese language instructor, Defense Language Institute; author _Population and America's Future_), September 5, 1985, _USA Today_, p. 44 [Sara Boblick]

America's population can not grow forever. Even technological optimists who hope that new innovations in energy and agriculture will allow us to pack our land with several times its present population recognize that. The important question then is not whether population growth will stop, but when and how? Will it stop through rational planning while there remain sufficient land and resources and a sufficiently clean environment for all to enjoy a reasonably high standard of living, or will it stop only after overpopulation has brought about an ecological—and, therefore, almost certainly a political—disaster?

The American people as a whole are still only marginally concerned about population, so it is no doubt premature to expect a debate on population policy to enter the realm of electoral politics, to compete for time and attention with more immediate economic and political concerns. However, it is time to plant wherever possible the seeds of awareness for such a national debate, for it can not be very far into the future before events force the majority of Americans to see population growth for what it is—a problem which, if ignored, will destroy any possibility of a prosperous and environmentally sound society for our children's and future generations.

In the years before widespread, inexpensive photocopying, debaters copied evidence from books and magazines by hand onto note cards. Today, most competitive debaters photocopy pages from the original source, cut the desired paragraphs out of the photocopied article, and tape the evidence onto regular-size paper. In this way, three or four pieces of evidence on the same subject can appear together on one page. The page is often organized as a *brief*, a sheet of paper containing arguments on the same issue. The briefs are then organized in folders or accordions, labeled by subject.

If your evidence is not a photocopy of the original source, or if it has come from an on-line information service, it is important to identify directly quoted material with quotation marks, omitted material with ellipses, and interpolated material with brackets rather than parentheses.

ETHICS IN RESEARCH

Finally, it is appropriate here to talk about the ethics of research. The requirement that you provide evidence for all your claims and arguments in a debate is one reason that debate is so educational. Debaters do more research and accumulate more files of evidence than just about anyone, especially on a voluntary, extracurricular basis. It is not uncommon for a high school debater to compile 2,000 or more pieces of evidence during the debate season.

On the other hand, the rule that you must provide evidence as proof in a debate has ironically set up an almost counterproductive situation. What if you need a piece of evidence to say something, and you don't have it? Chances are, you will lose the argument, especially if it is refuted by your opponent. Yet, if you just had that piece of evidence, perhaps you would be able to win the argument instead of losing it. The temptation is to lead the judge into believing that you indeed have the evidence by "doctoring" evidence or by simply making up a piece of evidence that says what you need it to say.

The misuse of evidence is the most serious breach of debate ethics. To misrepresent a piece of evidence is called *distortion*, and to make up evidence is called *fabrication*. The American Forensic Association recommends that the penalty for evidence distortion and evidence fabrication should begin with an automatic loss of the debate round. Also, it advocates that the debater who is guilty receive a score of zero speaker points, which effectively prevents her or him from receiving a speaker award in the tournament (such awards are based on the overall average of scores during the tournament). Beyond that, for evidence fabrication at the college level, in particular, a debater found guilty is barred from participating in the National Debate Tournament, and the American Forensic Association is instructed to write a letter of censure to the debater's home school. The National Forensic League also has strict rules in this area. As you can see, the forensic community takes this violation of debate seriously. So, as you record the evidence you discover in your research, do so accurately.

SUMMARY

The core of forensic competition is the research you do. Through research, you prepare the proof to validate your arguments.

Research is a careful process of determining what is available, using fully a wide variety of resources, and recording the results carefully and accurately. Once you have begun the research process, you need to turn your attention to the use of that information to establish proof.

Questions for Discussion

1. When preparing to research a proposition, why should you begin by developing a list of key terms?

2. Which type of evidence is considered to be the least educationally defensible? Why?

3. If the library near you has computerized indexes, why would it be to your advantage to use them?

4. If you need to determine how qualified a person is to speak to a topic, where can you find information?

5. Research goes beyond what is found in the library. On any given topic, there are numerous groups that print information concerning the topic. How do you tap these resources, and how do you determine their value?

6. What are the essential items of information that a piece of evidence should contain?

7. The reading and research skills learned for debate can be applied to other areas as well. Describe some of these other applications.

Activities

1. Using one of the following propositions, make a list of key terms. Use your imagination.

   Resolved: That academic achievement criteria should be applied to extracurricular activities for participation.

   Resolved: That the United States should significantly change its foreign trade policies.

   Resolved: That the federal government should establish a program to provide for aging American citizens.

2. Using one of the resolutions in Activity 1, perform the following tasks (be sure to use your list of key terms):

    a. Make a list of books of interest on the proposition.

    b. Using one of the indexes listed in this chapter, develop a bibliography of magazines or government documents available on the proposition.

3. Using one of the resolutions in Activity 1, identify any private interest groups that might have materials available on the resolution. Draft a sample letter to send to these interest groups.

4. The following facsimiles of evidence are flawed. In each, identify the flaw.

    Anita Johnson (Prof. of Medicine, MIT), *Environment*, March 1992, p. 9.

    "Flame retardants are not labeled, nor are the many extraneous ingredients in drugs, such as flavors and dyes."

    Edward Kennedy (Senator, Mass.), Hearings, Subcommittee on Health and Scientific Research, May 17, 1993, p. 4.

    "Most patients today are hopelessly uninformed about what drugs really do and cannot do. They therefore make excessive and irrational demands for drug treatment when they see their doctor."

    "Another Study Refutes Saccharin/Cancer Link," *Chemical and Engineering News*, March 17, 1995, p. 8.

    "Wynder and Stellman state emphatically, 'No association was found between use of artificial sweeteners or diet beverages and bladder cancer.' Alan S. Morrison and Julie E. Buring, who conducted the Harvard study, hedge only slightly by concluding that 'users of artificial sweeteners have little or no excess risk of cancer of the lower urinary tract.'"

    David Dickson, *Nature*, January 3, 1996, p. 2.

    "Such nonpropellant emissions could bring the total CFC emissions back up to previous levels within seven to ten years."

    Lewis A. Dunn (Prof., Harvard U.), *Controlling the Bomb*, 1992.

    "It also would lessen the chances of unauthorized use of nuclear weapons in local conflict, thereby dampening one flash point of Soviet-American confrontation."

Ted Greenwood (Professor of Political Science, U. of Vermont), "Supply-Side Non-Proliferation," *Foreign Policy*, Spring 1961, p. 131.

"In the absence of international acceptance of existing U.S. policy, Congress and the new administration should initiate movement toward a revision of the international nuclear regime. Such revision should be pursued through a process of broad negotiations and agreement. A wholesale dismantling of the regime—all too easy to bring about in the current political environment—would not be constructive and should be avoided."

A. M. Weinberg (Commonwealth Edison), "Can We Fix Nuclear Energy?" *Annals of Nuclear Energy*, 1996, p. 473.

"A one million KW pressurized water reactor contains 15 billion Ci radioactivity. This is about equal to the natural radioactivity in all the oceans; radioactivity that accompanies the decay of the 4 billion tons of uranium and its daughters dissolved in the seas."

Chemical Week, January 2, 1983, p. 16.

"Industry sources estimate that another 1,000 to 2,000 doctoral-level toxicologists will be needed by 1991, which is sooner than the nation can possibly generate them, warns Lange."

Health Benefits: Loss Due to Unemployment, Hearings before the Committee on Energy and Commerce and the Subcommittee on Health and the Environment, House of Representatives, January 24 and April 22, 1983, p. 16.

"Many working mothers and their children who under the harsh rules demanded by the Reagan Administration are no longer eligible for Aid to Families with Dependent Children (AFDC) have simultaneously lost their eligibility for Medicaid. Individuals who are losing social security disability benefits lose their entitlement to Medicare."

David A. Andelman (The Peace Movement), "Space Wars," *Foreign Policy*, Fall 1987, p. 102.

"...if the United States possessed an ABM system, the Soviets would inevitably acquire one too."

5. Discuss the role of ethics in debate competition and how a team can cope with pressure and loss, as well as victory.

THE SKILLS OF REASONING

OBJECTIVES AND KEY TERMS

After studying Chapter 4, you should be able to

1. Explain the meaning of *proof*,
2. Explain and demonstrate the relationship among evidence, claim, and reasoning in the establishment of proof, and
3. List the tests for credibility for generalizations, analogy, cause-effect, statistics, and authority as forms of reasoning.

After reading this chapter, you should understand the following terms:

analogy	refutation
correlation	sign
counter example	variable
empirical evidence	
proof	
reasoning from authority	
reasoning from scientific methodology	

Forensic events provide an educational laboratory in which to learn and practice the principles of analyzing a problem area in the context of debate and student congress. Methods of analysis were explained to you as the way you organize information. To find the information, you have seen that you must do research. The final task in this section is to explain how to integrate your information and analysis to create convincing proof.

ESTABLISHING PROOF

In any forensic event, you must represent your conclusions to others for their consideration. To do so, you make a *claim*, a statement of what you will be proving. You ask for belief in your conclusion. Suppose you are asked, "Why should I accept your claim?" What would you answer? It is not enough simply to say, "You should believe what I say because I said it." If, however, you say, "This is the *reason* you should accept it ...," and then you furnish a reason for accepting your claim, you have given the other person a basis for considering your conclusion. *Reasoning* is the process of providing support for a claim.

When your reason seems acceptable to the other person, and the person believes your claim on the basis of your reasoning, it is said that you have proved your claim. *Proof* is information which, when offered in support of a claim, presents sufficient reason to make a claim acceptable. If the other person fails to accept your reason as sufficient for belief, then you have not proved your claim, even though the person may understand your position better than before. You have given a reason, but not a good enough reason to constitute proof in the mind of that person.

What is the difference between good and poor reasons? The answer to this question is complex. To grasp the concept of proof fully, you must understand psychology and *persuasion* (what causes people to believe or to doubt a statement), and you must also understand the rules and standards applied to proof within various contexts. For instance, if you are making your argument in a court of law, you must realize that there are many rules of evidence to govern what proof may be introduced, in what form it can be offered, and at what point in the proceedings it may be presented. Similarly, other settings for argument have special rules of procedures and standards of proof.

You do not have to become an expert to prove your case in forensic events. You may use some widely shared principles of reasoning and proof. The primary rule in the events of forensics is that all arguments must be based on *evidence*. Evidence consists of those items of information discovered through research and offered as proof in support of your claim. The claims you make must be accompanied by a reference to evidence. Without evidence, a claim has no support and is called an *assertion* This label is used because you assert a claim based on your own belief and nothing else. In debate, an assertion is not accepted as proof. But a claim founded on evidence is always accepted as proof until it undergoes *refutation*, the process of exposing flaws in opponents' arguments.

You must also make clear the connection between your evidence and your claim. Go back to the initial question: "Why should I accept your claim?" Suppose your answer is, "Because I have this item of evidence." Now suppose you are asked, "How do you get your conclusion from that evidence?" You are asked to relate the evidence to your claim. If you fail to make the connection, your evidence will not serve as proof for your claim; it will be considered irrelevant, or unrelated, to the issue. So, in the final analysis, proof might be represented as the equation:

$$PROOF = EVIDENCE + REASONING$$

TYPES OF REASONING

The following diagram illustrates the process of providing reasons for your claims on the beliefs of other people. On the right, you have stated a claim on your belief. On the left, you have an item of evidence.

Evidence	*Claim*
Auto manufacturers are making cars about 500–750 pounds lighter each year.	Cars in the future will be more economical to run.

Reasoning
?????????

How do you get from the evidence to the claim? You must have some reason to believe that the evidence supports the conclusion. In the example, you must reason something like this: "Lighter cars require less fuel than heavy cars; if future cars are lighter, then they will burn less gasoline." If your reason (that lighter cars consume less gasoline) is correct, then the evidence supports the claim. Several types of reasoning are generally accepted in forensic events.

Generalization: Reasoning from Facts

One of the most common forms of reasoning assumes that, if individual members of a general class of objects share a characteristic, then the characteristics will apply to all other members of the class. If you draw a general conclusion based on some specific examples, you have made a *generalization*.

Evidence	*Claim*
My 1992 Buick station wagon gets about 15 mpg on the highway.	Big cars are gas guzzlers.

Reasoning

Generalization: I assume all big cars are like mine.

In reasoning through generalization, what are the major types of evidence used? The evidence offered in support of a generalization is the *example*. When you claim that all members of a class or category are alike in certain characteristics, and your audience asks you to furnish proof, your response should be to point to individual members of the class about which you are generalizing and say, "See, this example (or group of examples) has the exact characteristics I am talking about." Ideally, the more examples you can produce, the better your argument.

Beyond the technique of itemizing specific examples leading to a generalization, you may also select one instance from a general group. This procedure forms the basis of *survey research*, such as public opinion polls. Rather than surveying every member of the population, you look at the population sample developed in the polling process and then make the assumption that it represents the entire group. There are rigorous scientific procedures you must observe in survey research, but the basic form of reasoning involved is simple generalization.

Several tests help to determine whether your generalizations are sound: (1) *Are there enough examples?* If the generalization is well known and widely accepted as true, just a few examples may serve to substantiate the point. If the conclusion is not so well known, then you may wish to provide quite a few examples. For instance, the conclusion "Playing football is dangerous" might seem untrue. But if you look at the large number of people hurt each year in football games and practices, the conclusion can be proven. (2) *Are the examples typical of the group?* A typical example is one that represents the group as a kind of average case. To prove the generalization that most people on welfare are undeserving you would have to do much more than find one or two examples of people who did not need aid. You would have to show that the average person does not need welfare. (3) *Are there significant counterexamples?* In some instances, you might find enough examples to prove a claim, and these examples might represent the average case that supports a generalization. What might weaken the support of your claim, however, are a few significant counterexamples.

Counterexamples are instances in which the generalization does not hold true. If you were arguing that it is good to intervene in the affairs of another nation, for instance, you might contend that, on the average, intervention saves the lives of U.S. citizens. Historical examples might be used to support the conclusion. The Vietnam War, however, serves as an instance that, according to some people, denies the claim that U.S. military intervention is good. If you know that there are some important counterexamples to your generalization, you should be willing to modify your claim. For example, instead of saying all interventions are good, you must say that some or most are good.

In statistical survey research, the tests are very similar: (1) *Is the sample size great enough?* (2) *Is the sample representative of the whole population?* The process of survey research is guided by scientific rules of procedure. For instance, to insure representativeness, the sample is drawn randomly, which allows every individual member of the population the same chance to be selected. Random selection avoids introducing bias into the selection process, which would possibly yield a sample that does not represent the entire population. Testing this kind of evidence by these standards is referred to as looking at the methodology employed.

Analogy: Reasoning from a Similar Model

You also reason by *analogy*: You draw a conclusion about an unknown based on its similarity to a model that is known. An analogy, then, is a comparison. An analogy is somewhat like a generalization in that it uses a specific, known example as its basis. However, the generalization draws a conclusion about the whole class of objects from which the example is drawn. The analogy draws its conclusion about another specific example. The analogy makes the assumption "This unknown example is like that known example."

Evidence	*Claim*
The U.S. Postal Service is wasteful and inefficient.	The proposed new energy distribution agency would be wasteful and inefficient

Reasoning

Analogy: I assume the new federal agency, which is unknown, is like the U.S. Postal Service in the known areas of wastefulness and inefficiency.

The test of an analogy is this: Is the unknown example like the known example in the essential areas being compared? As long as the similarities lie in the areas about which the claim is being made, argument by analogy constitutes proof. If the analogy draws its comparisons in an area not relevant to the claim, the argument will be faulty. This fallacy is called the *false analogy*.

You must realize, however, that even the literal analogy is regarded as a weak form of proof—in fact, some authors have called it the weakest form of proof. There are many confounding factors that weaken the power of an analogy; there are always elements that are not comparable between the known and the unknown. To say that one thing is like another thing is not to say the two are identical. Differences between them exist. The closeness of fit between your model and the unknown example you are reasoning about is the most important consideration in evaluating the strength of an analogy. For example, both sugar and salt have comparable qualities of visual appearance and texture; however, many a bowl of oatmeal has been ruined at camp by pranksters who filled the sugar bowl with salt.

One form of proof is the extended analogy. The *extended analogy* moves from a detailed discussion of a known person, place, object, or event to a detailed examination of something not completely understood or perhaps even entirely unknown to the audience. The argument of the extended analogy proceeds by distinguishing points of essential similarity from characteristics that are circumstantial or nonessential. Consider an extended analogy that members of the United States Congress often use when discussing military affairs in Europe: Intervention in Bosnia would be similar to intervention in Vietnam. The congressional representatives who make this analogy do not want U.S. combat troops sent abroad. They hope to persuade the president to restrain intervention by suggesting that any intervention in an Eastern European country would be just like, or analogous to, U.S. intervention in Vietnam. They hope to prevent the United States from repeating the mistake. To extend the analogy, the representatives point out that like the war in Vietnam, the war in Bosnia is a revolutionary struggle, and the turmoil requires a political, not a military solution. They also note that differences are really not essential. Though Vietnam and Bosnia are in different parts of the world, what is important is the kind of war and the required solutions. To dispute an analogy, you must determine why the differences between the two things compared are significant. In this analogy, it might be maintained that the Vietnam intervention and a Bosnian intervention are essentially dissimilar because in Vietnam, China could easily supply military weapons to keep the war going, while in Bosnia, maintaining a supply of weapons would be far more difficult. The extended analogy, then, is an important and exciting form of reasoning.

The ability of an analogy to explain, illustrate, or clarify the unknown matter is great. For this reason, figurative analogies are sometimes used. A *figurative analogy* is a comparison of dissimilar persons, places, objects, events, actions, or ideas. For example: "The government is like a three-legged stool; it has an executive branch, a legislative branch, and a judicial branch, tied together with the system of checks and balances. If one of these branches were to be destroyed, the government could not stand." In this way, figurative analogies simplify complex ideas and make them vivid in the minds of listeners. To gain increased understanding and to establish your point of view may be as important to winning your argument as providing more factual and logical arguments.

However, if you rely too heavily on figurative analogy for support of your argument, you run the risk of easy refutation. Such refutation simply shows that you have compared the known model with your claim in the wrong dimensions for comparison; you have overlooked crucial differences that exist between the items you are comparing; or stronger forms of argument can be proved that contradict your figurative analogy. Thus, you need to exercise care in the construction and use of this form of argument.

Cause-Effect: Reasoning from Process Relationships

In concept, the cause-effect relationship is easy to grasp, and it is therefore a familiar form of reasoning. Basically, a *cause-effect* relationship is one in which two phenomena (objects, events) are observed interacting in some process, and it is assumed that one of them causes the other. The form of the argument is "If...then...."

Evidence	*Claim*
This is the coldest winter since 1907.	My heating bill will be outrageous.

Reasoning
Cause-Effect: I assume my
furnace will burn more fuel
than usual because of the
cold weather.

In forensic events, this reasoning form is very important. Most of the events deal with cause-effect relationships: What are the causes of the problem? What are the effects of the problem? What would be the result if this or that change were implemented in dealing with the problem? Understanding the nature of this form of argument is difficult, because it is the most complex form of reasoning. You need to examine it in a bit more detail.

As mentioned, the cause-effect relationship assumes that in the process of interacting, there is a connecting link between one phenomenon and another. It further assumes that this connection is so strong that the relationship is predictable. For instance, what will happen when a bowling ball strikes a pin? In this simple process, would you predict that the pin will fall down? You should, because there is a strong link between the two events of a bowling ball striking a pin and of the pin falling down.

The quality of predictability is very strong when one phenomenon acts regularly and directly on another. As long as other factors involved in the interaction process are unchanged, the results of the interaction between the two phenomena will be the same. For example, water will always boil at 100°C at sea level, unless other factors intervene, such as dropping a box of salt into the water.

There are also situations in which two phenomena interact not by virtue of a causal link, but by sheer coincidence. It is possible that your golf shot could hit the back of a turtle on the fairway and ricochet into the hole for an ace. Would you like to bet that you could do it again? Coincidences have the quality of unpredictability. They are in the realm of the possible, but not in the realm of the predictable. Even though you play on the same golf course every day and even though another turtle could cross the fairway just as you are hitting the ball, there are too many intervening variables to predict that such a freak event could ever happen again.

The notion of intervening variables is what makes the cause-effect relationship problematic. From a purely scientific point of view, it is next to impossible to create a closed system with only two components operating in an unvarying process of interaction totally immune from any outside variables. A *variable* is a condition that may change and alter the relationship. Some scientists are unwilling to predict with certainty that the sun will rise tomorrow morning, based on the principle that there are so many potential intervening variables in the open solar system.

To make matters even more complicated, many phenomena are linked by connections that are weaker than causality but stronger than coincidence. Imagine a spectrum ranging from zero linkage to total linkage. The coincidental occurrence would rest near the zero linkage end of the range; the cause-effect relationship, near the 100 percent linkage end. Between these extremes are other degrees of linkage. Scientists have conveniently labeled two of these positions association and correlation.

0% Linkage			*100% Linkage*
Coincidence	***Association***	***Correlation***	***Causality***
An expected outcome is highly unlikely.	Plausible or possible at one level.	Probable and within a confident level of predictability.	Certain and totally predictable.

The concepts of association and correlation allow you to reason about the relationships between phenomena and still take into account intervening variables. The *association* linkage merely establishes that where one phenomenon is found, the other is likely to be found. No attempt is made to prove that the one causes the other. In fact, in this instance the two phenomena may not be directly related anyway. Rather, each may be closely related to a third factor. Suppose that there are no pawn shops in Auburn, but there are several in Columbus, 30 miles away. Ft. Benning is adjacent to Columbus. Why are there pawn shops and finance companies in a town near a large military installation? It is not reasonable to assert that the military base causes pawn shops to locate nearby, any more than it would be reasonable to claim that the pawn shops cause the military base to locate there. Somehow, the large population of military personnel in a metropolitan area creates a demand for access to ready cash between paydays. Thus, pawn shops are *associated* with military towns.

A *correlation* linkage is stronger than an association linkage: Not only are two phenomena typically found together, but they vary together. That is, changes in the scope or magnitude of one are accompanied by corresponding changes in the other. (Note: When one phenomenon increases and the other increases, the correlation is called *direct*. When one increases and the other decreases, the correlation is called *inverse*.) Here, the phenomena in question are part of a larger, interlocking system. Although they are strongly connected, the phenomena are affected by other factors that complicate the relationship and prevent you from being able to make predictions with certainty. You can still make predictions, but you are allowing for some randomness, error, or intervening variables. These predictions have the quality of *probability*, or a high degree of confidence that falls short of absolute certainty.

There are traditional tests of cause-effect reasoning to help you distinguish between necessary and sufficient causes. The difference is easy to illustrate. Suppose you walk into a dark room. You want some light provided by electricity. You know that to obtain this light there must be wires, a lightbulb, a lamp, and electricity, all in good working order. These are the *necessary* components of an electrically lighted room, but they are not sufficient in themselves. The room remains dark unless another element is added: You must turn on the light. The act of turning on the light, in this context, is a necessary *and* sufficient cause of lighting the room. Remember that phenomena necessary to creating an effect may not be *sufficient* to bringing about the effect. Only when causes are both necessary and sufficient can the effect occur.

This test is important in judging the adequacy of value and policy claims. If someone argues that it is necessary to spend more money on a problem to bring about a solution, this claim can be granted, and you can still refute the argument. You can say that although it is necessary to spend more money, say, to relieve poverty, money by itself will not end the problems of poverty because other factors are involved. If you can find important factors that could prevent the cause and effect relationship from taking place, you can disprove the relationship.

Typically, resolutions that emerge from problem areas of significant social concern involve complicated causal analysis.

In debate analysis, the *stock issues* approach begins with the question "Is there a need for a change?" In traditional debate theory, you have to prove that the present system *causes* the problem and that no changes, short of those contained within the debate resolution, would solve the problem. The second stock issue is "Will the plan solve the need?" To prove this point, you are required to prove that the plan will eliminate the cause of the problem—that is, that the plan will *cause* the solution. The third stock issue, "Is the plan desirable?" calls for examining other possible results of adopting the plan. All these stock issues require a high degree of causality between policies or policy changes and results.

On the other hand, the *systems analysis* method investigates all the relevant factors within the present system and compares the predictable results of manipulating one or another of these factors. Since systems analysis allows for secondary causal linkages, the connections may be weaker. They may range within the realm of correlation between policy change and outputs of the system. In both the stock issues and systems analysis methods of determining solutions, you need to have a basic understanding of cause-effect reasoning.

Sign Argument: Reasoning from Related Observation

Another form of reasoning is argument from sign. *Sign argument*, in its most simple form, says that when one thing occurs so does another. The phenomena are not causally linked, but they always (or almost always) occur either simultaneously or in succession. The *sign* is the observed phenomenon or phenomena. The *signified* is the phenomenon referred to or predicted by the sign. Consider a basic example:

> You are out on a walk in late summer and you observe the following: The squirrels are running about gathering nuts. Many have grown thick fur. Further, you notice that all the birds seem to have flown south. You observe that winter must be coming early. You read from the signs of nature an event that is about to take place.

Notice that the relationship here is not causal. Birds flying south and squirrels gathering nuts do not cause winter to come early. They are merely signs, or symptoms, of early winter. And they allow you to predict that winter is coming soon.

Evidence	*Claim*
Leaves are falling.	Winter must be coming.
Squirrels have thick fur.	
Birds have flown south.	

Reasoning
These characteristics are
associated with the advance
of winter.

Sign arguments are reversible. This means that you can reason from sign to signified, or from signified to sign. If someone told you that Jesuit College Preparator was an excellent school, for instance, you would expect a number of characteristics or qualities that would signify a quality high school. If these signs were *not* there, then you would question the assertion. Conversely, if you could agree on the qualities of an excellent school, then you might look for these signs in investigating a school you desire to attend.

Some sign arguments are infallible, while others are not. An infallible sign argument is difficult to refute, but it is hard to find. Most infallible signs, in fact, do not seem to invite much controversy. Darkness is taken for granted as a sign of evening, even though an eclipse occurs once in a great while. This is an almost infallible sign argument.

Fallible sign arguments, while more controversial, allow greater freedom to speculate. It may be the case that a certain combination of symptoms is a sign that disease is setting in. Even if your certainty level about this conclusion is not great, it might be better to act to prevent the disease—even if there is some chance the sign argument is wrong. Note that a fallible sign argument is weak to the extent that you can find similar objects signified by the same sign or group of signs. A good win-loss record for your basketball team might be a sign that your school has an excellent team and will do well in the play-offs. But it may also be a sign that the team has been lucky, that it has an easy schedule, or that it plays in a weak league. To the extent that alternative explanations can be introduced, the relationship between sign and signified is weakened.

Statistics: Reasoning from Scientific Methodology

There are two typical approaches to explaining statistics in a book of this kind. The first approach is to treat statistics as merely a collection of examples, a survey sample. In this approach, the reasoning form is the same as that of the generalization. Instead of citing a specific example or group of examples, you insert a number into your evidence. You would say something like "Big cars are gas guzzlers because the average EPA gas mileage estimates are lower for the Chevy Sportvan than they are for the Chevette." The same tests apply: Are the figures based on a large enough sample? Is the sample representative (that is, typical of the population of all members of the class)? Is there another sample with contrary findings?

The second approach to statistics is derived from more advanced scientific methodologies. There are more types of experimental methods than the survey sample and the average score. The objective of advanced scientific research methodologies is to study the precise relationships that exist in a process interaction. Control procedures for conducting research in such process interaction relationships make the method more scientific and the results more precise. A specific explanation of any of the statistical methodologies is not the purpose here. Rather, the authors want to point out a few of the qualities required of statistical studies generally.

Evidence	***Claim***
Studies show that solar energy is economical only as a supplement to a regular heating system, only for heating water, only in certain geographical areas.	Solar energy is not the answer to the energy crisis.

Reasoning
Statistical: I assume the
methodology of the studies
meets scientific standards.

Notice that in this form of reasoning, the connection between the data and the claim is not an assumption about the facts themselves, but rather the method of the study. In this example, the method is not made explicit. Suppose the particular evidence is well known in the field, and you are familiar with how the evidence was obtained. Suppose further that it is derived from a computer simulation of future energy use and based on projections of further energy costs (assuming a certain rate of price increases) and on current solar technology. A computer simulation calculates with great precision, but it is limited to the data programmed into it. Hence, the calculations are subject to possible variations if energy prices do not behave in the field as predicted in the simulation or if solar technology achieves a presently unforeseen breakthrough. In other words, whenever reasoning is based on a method of statistical analysis, the important thing to remember is that what is claimed is not based so much on the results of the calculation as it is on the quality—and the limitations—of the method used.

In testing reasoning derived from statistical methodologies, it is not enough merely to ask, "What's your methodology?" Finding out what methodology was used is only the starting point. It is also important to know the assumptions used in conducting the experiment. Small variations in assumptions can produce large variations in the calculations. Therefore, it makes little sense to test the results of the calculation without first examining the assumptions used in the methodology.

The findings of any scientific study are strictly limited to the population tested, under the conditions that prevailed during the test. It is contrary to the scientific method to make extensive extrapolations of the findings into realms where the same conditions do not exist. For example, if a study were conducted specifically to test the effectiveness of air bags in front-end collisions at speeds less than 50 mph, it would be fallacious to expand the statistical results to apply to all automobile accidents.

Authority: Reasoning from Source Credibility

Up to this point, this treatment of the forms of reasoning has been based on the different kinds of reasoning about facts. Generalization, analogy, cause-effect, sign, and statistical reasoning all begin with concrete data.

Forensic events also use reasoning based on evidence drawn from the opinion and testimony of authorities. The principles of reasoning involved differ considerably from any discussed so far.

Evidence	*Claim*
The president said the nation should modify its policy toward the People's Republic of China.	The nation should develop a modified policy toward the People's Republic of China.

Reasoning
Authority—I assume that
the president knows what
he is talking about.

In this sample of reasoning, the claim is based entirely on what the authority said. This argument contains no generalization, no statistics, no analogies, no scientific studies. All that is presented to you is the testimony of an authority.

The tests of reasoning from authority are basically the same as the tests of source credibility in rhetoric. First, is the source quoted an expert? Is there reason to believe the person is competent to voice an opinion? Second, is the source quoted trustworthy? Is there reason to trust the sincerity, objectivity, and good faith of the person? Third, does the evidence agree with that of other authorities? This question is important because no data is given to support the testimony; therefore, an independent check on the claim must be made.

After making these tests of reasoning from authority, you then apply the routine tests of evidence: Is the quotation consistent with the context from which it was taken (or consistent with other known statements of opinion from the same source)? Is it the most recent evidence? Was the statement meant literally or figuratively? This test is especially important when the source uses figures in the statement, such as "Ninety-nine times out of a hundred, we would not have run out of coal in the city during the winter months."

Authoritative evidence is qualitatively different from empirical or factual evidence. Each kind of evidence has its strengths and liabilities. When your argument is over propositions of fact, *empirical evidence*—evidence based on observation or experience— is superior to testimony and opinion evidence. When proving the significance (that is, the measurable scope or magnitude) of a problem area, it is better to use concrete evidence. However, when the issue is over goals, values, or principles, the opinion of respected authorities is preferable. For example, if you want to prove the extent of unemployment among African American youth in the nation's cities, simply cite the statistics given by the Department of Labor's Bureau of Labor Statistics. This form of evidence is better than a quotation from an authority who believes that "very high" unemployment exists. However, if you want to prove that unemployment rates among urban African American youth is "the worst social problem confronting America," this is a value judgment and would be more persuasive if quoted from civil rights leader Jesse Jackson or another respected authority.

SUMMARY

When research provides data relevant to the problem you are analyzing, your real task is to integrate your data and analysis into proof. This proof is necessary so that you can support the conclusions you draw about problems and solutions. In all forensic events, reasoning skills hold the key to eliciting the belief of others.

QUESTIONS FOR DISCUSSION

1. Explain the concept of proof.
2. Why is it important that an argument be based on evidence?
3. In reasoning by generalization, what are the major types of evidence used? Describe three tests that help to insure that your generalizations are sound.
4. How is reasoning by analogy helpful to someone who is listening to your argument? Define a false and an extended analogy.
5. Most events in forensics deal with reasoning from cause and effect relationships. Define reasoning based on cause-effect sequences. Provide an example. In your example, are there any intervening causes?
6. In the argument "Our school has a great football team and therefore should do well in city competition because it has lost only two of its last ten games," what type of reasoning is used? How could such an argument be challenged?
7. What is the value of using statistics to support your reasoned conclusions?
8. When examining statistics for use as evidence, why is it important to understand the methodology?
9. Forensic events often use evidence drawn from opinion, testimony, or both. To support the claim "The United States should maintain a balanced budget," find two pieces of evidence that rely upon authority. How do your authorities meet tests of source credibility suggested by rhetorical considerations? Next, apply routine tests of evidence.

ACTIVITIES

1. Using the claims provided below, demonstrate how you would prove or disprove each. At the end of the activity, be sure you have used all the forms of reasoning covered in this chapter.

   Claim: In the future, most Americans will drive small cars.

   Claim: The cost of houses has kept many first-time buyers out of the housing market.

Claim: A college diploma is a prerequisite for a good job.

Claim: A two-income family is becoming a necessity in today's society.

Claim: Sending U.S. combat troops on a peacekeeping mission to Bosnia will help the administration when negotiating a truce with Serb, Croat, and Muslim leaders.

Claim: Pollution is destroying the ozone layer.

2. Using a current issue, find examples of reasoning through generalization. Use magazines such as *Time, Newsweek,* and *U.S. News & World Report.* Diagram the generalizations.

3. Develop an analogy, an extended analogy, and a false analogy on each of the issues to follow:

Issue: The rise of juvenile delinquency and gangs in the United States.

Issue: The U.S. Postal Service versus private mail service.

Issue: The increasing federal deficit.

Issue: Student dress codes in secondary schools.

Issue: Funding of elementary and secondary education.

4. Using an issue affecting your personal life (for example, curfew, car privileges, allowance, and phone use), outline your position using cause-effect reasoning. Outline a refutation of your position. Be sure to look for flaws in the cause-effect relationship.

5. Using one of the following issues, develop an argument (for or against) with statistics. Use your local newspaper, the *New York Times, The Wall Street Journal,* or *Newsweek.* Demonstrate the validity of the statistics.

Issue: The relationship between U.S. trade policies and unemployment.

Issue: Decreasing inflation is indicative of a healthy economy.

Issue: Decreasing energy prices have increased the use of foreign oil.

Issue: Storage of toxic wastes—effects on the environment.

Issue: Safety of nuclear power plants.

6. Using a current issue, look for evidence drawn from opinion or testimony. Find three credible statements and three statements that do not meet the tests of credibility. Explain the differences between the two sets of statements.

PART TWO

DEBATE

WINNING DECISIONS IN ARGUMENTATION

Every year, thousands of students in junior and senior high schools, colleges, and universities participate in academic debates. They have different levels of success depending on many factors—motivation, dedication, and talent. The fact that you are studying this book is an indication of your desire to acquire or improve the skills necessary for success.

The preceding section of this text discussed the basic skills of analysis, research, and reasoning, which are applicable to many forensic activities. This section introduces the rules and strategy of policy debate.

FUNDAMENTAL CONSIDERATIONS IN DEBATE

OBJECTIVES AND KEY TERMS

After studying Chapter 5, you should be able to

1. Explain "burden of proof,"
2. Understand what is required for a *prima facie* case,
3. Explain "stock issues,"
4. Explain "systems analysis," and
5. Understand how to design a plan of action in response to the resolution.

After reading this chapter, you should understand the following terms:

affirmative	**systems analysis**
burden of proof	**topicality**
burden of refutation	
fiat power	
negative	
plank	
prima facie case	
status quo	
stock issues analysis	

A cademic debate is a forum for developing the skills of advocacy. Within clearly prescribed limits, you are encouraged to analyze complex issues, reason from your evidence to solid conclusions, think quickly in the face of your opponents' arguments and refute them logically, and defend your case all the way through to the end of the final rebuttals. Hence, debate offers an ideal setting in which to develop your ability to advocate public policy, to dispute values, and to learn how to test propositions of fact.

Debate is an intensive activity. The breadth of the debate resolution requires you to gain a great deal of knowledge about the facts and issues involved. Moreover, in competition with debaters from other schools, you are required to be well informed to be able to refute their arguments as well as to be prepared to prove your own. Since policy debate is a team contest, you have a partner to help you, and of course the whole squad in your school will work together in preparing for tournaments. Even so, if you want to succeed, debate requires a significant investment of time, thought, and work. It takes both time and experience to master all the elements necessary to be a championship debater. Mastering the knowledge and skills involved in activities such as band or chorus, athletics, or drama involves high levels of determination and commitment. This level of involvement is no less true in debate and other forensic events.

You will find that debate pays off in personal achievement and satisfaction. Even one year's participation will provide you with valuable skills for organizing your thoughts, thinking logically, and speaking with confidence and impact. The longer you stay involved in debate, the more you will learn—and win. Debate serves another important personal function: Your association with a group of people working together toward the common goal of excellence in debate can be very satisfying. You will enjoy a sense of belonging and acceptance, a sense of worthwhile achievement and personal growth as a part of an important activity, and a sense of contribution. Even if the tangible results of a season of competition seem modest in terms of trophies and awards won, the intangible satisfactions will ultimately loom large in your feelings. For these reasons, many adults recall their experiences as debaters with pride and warmth.

DEBATE AS CONFRONTATION

There are two sides in a debate: the affirmative and the negative. The side in favor of the resolution affirms it, and the side opposed to the resolution negates it. These two sides confront one another in the debate and place their arguments about the resolution before the judge. Based on the arguments developed in this confrontation, the judge decides the winner of the debate. The judge is an impartial person with regard to the resolution. The decision is not based on how the judge feels about the resolution personally, but strictly on whether your arguments have adequately supported your position. Thus, the debate is won or lost on the basis of your skills in analyzing the resolution for the judge, proving your arguments with superior reasoning and evidence, and refuting the arguments and case presented by your opponents.

When you participate in a debate, the confrontation emphasis is always on the issues and evidence presented. Debate is a confrontation of ideas rather than personalities. For this reason, debate permits you to argue and disagree with your opponents without being personally disagreeable. In fact, sarcasm and insults have no place in debate, and most judges will severely penalize you if you resort to such behavior. By keeping the debate on an intellectual level, you learn to make decisions about the significant problems and proposed policies of your time through reasoning and facts, rather than emotions.

Debate is the most competitive of the forensic events. In student congress, debate is used as a decision-making tool, but the objective of that debate is to win the support of the other members of the congress. To this end, the bills and resolutions may be amended either to remove barriers to agreement or to add elements designed to make them more acceptable to the majority. Cooperation is key.

This objective does not exist in debate. The affirmative and negative sides are expected to remain firmly committed to their side of the resolution to the very end of the debate. It is not your task to come to an agreement with your opponents over whether the resolution should be accepted. It is your task to convince the judge of the reasonableness of voting for your side and against your opponents. The rules and procedures of debate are designed to provide you with a fair, equal opportunity to win the judge's decision. The debate format, which emphasizes confrontation of evidence, ideas, and arguments, allows you to take this competitive stance with dignity, respect for each other, and, ultimately, zest and enjoyment. Although competing debate teams are adversaries during the debate, it is possible for them to remain friends both during the round and afterward. In much the same way, the prosecutor and the defense attorney in a courtroom can remain friends despite their opposing roles in the trial. Indeed, friendships frequently grow among debaters as they gain mutual respect for the forensic skills each possesses.

ANALYSIS IN DEBATE

In academic debate, as in other forensic events, analysis is a crucial skill. To understand the methods of analysis in debate, you should first have a clear idea of the aim or objective of the contest. Most important, it should be noted that policy debate involves some special assumptions about how argument emerges and how it should proceed. By understanding these rules, you will be able to begin to construct speeches and take sides in the argument.

A resolution of policy requires an affirmative and a negative. The *affirmative* is the side championing the resolution. The *negative* plays devil's advocate, closely questioning the resolution's necessity and desirability. As policy debate is presently set up, all resolutions are designed to call for a change from the present system. To affirm the resolution is to say in effect that the status quo is in some way defective and a better alternative is possible. The reason for creating resolutions that mandate change is that debate itself is thought to be a policy-testing process. A good policy should be able to withstand severe criticism. Although it is possible, and even desirable, to debate the value of existing policies, the educators who created academic policy debate believed that it is better to discuss new alternatives. The affirmative, then, proposes. The negative opposes.

Debates are judged by a neutral third party. The affirmative resolution is submitted to a judge for approval. On the other hand, the negative argues that the judge should not grant approval or even that the judge should render firm disapproval. Note that a judge need not believe the resolution is a bad idea to vote negative.

He or she may simply say that there is not enough proof to tell whether it is good or bad and so may withhold consent.

The Burden of Proof

How does the judge know when an affirmative has presented enough proof to justify assent? Debate theory provides guidelines for making a fair allocation of responsibility between the affirmative and the negative. Because judges disagree about proof standards, however, the guidelines for determining the minimal level of proof required to earn a decision vary. Current opinion on this subject is explained briefly here; additional explanations will be provided later, as you explore case strategies available to both the affirmative and the negative sides in a debate.

A good starting point is to realize that to deserve the judge's decision for a proposed debate resolution, the affirmative must prove that the resolution merits adoption. It is not sufficient merely to suggest a change in the present system of dealing with a problem area. Traditionally, change is not a good in and of itself. The responsibility to prove a case for the resolution is known as the affirmative *burden of proof*. The affirmative must prove something before it can hope to win the judge's decision.

The phrase "burden of proof" has a special meaning here. You understand, of course, that each debater in the round, whether affirmative or negative, has the burden to prove any asserted argument with evidence. The mere assertion of a claim is rarely accepted as a valid argument. In this broad sense, all debaters have a burden of proving.

Beyond this general burden, however, the affirmative has a specific requirement to prove its case for the resolution. Unless the case is proven by the affirmative, the negative has every right to expect the judge's decision. To turn this equation around, the negative does not have to prove that the resolution should be rejected. If the judge were asked to render a decision prior to hearing either side speak, the decision would be for the negative because no case has been offered to support the resolution to change the present policy.

What must the affirmative prove? The usual answer to this question is that the affirmative must present a case sufficient to convince a reasonable and prudent person that the proposed resolution merits her or his acceptance. Such a convincing case is called a *prima facie* case, one that is convincing on its face, or at first glance. If the affirmative fails to offer a prima facie case for the resolution, then the impartial judge cannot give assent. On the other hand, if you succeed in presenting a prima facie case, then the negative has the burden to refute it and convince the judge not to accept the resolution. Just as the affirmative has the burden of proof with regard to the resolution, the negative has the burden of refutation with regard to the affirmative case.

What constitutes a prima facie case? Analysis. In debate, *analysis* means breaking the suggested proposal into the essential elements that enable a judge to see the reasons the proposal should be accepted.

Stock Issues Analysis

One form of debate analysis is called *stock issues analysis*. A series of questions about the resolution under debate makes up the stock issues. This is the most traditional and most widely understood form of analysis because it has been used in academic debate for decades. To understand the logic of the stock issues, recall that the debate *resolution* is a proposed action to change the present system of dealing with the problem. You assume that the debate judge does not know why the change is being proposed, and then you use the following questions to reveal the information necessary to convince the judge to accept the proposal:

1. *Is there harm in the present system?* This is the first stock issue. You must show that a harmful condition exists in the status quo. Unemployment, risk to national security, disease and death, or the violation of fundamental rights might all be claimed as harms. Most stock issues judges believe that the problem in the present system must also be proven to be *significant.*

2. *Is the harm inherent in the status quo?* One might find a significant problem, but if it is likely to go away of its own accord, no alternation in the status quo would be necessary. For instance, a large public works program to solve unemployment might be ill advised if the unemployment problem is cyclical or temporary. If the status quo is capable of solving its problems through existing mechanisms, then the resolution is not necessary.

3. *Will the proposal solve the problem?* Once you have shown that the problem exists and will continue despite every effort to correct it, you must show how the proposed change would work to remove the causes of the problem and thus allow for a solution.

These three questions create the stock issues in debate. Notice that the affirmative must prove all of them because if any one of them is answered in the negative, then the judge will not accept the proposal. Who would want to make a change without justification?

The stock issues approach assumes that the judge has an initial presumption that the present system is dealing adequately with the problem area. You overcome this presumption by using the stock issues to show the following: There is a need to change the present system; your proposed change is the only way to achieve the best solution to the problem; the program would work; and it would be desirable to make the change. If you fail to prove any one of these arguments, then the presumption is that the present system should not be changed, and things should continue exactly as they are.

The stock issues method of analysis is criticized largely because of its basic presumption that the present system for dealing with problems can and will continue unchanged unless a positive decision to change it is made. In reality, the present system itself is undergoing changes all the time due to changing conditions. For instance, as the population grows, the economy alters, and the *status quo*—the current situation—changes accordingly. New problems arise and old problems change in character, so national policies are constantly being adjusted to accommodate natural changes in the environment.

Systems Analysis

Systems analysis is a method used to determine what changes should be made in laws and policies dealing with problems. Rather than presuming a static, unchanging environment, systems analysis presumes that everything is in a state of constant change. By keeping a careful watch on the situation, it is possible to make predictions and projections about where evolving problems are likely to arise within the system. Thus, the underlying principle of systems analysis is to try to make ongoing decisions about the kinds of changes you want, rather than the simple decision about whether you want to make any change at all. If change is inevitable, it would be better to adjust the policies to control the direction and extent of change, rather than do nothing and allow the situation to undergo changes on its own.

As a method of debate analysis, the systems analysis approach calls for each side to uphold a particular system for controlling the changes the present system is undergoing. The debate resolution upheld by the affirmative represents only one possible method of dealing with the problem posed by the resolution. The negative must oppose the affirmative approach to the problem. It may do this by defending the status quo, making a counterproposal, or some combination of the two.

A critical difference may now be observed between the logical requirements for a prima facie case using the traditional stock issues method of analysis and the more recent case form using systems analysis. In the former, the affirmative has the burden of proof to overcome an initial presumption in favor of the present system. Unless this presumption is overcome, the judge must vote for maintaining the present system. However, in systems analysis, the prejudgment in favor of maintaining the present system is greatly diminished. This does not mean that the judge has no standard criteria for accepting or rejecting the resolution; presumption still exists in the debate. However, instead of initially presuming that the present system should be maintained, the judge reserves presumption for the proposed system that affords the greatest probability of benefit against the least measure of risk. The one with the most favorable cost-benefit ratio becomes the one that the judge presumes is deserving of the decision in the debate.

INTERPRETING THE RESOLUTION

So far, you have seen that the objective of debate is to convince the judge that the resolution should be accepted or rejected. The resolution represents a proposed changed in the present system for dealing with a problem area. The method of analyzing the resolution is to narrow it to its essential elements or issues.

Limiting the Resolution

The national high school debate resolution is always stated broadly. For instance, the 1995–96 debate resolution is "Resolved: That the United States government should substantially change its foreign policy toward the People's Republic of China."

This is a broad resolution. Who should be able to interpret what changes are required? There are quite a few possibilities, and not all of them are consistent. Increases and decreases in economic assistance to China might both be "substantial changes." Another question concerns the meaning of the term *foreign policy*. Would it include changes in immigration policy, or trade policy, or are those distinct areas? Finally, who is to determine what a "substantial" change might be, and how it is to be measured?

The affirmative has the opportunity to interpret the resolution and establish the grounds for debate. It need not defend all possible interpretations of the resolution; there is no time to do so, and the different interpretations might well be contradictory. So long as the affirmative interpretation is reasonable, the debate should proceed without objection. Even if the judge does not agree completely with how the affirmative has defined its terms, the question of adherence to the topic (or what is called *topicality* by debaters) should not be at issue. However, once the negative claims that an affirmative interpretation of the resolution is unreasonably narrow or even completely incorrect, the question of the meaning of the topic is as debatable as any other issue.

Designing the Plan

The affirmative team also has an obligation to present a specific plan for consideration. It is not enough for this team to focus on existing problems in a reasonably limited area; it must also provide a plan for a solution that could be implemented. The plan must include certain minimal components, or *planks*. These include 1) the *principle*, or the policy goal that the plan is designed to accomplish; and 2) the *mechanisms*, or the specific actions that must be taken to implement the policy goal. The mechanisms may include the establishment of a new agency that has the power to implement the plan; the revision, reinterpretation, or amendment of an existing statute, legal procedure, or treaty; or a change in executive or administrative action.

How can the affirmative team ensure that its plan would be adopted? After all, it has offered the plan partly because the present system has *not* responded to the problem. Fortunately for the affirmative, policy debate revolves around the question of whether the plan *should* be adopted, not whether it *will*. Most judges accept that, in offering its plan, the affirmative operates under the scope of *fiat power*. The word *fiat* is Latin for "let it be done," so *fiat power* means that the affirmative is able to "command" its plan into operation. Generally, the affirmative has the power to do whatever the agent of the resolution, usually the U.S. government, would normally do to put a policy in place. Ordinarily the plan is presented in the form of a proposed law for Congress to pass, but it might also include judicial action or executive orders where appropriate. The affirmative may also mandate funding and enforcement provisions for its plan, just as the government would.

Beginning debaters are sometimes confused by the concept of fiat. It is important to remember that the affirmative's fiat power has limits. The affirmative may assume that its plan will *come into existence*, but not that it will necessarily solve the problem. Reasonable negative objections to the workability of the plan, or arguments that the plan will cause significant disadvantages, cannot be answered with the "magic wand" of fiat power. Furthermore, while the affirmative can certainly ensure the "passage" of its plan, they cannot ensure that public or political attitudes against it will change once it has been adopted.

SUMMARY

Regardless of how much or how little experience you have with debate, you will quickly recognize that debate deals with argumentation and that it involves confrontation. The formats and time elements that control debate have a definite purpose. The side that each team assumes in a debate has clearly defined obligations. Your debate skills are built on your understanding of basic concepts, such as the burden of proof, types of analysis, and the function of the resolution. As you move into building cases, these are the fundamental considerations that will guide you.

QUESTIONS FOR DISCUSSION

1. What is the difference between a resolution and a plan? If a resolution is a call for action, why is a plan necessary?

2. In debate, the affirmative and negative present their arguments about a resolution before a judge. How does the judge make a decision about the resolution? What is the advantage of being evaluated on the confrontation of ideas rather than personalities? What role should personal prejudice play in the evaluation of a debate?

3. In a debate, what is the fundamental difference between the affirmative and the negative?

4. In debate, the affirmative is said to have the "burden of proof." What does this mean? What is it that the affirmative must prove?

5. What does prima facie mean? What happens if the affirmative does not present a prima facie case?

6. In the stock issues form of debate analysis, a series of basic questions are raised about the resolution. What are these three questions?

7. What is systems analysis? In systems analysis, how is the negative's responsibility changed? How are the requirements for a prima facie case different under systems analysis from under a stock issues model?

ACTIVITIES

1. Listen to a debate and be sure to take notes on the arguments. What type of debate analysis (systems analysis or stock issues) was used by the affirmative? Did it work well for the affirmative? Why?

2. Watch a segment of *60 Minutes, 20/20,* or a similar news magazine program. By academic debate standards, did the reporter meet the burden of proof when presenting the news story? Why?

3. Using stock issues analysis, look at the following examples of problem areas and proposed solutions. Do the examples meet the three stock issues? Why?

    Problem area: Unemployment is increasing because of increased foreign imports.

    Solution: Tighten restrictions on imported products that compete in industries in the U.S. experiencing increased unemployment.

Problem area: Population in developing countries is increasing faster than these countries can provide for their new people.

Solution: Family size would be restricted to two children per family in developing countries in order to stabilize population growth.

Problem area: Illegal immigration is on the rise.

Solution: Implement new programs for stemming illegal immigration at international borders and entry points.

A REMINDER ABOUT ETHICAL ARGUMENTATION

Before you go on to the next chapter on debate presentation, review the guidelines debaters and advocates in general are expected to follow.

- **Do** summarize an opponent's arguments.
- **Do** state objections to a contention.
- **Do** consider what will happen if neither side wins a particular argument.
- **Do** deal with opposing arguments in a calm, efficient, and respectful tone.
- **Don't** practice refutation with the childlike "Yes, it is, No, it isn't, Yes, it is..." argumentation strategy.
- **Don't** employ shallow tactics such as overwhelming your opponent with a flood of questions. (This tactic may come back to haunt you.)
- **Don't** get in a rut. (Reassess your strategies periodically. Change tactics occasionally.)
- **Don't** forget to be critical of your own constructive arguments.

From *Strategic Debate*, Roy V. Wood and Lynn Goodnight, 5th Edition, 1995, National Textbook Company.

CHAPTER 6

PRESENTATION OF THE DEBATE

OBJECTIVES AND KEY TERMS

After studying Chapter 6, you should be able to

1. Describe the different debate formats,
2. Describe the concept of preparation time,
3. Explain the obligations of each speaker in a debate round,
4. Organize a speech for presentation,
5. Explain the concept of and formulate an affirmative or negative brief,
6. Understand the concept of flowing a debate, and
7. Use a system of abbreviations for flowing a debate.

After reading this chapter, you should understand the following terms:

briefs	rebuttal speech
constructive speech	solvency
cross-examination	speaker responsibilities
flowing a debate	standard debate
negative block	tags
preparation time	

In traditional academic debate, a team is composed of two speakers. In a round of debate, there are two teams—one designated as the affirmative side and the other as the negative. Four constructive speeches and four rebuttals are presented during the debate. Each speaker, then, is obliged to give a constructive and a rebuttal speech. Cross-examination debate builds on traditional academic debate, providing each debater the opportunity to question his or her opponent between the constructive speeches. The duties of the affirmative and negative during constructives and rebuttals are the same for traditional and cross-examination debate. Other duties that cross-examination debate entails are discussed in Chapter 9.

The *constructive speech* is the longer of the two designated speeches each team member gives. Its name indicates the fact that all case building (construction through the introduction of arguments) must be done during that speech. In the affirmative constructive speeches, the justification for change and the method of change must be presented. The negative, on the other hand, must set up the negative philosophy, any defense of the present system, and objections to the affirmative plan during the constructive speeches.

Rebuttal speeches are delivered after the constructive speeches have been completed and are much shorter than constructive speeches. Their purpose is to attack and defend contentions introduced into the debate during the constructive speeches. The traditional rule of debate is that no new arguments may be introduced in rebuttal speeches. Beginning debaters sometimes misunderstand this rule to mean that nothing can be said during rebuttals that has not been said before. This is not true. Additional *evidence* not only may but should be heard. Extensions of arguments already introduced should be made. However, a whole new line of argumentation cannot be introduced in the rebuttal speech. For example, if the negative has not debated the topicality of the affirmative case in one of the two constructive speeches, it may *not* be discussed in rebuttal. If, however, topicality has been introduced as an issue in a constructive speech, it can be developed and extended in rebuttal.

PURPOSE OF POSITIONS

Affirmative

In any debate, the affirmative position should affirm the resolution. Speeches given by the affirmative are designed to explain what the resolution means and to show that its adoption will be advantageous to society. The affirmative supports the resolution calling for change by showing how the status quo is lacking. In this way the role of the affirmative is comparable to that of the prosecuting attorney in a court trial. The affirmative charges that the present system is failing to accomplish a desired outcome. Because of its attack role, the affirmative must speak first, for the negative cannot defend the present system until it knows the charges against the system. By the same token, since the affirmative attempts to prove guilt, it is allowed to make the final summation to the judge. Thus, the affirmative speakers begin and end the debate.

Negative

The negative role in the debate is to deny that the affirmative rationale is true. Once the affirmative introduces its charges against the innocence of the status quo, the negative must immediately employ a number of alternative strategies to defend the present system and to impeach the advisability of the proposed change. This basic position in the debate also determines the order and sequence of the negative speeches.

FORMATS OF DEBATE

In academic team debate, two formats seem to be popular. The first is the traditional time and arrangement that is sometimes referred to as *Oxford* or *standard debate*. Some state activities leagues and invitational debate tournaments still use this format, in which there are speeches and rebuttals, but no cross-examination. A few tournaments offer standard debate for novice teams, enabling beginners to work on debate fundamentals before adding in the cross-examination periods. Usually after one semester (or at the most, one year), the debater will begin participating in cross-examination debate. In standard debate format, the speeches occur in the following order and times:

First Affirmative Constructive	8 minutes
First Negative Constructive	8 minutes
Second Affirmative Constructive	8 minutes
Second Negative Constructive	8 minutes

First Negative Rebuttal	5 minutes
First Affirmative Rebuttal	5 minutes
Second Negative Rebuttal	5 minutes
Second Affirmative Rebuttal	5 minutes

The second format used in academic debate is called *cross-examination*. At the high school level, the cross-examination format has been used for a number of years by the National Forensic League. In this format the speeches occur as follows:

First Affirmative Constructive	8 minutes
Negative Cross-Examination of First Affirmative Speaker	3 minutes
First Negative Constructive	8 minutes
Affirmative Cross-Examination of First Negative Speaker	3 minutes
Second Affirmative Constructive	8 minutes
Negative Cross-Examination of Second Affirmative Speaker	3 minutes
Second Negative Constructive	8 minutes
Affirmative Cross-Examination of Second Negative Speaker	3 minutes

Rebuttal speeches are in the same order as they are in standard debate, and they are generally five minutes in length. Specific information on cross-examination debate can be found in Chapter 9.

PREPARATION TIME

Most leagues and tournaments permit each team a certain amount of *preparation time* to be used as it sees fit between speeches. The most common practice is the *eight-minute rule*, the allotment to each team of a cumulative total of eight minutes between speeches during the debate that can be used for preparing to speak. Time is tallied by the timekeeper, who informs each team of the passage of its preparation time. There is no specification as to how the debaters may allocate their time. Thus, the negative may choose to use two, four, six, or eight of its eight minutes before the first negative speech, giving that speaker whatever preparation time he or she needs. The affirmative may choose to use most of its preparation time before the first affirmative rebuttal so that this important speech can be carefully planned and organized. This practice has also been used with five or ten minutes of prep time instead of eight minutes. Always check the tournament rules to determine which practice is to be followed.

OVERVIEW OF SPEAKER RESPONSIBILITIES

Details concerning the duties and opportunities of each side and each speaker position in a debate will be presented later; what follows is an overview of the speakers' responsibilities to help you understand the rules of the game. After all, as complex a game as chess may be, it must be learned by understanding the initial movement of the pieces.

During constructive speeches, the affirmative and the negative speakers have a chance to develop and critique contending positions. Rebuttal speeches follow the constructives and are much shorter. Rebuttals are used to extend criticisms already begun in constructives and to sum up the affirmative and negative positions.

Note the sequence of speeches in a debate. The affirmative always goes first. The debate is commenced by the affirmative asserting that a resolution is true, and by its presentation of a prima facie case, including the plan. In most parts of the country, the first negative constructive follows by presenting the entire array of negative arguments against the affirmative case: attacks against the affirmative stock issues or advantage; possible disadvantages or counterplans to the affirmative proposal; and, if necessary, attacks on the affirmative's topicality. (In some regions the first negative attacks only the affirmative case, with disadvantages reserved for the second negative constructive.) The second affirmative constructive speech attempts to rebuild the affirmative case and to offer responses to the other negative positions.

The second negative constructive and the first negative rebuttal, taken together, are known as the *negative block*. Properly used, this thirteen-minute block of time, interrupted only by the cross-examination of the second negative constructive, is a powerful weapon. It is important that members of the negative team *divide the labor of argument* so that they do not duplicate each other's efforts. For instance, the second negative constructive might concentrate on extension of the disadvantage arguments, while the first negative rebuttal might focus on the lack of *solvency*—the issue of whether a plan will meet its goal—in the affirmative case.

The first affirmative rebuttal must respond to all the negative argumentation. Note that by the time of the first affirmative rebuttal, the negative will have had 13 minutes to develop the opposing position. Obviously, the first affirmative rebuttal must respond succinctly to new arguments and also respond to important arguments made in rebuttal.

The last two speeches in the debate sum up final positions. The second negative rebuttal selects, from all the objections to the affirmative proposal made in the round, the few that are most important. The second affirmative rebuttal answers the remaining negative objections and returns to the affirmative case to remind the judge of its merits.

General Considerations of Presentation

Planning

Affirmative and Negative Briefs

Debate is a unique and exciting combination of speaking from both a prepared and an extemporaneous stance. Of the eight speeches in a debate, only the first affirmative constructive speech should be totally prepared in advance. All other speeches, although they may contain elements that have been prepared in advance, must be responsive to what has gone before them in the debate. If this is not the case, the debate will lack the essential element of clash. It will not only be dull; it will be almost impossible for the negative to win.

Even so, teams can prepare a great deal in advance for use in the debate. The affirmative should have attempted to anticipate every possible line of argumentation against its case. The team should have thought through its own analysis in response to these arguments, located evidence to prove that analysis, and organized that material in advance. Affirmatives frequently develop affirmative briefs. Advance preparation can also be done by the negative in the form of negative briefs, analysis, and evidence organized in advance for cases that the team has already met on that year's topic. Such advance preparation is a good way to guarantee organized, thoughtful responses to the opposition.

When making preparations for a debate, remember that no two teams will argue in exactly the same way on a given issue. Therefore, be sure that you relate your prepared materials to the specific case you are debating during a given round. If your responses sound canned, most judges will rank you very low on analysis, and you will probably miss vital points and argue off-center to the voting issues in the debate.

A *brief* is a method of organizing issues and evidence. On some topics there will be arguments recurrent enough that they will appear in almost every round of a debate. The negative should always be able to question affirmative arguments spontaneously, but it also helps to prepare thoughtfully. This is the function of a brief. To prepare a brief, three things must be done. First, the debater should find evidence pertaining to the general topic. If the resolution calls for a universal system of employment guarantees, for example, the negative will almost certainly have to prove that unemployment is not harmful. Evidence stating that unemployment does not cause harm is thus useful. This evidence should be categorized by specific type of harms: unemployment does not cause (1) stress, (2) alcoholism, (3) mental illness, or (4) spouse abuse—to name just a few. Second, the categorized evidence should be placed with its appropriate label on a sheet of paper. Only one or two of the best pieces of evidence should be written under each point because time is limited. Third, the brief should contain a short explanation as to why the negative evidence is conclusive. Again, the more concise the brief, the better. (See the illustration of a topicality brief on the healthcare debate, page 92.)

Many debaters find it useful to develop briefs with first, second, and third lines of evidence and responses. Some go as far as rebuttal responses. As the brief grows longer and more complicated, a system must be devised for easy use. Not all the evidence or responses on a brief will be read in every round. To stay organized and not waste precious speaking time, the debater can do one of two things. The first is to enclose all briefs in plastic sheets. Once this is done, the debater can then mark the evidence and responses to be read with a grease pencil or with paper clips. At the end of the round, the marks can be wiped clean or the clips can be removed, and the brief will be ready for use in the next round.

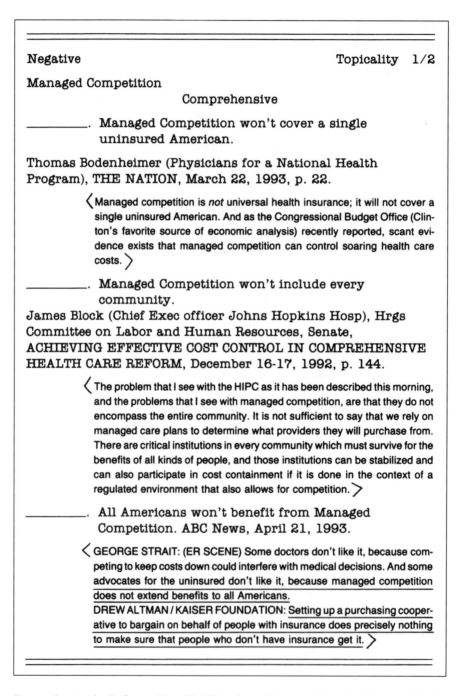

Negative   Topicality   1/2

Managed Competition

Comprehensive

_____. Managed Competition won't cover a single
                uninsured American.

Thomas Bodenheimer (Physicians for a National Health
Program), THE NATION, March 22, 1993, p. 22.

> Managed competition is *not* universal health insurance; it will not cover a
> single uninsured American. And as the Congressional Budget Office (Clin-
> ton's favorite source of economic analysis) recently reported, scant evi-
> dence exists that managed competition can control soaring health care
> costs.

_____. Managed Competition won't include every
                community.

James Block (Chief Exec officer Johns Hopkins Hosp), Hrgs
Committee on Labor and Human Resources, Senate,
ACHIEVING EFFECTIVE COST CONTROL IN COMPREHENSIVE
HEALTH CARE REFORM, December 16-17, 1992, p. 144.

> The problem that I see with the HIPC as it has been described this morning,
> and the problems that I see with managed competition, are that they do not
> encompass the entire community. It is not sufficient to say that we rely on
> managed care plans to determine what providers they will purchase from.
> There are critical institutions in every community which must survive for the
> benefits of all kinds of people, and those institutions can be stabilized and
> can also participate in cost containment if it is done in the context of a
> regulated environment that also allows for competition.

_____. All Americans won't benefit from Managed
                Competition. ABC News, April 21, 1993.

> GEORGE STRAIT: (ER SCENE) Some doctors don't like it, because com-
> peting to keep costs down could interfere with medical decisions. And some
> advocates for the uninsured don't like it, because managed competition
> does not extend benefits to all Americans.
> DREW ALTMAN / KAISER FOUNDATION: Setting up a purchasing cooper-
> ative to bargain on behalf of people with insurance does precisely nothing
> to make sure that people who don't have insurance get it.

From *Strategic Debate*, Roy V. Wood and Lynn Goodnight, 5th Edition, 1995, National Textbook Company.

Flowing the Debate

Vital to successful debating is your ability to listen carefully, flow arguments accurately, analyze your own responses, and organize needed materials. These tasks must all be accomplished during the time in which the opposition is speaking and during any additional preparation time that the rules of the particular tournament allow you. Nothing can substitute for accurate *flowing* of a debate—that is, taking notes. You cannot maintain an organized response to the opposition if you do not have its arguments accurately recorded. (See the sample solvency flow on the next two pages.)

There are as many methods and arrangements for flowing a debate as there are debaters. Your own coach and members of your squad can show you how to place your notes of the debate arguments on a *flow sheet*. But there are important guidelines that any beginning debater needs to remember.

1. *Use a page of paper for each major issue in the round.* It is best to have room for as many arguments on a disadvantage or topicality (for example) as your opponents may wish to generate. Try to leave lots of margin at the top and bottom of each page; leave as much space as you can between arguments.

2. *Flow speeches vertically, in the order in which arguments are made* (but remember to change pieces of paper when a new issue is introduced).

3. *Flow arguments horizontally, opposite what they answer.* This is the best way to preserve a record of the clash on any particular issue.

4. *Listen first for headlines or "tags," then for evidence.* Novice debaters are sometimes overwhelmed by the volume of arguments in competitive debate. If you begin by trying to take down too much at once, you may fall behind and miss crucial arguments. If you miss an evidence citation, you can usually ask for it later, but it is impossible to refute arguments that you have failed to flow.

Certainly, it is important to learn to listen carefully to evidence. Listen particularly well to vital elements, such as the date, the qualifications of the source, and any limiting words, such as *may* or *projected*. Flow these evidence characteristics; they often become

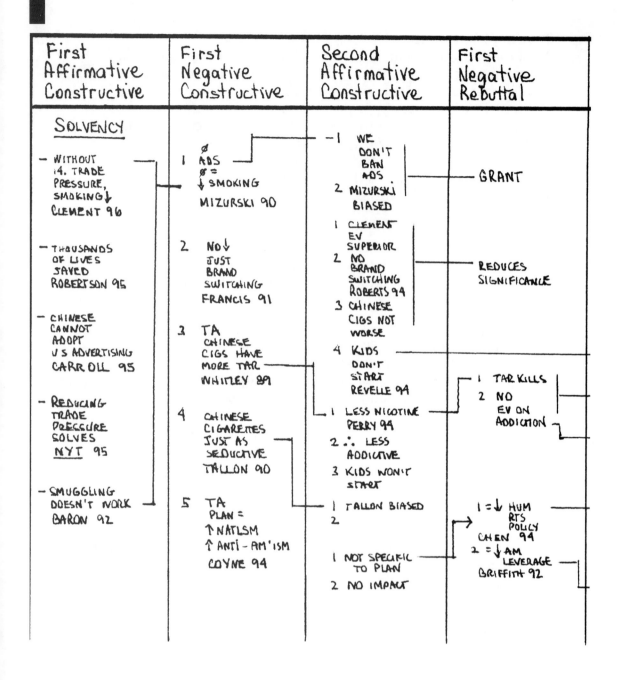

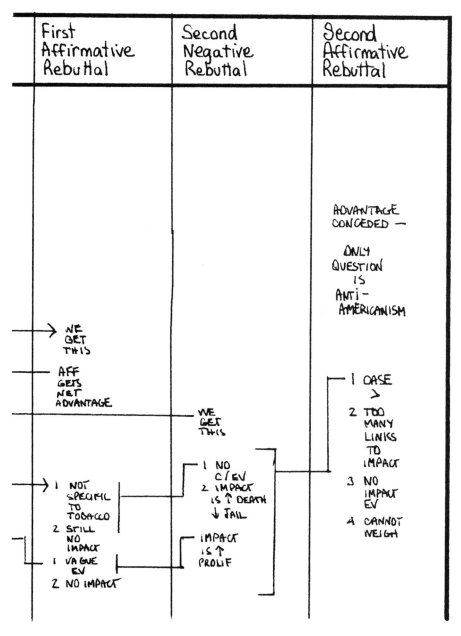

First Affirmative Rebuttal	Second Negative Rebuttal	Second Affirmative Rebuttal
		ADVANTAGE CONCEDED — ONLY QUESTION IS ANTI-AMERICANISM
WE GET THIS		
AFF GETS NET ADVANTAGE		1 CASE >
	WE GET THIS	2 TOO MANY LINKS TO IMPACT
1 NOT SPECIFIC TO TOBACCO	1 NO C/EV 2 IMPACT IS ↑ DEATH ↓ JAIL	3 NO IMPACT EV
2 STILL NO IMPACT	IMPACT IS ↑ PROLIF	4 CANNOT WEIGH
1 VAGUE EV 2 NO IMPACT		

Resolution under debate:
RESOLVED: That the United States government should substantially change its foreign policy toward the People's Republic of China.

Symbols and Abbreviations

T	topicality
Inh	inherency
DA	disadvantage
PMA	plan-meets-advantage
PMN	plan-meets need
Circ	circumvention
PS	present system
SQ	status quo
TA	turnaround
CP	counterplan
Sig	significance
OBS	observation
U	unique
NU	non-unique
thr	threshold
$	dollars, money, finance, revenue, funding
MR	minor repair
EXT	extratopicality
x	dropped argument
EV	evidence
Pop	popularity
CD	card (evidence)
Ø	no evidence; dropped
NE	no evidence used
??	(used before an argument or card to show you're not sure you flowed it correctly)
CX	statement from cross-ex.
>	greater than
<	less than
↑	increase
↓	decrease
⇏	causes does not cause
=	equals, is
≠	is not
w/	with
w/o	without
w/in	within
b/c	because
avg	average
∴	therefore

crucial in the debate. To get as much information as possible you will need to develop a system of shorthand (or abbreviations). Using symbols such as = for equals or > for outweighs will enable you to get down more information.

If you are new to debate, you should not expect to be able to take a perfect flow at your first tournament. Flowing is a complex skill; it takes months or even years of debating to learn to do it well. A good way to develop the skill quickly is to do flowing drills with your partner or a colleague. Begin with simple speeches, then graduate to speeches that are faster or have a larger number of arguments. Compare your flow with the actual material in the speech that has been given.

The cardinal rule is that you must flow the debate. If you can interpret the flow accurately, you have done good work.

Organizing

No single debate skill is more important than organization. No matter how brilliant your argument or how cogent your evidence, if neither the judge, the opposition, nor your partner can decipher which of the opposition's contentions you are addressing, then you have not advanced a coherent position and have lost most of the impact of the points presented.

Headline Value
The first step in making arguments clear is to word them with headline value. Imagine for a minute what the morning newspaper would look like without the presence of bold, concise headlines. None of the news articles would stand out, so most of the news would be "lost" in a great mass of black print. By the same token, if you begin speaking and reading evidence in a debate without labeling arguments with brief, specific headlines (or "tags"), then you may not be able to distinguish one argument from another. You should word contentions concisely, and you should use that form each time you refer to that argument. This headline becomes a point of reference for both teams and for the judge. The argument is less likely to get lost if it is properly headlined.

Internal Structure
In addition to headline value, each argument should have internal structure. You should use numerical and alphabetical designations

for the arguments you present so that they are easy to flow and to relate to the case of the opposition. For both the affirmative's constructive presentation and for negative and affirmative refutation, the internal structure of arguments is vital. The affirmative construction of each contention should (1) state the contention headline, (2) explain the contention, (3) evidence the contention, and (4) restate the contention. In refutation, both teams should (1) state the contention to be addressed, (2) structure answers as subpoints and evidence each one, (3) relate answers to the total impact of the opposition's case, and (4) restate the contention briefly.

External Structure

The external structure of your speech is important, too. Not only must each argument presented be well organized, but the total speech must have a structure—and you must make the judge aware of that structure in advance. A statement such as "In this speech, I am going to examine three major issues: topicality, significance, and inherency" gives the judge advance notice of where to look on the flow and identifies for him or her the issues in contention. If your topicality argument, for example, is composed of three basic responses, indicate this, enumerate them with headline value as you present them, and remind the judge at the conclusion that you had three responses to topicality. Too many beginning debaters seem to adopt the motto "If you can't beat them, confuse them." Unfortunately, the person most often confused is the judge, and few ballots are won by unorganized debaters. You are always ahead if everyone in the round—judge, opposition, and most of all, you—can accurately place your arguments on a flow sheet.

Delivering

Debate is an oral activity. It differs from events like original oratory or dramatic acting insofar as it contains more intellectual content and spontaneous commentary. However, if the debater or the coach forgets that information must be communicated in a limited amount of time through oral means, the event can become quite frustrating. Anyone who has gone to a debate tournament has seen speakers talking at a rapid rate of speed. These are usually experienced debaters who have learned to think fast while talking quickly. You may be tempted to imitate this practice. Don't. What will come out is only a jumble of words. Just as you had to learn to walk before you could run, so you must practice speaking *clearly* before you can speak *quickly*.

There is no substitute for practice in preparation for debate tournaments. Practice includes participation in rounds of debate with your classmates. These rounds offer you the opportunity to give a speech once and then to deliver it again, with improvements. Practice should aim at reducing the number of nonessential arguments. Eliminate the weakest arguments and you will be able to slow down to a reasonable rate of speed and still say all that is important.

One thing that may be difficult for you is to seek advice on public speaking. No one likes to be criticized, but it is possible that you have annoying habits of speaking simply because you have never been informed of how to speak well. Ask your teacher or your debate coach about your speaking. Make sure that you have the right tone, pitch, and level of articulation for debate. Rather than tarnishing your ability to speak well, debate should enhance it. The best debaters are not necessarily the fastest; they are the ones with the ability and experience to argue essential points and persuade the audience.

SUMMARY

This chapter has examined the basics of academic debate. You should now be able to identify the elements of an academic debate, the duties of each speaker, the obligations and opportunities of the affirmative and the negative, and some of the typical kinds of arguments that are made. You should also be able to identify ways to prepare for a debate, plan arguments, arrange briefs, and structure specific arguments and entire speeches. Finally, you should be aware of the need to practice these arguments in developing skills of oral presentation. The following chapters present some strategic considerations for fulfilling these requirements in rounds of debate in which diverse arguments are made.

QUESTIONS FOR DISCUSSION

1. Even though most of each debate round is an extemporaneous activity, you must spend some time organizing your

thoughts. Explain the rules governing preparation time. Why are such rules necessary?

2. Define a constructive speech and a rebuttal speech. What is the difference between the two?

3. What are the parts of a first affirmative constructive speech?

4. What is the purpose of preparing affirmative and negative briefs prior to a debate?

5. What is the value of taking a flow in a debate round?

6. What is to be gained by keeping each speech organized?

ACTIVITIES

1. Using the current national debate topic, organize and prepare an affirmative or negative brief. The brief should deal with a single issue.

2. Develop a list of abbreviations and symbols for taking a flow (notetaking) during a debate. You may use the list with the sample flow sheet in this chapter as a basis for your own.

3. For the next week, use the list developed in Activity 2 as you flow speeches while listening to class lectures, the nightly news, or a news radio station.

4. Collect five articles dealing with the current topic chosen in Activity 1. Using headlines and internal structure, organize the issues contained in the articles.

AFFIRMATIVE CASE CONSTRUCTION AND STRATEGY

OBJECTIVES AND KEY TERMS

After studying Chapter 7, you should be able to

1. Explain the essential characteristics of each type of affirmative case construction,
2. Explain how one decides which case type to use,
3. Produce an affirmative case and plan, complete with evidence, and

After reading this chapter, you should understand the following terms:

advantage

caseside

case turns

comparative advantage

contention

duration of significance

harm

inherency

need-plan case

turn around

There are numerous methods of constructing an *affirmative case*, the arguments an affirmative team presents to support the resolution. Generally, all the recognized affirmative case forms are derived from sound theories of logic and persuasion. Affirmative cases are built by applying the principles of organizational structure to the information you have obtained from your research. In this book you will learn some good ways to build affirmative cases. Specifically, this chapter will cover the traditional need-plan case and the comparative advantage case.

The Traditional Need-Plan Case

The traditional need-plan case format is appropriate for debating whether a new policy should be initiated in an area where no policy exists. In resolutions dealing with adjustments in the level or direction of an existing federal policy, the traditional need-plan case is less suitable for supporting the resolution.

To understand the traditional need-plan case, you need a bit of historical perspective. School debating has been going on for a number of decades. When it first became popular to use a national policy as the subject of the debate resolution each debate season, the federal government had little responsibility in domestic social areas. Consequently, most school debate resolutions called for the federal government to initiate some new policy in an area where there *was* no federal policy. Some of the actual resolutions debated in intercollegiate tournaments were these:

> 1931: Resolved: That Congress should enact legislation providing for the centralized control of industry.

> 1936: Resolved: That Congress should be empowered to fix minimum wages and maximum hours for industry.

> 1940: Resolved: That the nations of the Western Hemisphere should form a permanent union.

> 1949: Resolved: That the United States should nationalize the basic nonagricultural industries.

As recently as 1965, high school debaters were debating "Resolved: That Social Security benefits should be expanded to include medical care." A key factor that these and similar resolutions shared was the call for a federal action in an area where the national government was not already involved. It is difficult for many of us to recall a time when the federal government was not integrally involved in social areas and international organizations. But in a larger view, it really wasn't that long ago that there was no Social Security, no Medicare, no United Nations.

From such a perspective, it is clear how a need for federal action could be a regular subject for policy debate. In that climate the stock issues form of analysis was the only acceptable form in a debate. There was either a *yes* or a *no* answer to the debate resolution—the federal government either should or should not initiate a policy in a given problem area. This perspective is important to keep in mind, because when more recent developments in case forms are discussed, such as the comparative advantage case, the resolution for debate will assume that the federal government is already involved in the area of concern. The issues will be over the degree or kind of involvement that is desirable.

With this historical context understood, you are in a better position to examine the defining characteristics of the need-plan case. The basic format of the need-plan case is the same as the statement of the stock issues: First, the case develops the argument that a need for a change exists. Next, the case develops the plan and shows how the plan meets the need. Finally, the case develops the argument that the plan would be beneficial.

The heart of the case is that there is a need and that the plan will meet the need. In this emphasis, plan benefits assume a role of secondary importance. Judges are not asked to vote for a plan that fails to meet the need, even if it is a beneficial plan.

As a logical theory, the traditional need-plan case is the same as a problem-solution outline. Much of the underlying theory of the case is very similar to the Dewey method of critical thinking: Identify and analyze the problem; select the best solution. However, in debate, there are a few distinctive twists on the theory.

Characteristics of the Need

First, the need or problem has to be *compelling*. This means that you have to select an area in which the present system is woefully inadequate, and as a result, people are suffering, economically or physically.

Next, the need has to be *inherent*. In traditional need-plan analysis, *inherency* typically means a logical relationship between a specific condition existing as an effect of the present system and the specific characteristic of the present system that causes it. To prove that a need is inherent, you must demonstrate that the harmful condition you isolate is caused by that part of the present system that your plan is designed to correct. If the harmful condition or need can be remedied by measures other than your plan, it is not considered an inherent need, according to this analysis.

What could constitute such a characteristic of the present system? The law itself. If the law requires the present system to operate in such a way that the harmful result inevitably occurs, then the need is inherent. The need is created by the structure of the present system, the body of law. Only a plan to change the law can solve such a problem. An example of a structural inherency during the 1950s and 1960s was segregation and the discriminating body of laws regarding public accommodations, jobs, housing, and voting. Only a change in the law could remedy racial segregation; nothing else could solve that need.

Of course, in keeping with the historical analysis of the growth and development of the traditional need-plan case, inherency also is created by the *absence* of necessary legislation. The problems that exist because of the inability of government to act without any legislative authority can only be remedied by the creation of enabling legislation, together with its agencies and adequate resources to fulfill the intent of the law.

Characteristics of the Plan

Quite simply, the plan has to meet the need. The inherent and compelling need has to be completely solved by the affirmative plan. Judges will not accept a proposed federal policy that cannot overcome the causes of the problem and meet the need entirely. Partial solutions will not do.

The plan has to be *practical*, feasible. Even if a plan could theoretically meet the need totally, judges will refuse to accept it if it seems to be an impractical solution.

Originally, as the need-plan case developed in school debates, judges expected the affirmative speeches to be organized in a particular way. The first affirmative speaker presented the need, and the second affirmative speaker presented the plan and made the arguments about its workability, practicality, and extra benefits. Judges seldom voted for a plan because of its benefits, but they expected the affirmative to point out the benefits just the same. Currently, however, affirmative teams have begun to reveal the entire case—need, plan, and benefits—in the first constructive speech.

It is difficult to adapt the requirements of a need-plan case to a topic calling for incremental reform. If the United States is increasing or decreasing welfare, arms control, or environmental protection, the direction of policy may create more or fewer benefits, but the policy itself cannot be said to be a solution to a need. At best, it is only an incremental adjustment to the present situation.

The traditional need-plan case is designed to fulfill the affirmative team's burden to prove a *case*—an organized, persuasive series of arguments—for a new policy. Essentially, it is a problem-solution construct. The distinctive arguments required in proving the need-plan case are that the need or problem is compelling and inherent; the plan will meet the need entirely because it is workable and practical; and the plan promises added benefits. In terms of organization, the need is always presented before the plan because it constitutes the mandate for the plan.

THE COMPARATIVE ADVANTAGE CASE

The transition from the traditional need-plan case to the comparative advantage case was a gradual one that took place during the 1960s. Today the *comparative advantage case*—a case showing that the affirmative plan achieves an improvement over the present situation—is the most popular and widely known form of affirmative case analysis. Examining some of the factors involved in the transition from need-plan to comparative advantage cases will help you grasp the reasoning and theory behind the comparative advantage case as it is now used.

Again, remember the historical perspective we have already examined. In the 1930s and 1940s, the federal government could be described as low profile. The Great Depression of the 1930s and U.S. involvement in World War II in the 1940s combined to generate a much more active and powerful federal presence in both domestic and foreign policy. Consequently, the wording of debate resolutions began to mirror that change. No longer did they call for establishing a new federal policy where none had existed previously. Instead the resolutions called for increasing or decreasing government influence in a problem area where federal policy already existed. Some actual resolutions debated in inter-collegiate tournaments during this period were as follows:

> 1965: Resolved: That law enforcement agencies in the United States should be given greater freedom in the investigation and prosecution of crime.

> 1966: Resolved: That the United States should substantially reduce its foreign policy commitments.

> 1968: Resolved: That executive control of U.S. foreign policy should be significantly curtailed.

> 1971: Resolved: That greater controls should be imposed on the gathering and utilization of information about U.S. citizens by government agencies.

As you can see, the common feature in these resolutions is a call for modifying an existing federal policy, in contrast with the earlier period, when the common feature of debate resolutions was the call for initiating some new policy where none had existed previously. The shift in the wording of debate resolutions created a new way of looking at affirmative obligations.

In large part, the movement away from the need-plan case to the comparative advantage case was generated by the difficulty many affirmative teams had in winning debates. During this period, American federal involvement mushroomed in public problem areas. It became very difficult to establish an inherent (or unique) need to solve a problem through a new federal program when there already were a number of such programs in place. The negative could easily show that the existing programs could be effective if sufficient money, staffing, or enforcement were used. Or, the negative could take the position that the federal government could never solve the problems if existing programs were not able to do so. As a consequence, negative teams simply repaired existing programs or destroyed the credibility of government efficacy.

The comparative advantage case developed as an affirmative strategy to counter this strong negative position. Affirmative teams showed that, although existing programs could possibly be modified in the present system to achieve a solution to the problem area, the affirmative proposal could do the job better. On a comparative basis, then, it would be more advantageous to accept the affirmative resolution than to stay with the present system, even if it were modified a bit. Inherency became a major difficulty because of changes that occurred in the actual political events of the nation.

Inherency was not the only major difficulty for affirmative teams during the transitional period for affirmative case analysis techniques. *Solvency,* the ability to correct the demonstrated problem, also became difficult under the traditional stock issues analysis. In the need-plan case, it was imperative for the proposed plan to solve the need completely. However, changing social and cultural patterns in our society made such a burden almost impossible. Experts began to characterize social problems as highly complex with multiple causes. Increased mobility and density of population, intensified family pressures, and the emergence of economic ties and industrial conglomerates all served to complicate solutions to problems. Yet, if today's problems cannot be totally solved, they can at least be ameliorated through the constant review and correction of the policies that govern them. It was not always possible for the affirmative to prove that a plan would eliminate a problem completely, at least not at a feasible cost. Affirmative teams made the argument that this stock issues requirement was too rigid—that, in real-world decision making, policy changes are accepted if they seem to be advantageous. Even if adopting a policy does not totally solve a problem, if it produces benefits, it ought to be accepted. This argument focused debate on the comparison between the affirmative plan and the present system. If the plan offers the greatest advantage possible, it should be considered worthy of acceptance.

A homely analogy was argued: Why do people trade cars? If your family already has a car, there is no need to buy another one when you use the need-plan case as your rule for decision. However, if your family can get a *better* car—newer, nicer, more comfortable, and more economical—then, in all probability, a trade will be made. Likewise, why buy a word processor when you have a typewriter? Not because you have an inherent need for a personal computer, but because of the advantages that come from acquiring a faster, easier way to write papers.

Although such arguments were not completely convincing, they made enough sense to sustain the shift in affirmative case analysis techniques from the need-plan to the comparative advantage. However, some people still objected to the comparative advantage case as a theoretical framework because it dilutes the logical rigor that was the hallmark of stock issues analysis. For this reason. the comparative advantage case incorporated, with modifications, many of the same logical requirements of the stock issues or the traditional need-plan case.

The basic idea of the comparative advantage case is to show that in comparison with the present system the affirmative plan is advantageous—hence the name, comparative advantage. In order to make the comparison, the affirmative team presents its plan first and the advantages later. This is one major difference from the traditional need-plan case. Moreover, since the plan is no longer withheld from the negative until late in debate, the current practice is for the affirmative to present its entire case in the first affirmative constructive speech, regardless of which case structure is used.

CHARACTERISTICS OF THE ADVANTAGE

The *advantage* constitutes the rationale presented to support adoption of the plan. Because the concept of the advantage is the most important difference between the comparative advantage and the need-plan case, you should understand the arguments necessary to prove the comparative advantage case with regard to the claimed advantages.

First, the structure of the case remains essentially a problem-solution outline, except the solution is presented first and its effects are presented later. The proposed plan is the solution. By increasing or decreasing federal action in a problem area, the plan causes certain changes in the effects of the present system. These changed effects represent the advantages of the plan. Since the comparative advantage case is derived from the stock issues, as modified during the transitional period for affirmative case analysis, the advantage must be shown to be related to the plan along the same lines as the relationship between a need and a plan. For sound organizational structure, the affirmative case must give a direct comparison between the present system and the proposed change. Specifically, an advantage must be shown to be *significant* (corresponding to the requirement that a need be *compelling* in the traditional need-plan case). It must be *unique* to the plan (corresponding to the requirement that a need be *inherent* in the traditional need-plan case).

An advantage is said to be *significant* whenever it is an important outcome of the plan. Significance has a quantitative and a qualitative dimension. Ideally, an advantage should represent a plan outcome highly valued by society and applicable to a large number of people for a long time. Here are some ways to discuss significance.

Significance may be demonstrated by four different methods of measuring the amount or degree of change (1) *Absolute significance* means the total number of units affected by the change wrought by the affirmative plan. How many more people will be employed, how many lives saved, how many units of energy or dollars conserved? (2) *Risk significance* means the fractional proportion of the population that could be exposed to jeopardy by the policy system. For example, major medical expenses affect relatively few individuals in any given year. However, the *potential* risk of major medical expenses affect relatively few individuals in any given year. However, the *potential* risk of major medical expenses affects virtually everyone because serious illnesses and accidents can and do occur. Moreover, when considered over a longer time span than a year—say, over a generation or a lifetime—the percentage of people actually affected by financial catastrophe resulting from major medical expenses escalates, posing a significant problem area.

Where risk to human life is involved, public policy change may also be warranted. Experimental findings that common sugar substitutes may be carcinogenic (cancer causing) led to tighter restrictions on the sale and use of saccharine, even though not one person could be found to have cancer that could be directly linked to the product. The degree of risk was considered great enough to motivate policy change, especially since significant negative impact to tightening such restrictions was absent.

(3) *Degree of significance* means the relative value of the advantage. Public policy deliberation is affected by minor problems only when great numbers of people are involved, but a problem area involving great consequences in terms of values (either beneficial or costly) receives prompt attention even when relatively few individuals are subjected to the harm. The greater the consequences of benefit or harm, the greater the relative value attached to the policy. In fact, the degree of significance directly affects the required magnitude of the scope of the problem needed for policy action. Suppose a large number of people might feel irritable as a reaction to a specific prescription drug. This probably would not constitute a significant justification for a policy change. However, if that same drug had some powerful side effects (such as the drug thalidomide had on pregnant women), immediate withdrawal of

the drug from the market would be ordered by the Federal Drug Administration. Hence, the harm of the drug could be said to be significant in degree.

(4) *Duration of significance* means the persistence of a problem. In this sense the condition of inherency overlaps the issue of significance. Temporary problems (or temporary advantages) constitute much less of a rationale for policy change than permanent ones.

An advantage is shown to be *unique* to the plan whenever the advantage can be achieved best by the affirmative plan and not by any other means. This quality represents a major change in emphasis from the logical requirements for establishing inherency in the traditional need-plan case. There the need had to be created by the structure of the present system, and it could not be susceptible to a solution by any measure other than the plan. In the comparative advantage case, the issue is not whether other means of achieving the advantage exist, but whether the affirmative proposal is the *most* advantageous means. The advantage is considered unique to the plan when only the plan can achieve the advantage to the same extent of cost, efficiency, speed (rate of achieving the goal of the present system), or effective coverage.

By being relieved of the burden of identifying a law on the books that causes the problem or pointing out the absence of a law to solve the problem, the affirmative was free to describe other hindrances to the best operation of the system. Hence, there arose a new line of argument in affirmative case analysis called *attitudinal inherency*, the tendency of agents charged with creating or carrying out the law to avoid their responsibility. The condition of attitudinal inherency exists in such features of the present system as corrupt officials (as in organized crime), pressure groups and lobbies, conflicting laws and goals, and even general apathy. As long as the affirmative plan contains provisions to change or circumvent such attitudes, and the present system has no such mechanisms to step up its ability to do so, the affirmative can claim the advantage as being unique.

A second area of argument relates to the comparisons made between the proposed plan and the present system in relation to their relative success in achieving the goal in question. When the focus of agreement is over increasing or decreasing federal action in an area in which the federal government is already active, the first step is to identify the goal that the present policy seeks to achieve. Once the goal is identified, it is possible to compare the operation of the present system with the projected changes in operation made by the proposed plan in terms of achieving the goal.

The primary areas in which relative comparisons are made in debate analysis include cost, speed, and efficiency. A plan is advantageous if it can achieve the goal more *economically* than the present system, more *quickly* than the present system, or more *efficiently* than the present system.

Other Aspects of the Case

Two additional points should be made about the comparative advantage case. First, the case may include more than one advantage for adopting the plan. If the affirmative team shows that two, three, or more advantages stem from the adoption of the plan and, moreover, that each of the advantages is independent (capable of achievement without a necessary connection to whether other advantages are achieved), then any one of the advantages can stand as the rationale for adopting the plan. This argument is strategically important, because the affirmative could be defeated by negative refutation on one or more of the advantages and still win the judge's decision, provided there is still at least one advantage to adopting the plan. This strategy is a refinement of the transitional argument that an acceptable proposal is not required to solve the need totally.

The second point is that there is a second level of comparison to be made. Not only is the plan compared with the present system (which is the focus of the affirmative case), but also the advantages of the plan are compared with its disadvantages (which is the focus of the negative attack). This point will be developed more completely in Chapter 8, where negative strategies are discussed. The affirmative should be aware that the comparative advantage case must have advantages that not only outweigh the present system but also outweigh potential disadvantages of the plan.

The comparative advantage case grew out of the need-plan case to become the most popular form of affirmative case analysis. As a form of problem-solution argument, the comparative advantage case presents a proposed plan to change existing policy and bases its rationale on the ways in which the results of the policy change (the plan) would be improvements over the present system. Comparisons are made between the proposed plan and the present system in achieving a specific goal. To justify the proposed plan, the claimed effect or advantage must be significant and unique to the plan when compared with the present system or any other alternative policy. Comparisons are made between the proposed plan and the present system on the dimensions of cost, speed, and efficiency. More than one advantage may be presented to support the proposed plan, and if the advantages are shown to be independent reasons for adopting the plan, only one of the claimed advantages need be carried by the affirmative to win the judge's decision.

AFFIRMATIVE STRATEGY

Defending against Negative Case Arguments

Much of your success in debate will depend on your ability to anticipate potential negative objections to your affirmative case. No one will be more aware of weaknesses in an affirmative proposal than the debater who has had to painstakingly research, construct, and revise the case. An affirmative team should have a very good idea of the ways in which it is most likely to lose an issue, as well as the ways in which it is most likely to win.

Preparation against negative arguments should begin with the choice of arguments and evidence to be included in the first affirmative constructive. When you describe the *harm*—an undesirable result—in the present system, choose the most powerfully worded evidence presenting the strongest possible impact for your harm. In constructing your solvency contention (*contention* being a major claim), it is important to anticipate possible negative objections to the effectiveness of the plan and to incorporate evidence answering such objections. For instance, an affirmative team attempting to reduce the influence of American tobacco companies in China (thereby reducing deaths of Chinese who smoke American cigarettes) will expect the negative to argue that Chinese will simply switch to other cigarettes if American cigarettes are not available. It would be wise in this instance to include evidence in first affirmative constructive that explains why American cigarettes are uniquely attractive. Including such evidence presents the judge with a strong, sophisticated solvency position from the beginning. It also saves the second affirmative debater time if he or she can refer to evidence already presented, rather than read it.

The second affirmative constructive should attempt to answer every negative argument against the case. Backup evidence on the case issues should be prepared against common negative objections, and it should be briefed well in advance of the tournament. In general, the affirmative should be most careful in covering its solvency contention; it is increasingly rare for the negative to base a strategy on the argument that there is no harm in the present system, or that the current system will solve whatever harm exists. The second affirmative should be especially wary of *case turns*: negative arguments, usually made in response to the solvency contention, claiming that the plan worsens rather than alleviates the harm in the present system.

Affirmative teams should take particular care to learn their judge's preference concerning affirmative case approaches. (Your coach or more experienced debaters can help you prepare for particular judges.) For instance, a stock issues judge is likely to view harm, inherency, or solvency as *zero-sum issues* or non-issues. In other words, the affirmative might lose the round even though the negative has only cast doubt on a stock issue. A comparative advantage or policy-making judge, on the other hand, is not likely to vote negative on case issues unless he or she is convinced that the affirmative team presents no advantage at all over the present system.

Defending against Topicality and Disadvantages

Even affirmative cases that seem to aim at the heart of the debate resolution may be subjected to topicality arguments. Topicality is one of the few issues in debate on which judges everywhere seem to agree—if the affirmative loses topicality, it loses the round. Preparation for topicality, therefore, is crucial to affirmative success.

There are three essential strategies for responding to topicality arguments. First, you may be able to explain that your plan does, in fact, meet the negative's interpretation of the resolution. (This is a common approach against a negative team that has misinterpreted or misunderstood the affirmative plan.) Second, you should be able to present a competing definition or interpretation of the resolution and defend it as the superior interpretation. If a negative team, for example, defines a "substantial change" as "a complete reversal," the affirmative might counterdefine "substantial change" as "altering all of one subset," and show why its changes in trade policy meet that definition. Finally, the affirmative may choose to argue that, while it may not be in compliance with the negative's interpretation of the resolution, no harm or abuse to the negative has occurred. This line of argument assumes that the essential function of the topicality burden is to ensure a solid, balanced debate for which the negative has had a fair opportunity to prepare. A negative team that is well prepared on issues besides topicality will add strength to this response!

Affirmative teams must also prepare to answer negative disadvantages. Essentially, four types of response should be brainstormed, prepared, and supported with evidence, where necessary. First, the affirmative should attempt to explain why it does not link to the particular negative disadvantage. Affirmative teams may avoid economic disadvantages, for instance, by avoiding tax increases or deficit spending as funding mechanisms. Second, the affirmative might argue that the disadvantage is not *unique*; that is, it will result in the present system regardless of whether the affirmative proposal is adopted. If the negative claims that the affirmative proposal will cause new spending, leading to adverse economic impacts, the affirmative might respond that Congress already plans significant new spending; the impact will occur anyway. Third, the affirmative might argue that the impact of the disadvantage is insignificant or indeterminate, compared with the advantage claimed by the affirmative.

The fourth and most powerful method of answering a disadvantage argument is the *turnaround*. A turnaround argument, quite simply, reverses either the link or the impact of a disadvantage, thus producing a new advantage for the affirmative. Assume, for instance, that the negative claims as its link new spending by the affirmative team. It further argues that the risk of recession or even depression rises with new federal spending. If the affirmative team can establish that it in fact reduces spending, it might claim the reduced risk of economic setback as an additional advantage for its proposal.

Affirmative responses to topicality and disadvantages should be well prepared and briefed in advance. Debaters should not, however, become so dependent on their briefs that they fail to listen carefully to the details of their opponents' arguments. They should be ready to add to or subtract from their prepared briefs as circumstances warrant.

Affirmative Rebuttals

Most beginning debaters believe that the first affirmative rebuttal is the most difficult speech in debate. Indeed, answering thirteen minutes' worth of negative argument in only five minutes requires not only conciseness and speed, but also significant wisdom in selecting arguments.

The first affirmative rebuttalist should remember that although he or she probably cannot afford to lose an issue (such as topicality or a disadvantage), losing or conceding individual arguments is not as serious. It is usually good practice to attempt to win or extend the strongest arguments made by the second affirmative constructive on each issue, with particular attention to arguments that may have been dropped or mishandled in the negative block. It is also important to understand that, given the severe time pressure, the order in which the issues are addressed may be crucial. No affirmative rebuttalist should be forced to speed up his or her discussion of a vital issue (topicality, especially, or a disadvantage) because time is running out.

The second affirmative rebuttalist has the luxury of the last word. Although every argument made by the second negative rebuttalist should be addressed if at all possible, it is important in this speech also to consider what the negative has *not* addressed. This is especially true if the negative has spent time arguing its disadvantages and neglected the flow of the *caseside*—the debate arguments centering on issues directly raised by the affirmative case. The affirmative should always maximize the importance of its advantages and minimize the probability or significance of the negative team's disadvantages. It is particularly crucial that the second affirmative rebuttalist leave a significant amount of time—as much as a minute and a half or two minutes—for a summary or "story" that "stands back" from the details of the round and presents the judge with a clear calculus of how the affirmative advantages outweigh the negative disadvantages.

SUMMARY

Two methods of affirmative case construction have been described in this chapter: traditional need-plan and comparative advantage. Each has been examined within a context of historical and theoretical perspectives.

Imagine that instead of examining methods of proving that a debate resolution should be adopted, you have been examining how to sell real estate. The traditional need-plan case is comparable to persuading the judge that a trading post should be built in a remote region where no settlements have penetrated. In the absence of any policy, a new policy should be implemented. In order to build the outpost, you must show that a need exists, that the settlement would meet the need, and that it would be desirable.

The comparative advantage case would be comparable to persuading the judge to buy a store on Main Street because it does an impressive gross business. You would wait for the negative team to bring out the overhead costs and other disadvantages.

The keys to affirmative strategy are anticipation, preparation, and selection. The affirmative begins the round with the advantage of establishing the ground; it should build on this advantage by anticipating negative objections and preparing responses to them. Although the negative can often win the round by winning one issue, one or two good arguments refuting the negative position are sufficient if they are accurate and well supported.

QUESTIONS FOR DISCUSSION

1. Why is inherency the key term in the need-plan case?
2. What brought about the emergence of the comparative advantage case? In the comparative advantage case, how have the concepts of inherency and solvency changed?
3. What are the three essential methods of responding to a negative topicality argument? Which should an affirmative team use?

ACTIVITIES

1. Using one of the resolutions listed below or the current national debate topic resolution, identify a case area caused by attitudinal inherency. Outline the problem and tell why the present system cannot solve it.

    Resolved: That the Congress should provide financial support for all private elementary and secondary schools.

Resolved: That the method of selecting presidential and vice-presidential candidates should be significantly changed.

Resolved: That the federal government should establish a comprehensive program to increase significantly the energy independence of the United States.

Resolved: That schools should establish criteria for exemption from final examinations.

Resolved: That the federal government should provide employment for all U.S. citizens desiring work.

Resolved: That all U.S. citizens are entitled to a home and minimal nutrition.

2. Using one of the resolutions in Activity 1, define the terms of the resolution and decide on a case area for debate. What case format should be used and why?

3. Outline the affirmative case chosen in Activity 2. Research the contentions and gather evidence to support the case claims. Write a two- to three-minute speech on one of the contentions or advantages.

4. Draft a two- to three-minute speech covering the remaining contentions or advantages. Do not include a plan in this speech. At the end of this activity, you should have the body of a first affirmative constructive speech, short of the affirmative plan.

5. Using your affirmative case outline, draft an affirmative plan. Be prepared to discuss the plan in class and any potential problems in supporting the plan.

6. Examine the text of your first affirmative. Identify the most likely negative objections to your case analysis; then make a list of arguments and/or evidence to add to your speech to strengthen it against these possible objections.

7. Examine a flow of a second affirmative constructive speech from a practice round. Determine which arguments are most important and which could be omitted without creating much danger of losing an issue.

NEGATIVE ANALYSIS AND STRATEGY

OBJECTIVES AND KEY TERMS

After studying Chapter 8, you should be able to

1. Explain and present the arguments a negative should use against each type of affirmative case,
2. Explain topicality as an issue and demonstrate the ability to argue both for and against the topicality of a particular case approach on a topic,
3. Explain the characteristics of a counterplan and the guidelines for presenting one, and
4. Explain and demonstrate the use of disadvantages.

After reading this chapter, you should understand the following terms:

brink disadvantage	**permutation argument**
case refutation	**presumption**
counterplan	**voting issue**
linear disadvantage	
link	
minor repair	
net beneficial	

In any debate, the negative has a single burden: to refute the affirmative case. The negative does not construct its own interpretation of the resolution and then show how that interpretation should be rejected. The affirmative's burden is the successful defense of its own case. It is not obligated to defend any and all conceivable interpretations of the resolution. Consequently, the starting point for negative analysis is to realize that negative responsibilities are fundamentally linked to what the affirmative does in the debate.

NEGATIVE ANALYSIS

The negative's obligation to come to grips with the affirmative case has traditionally been lightened somewhat by various assumptions about the nature of debate. One assumption is that a debate is like a courtroom trial. The affirmative is assigned the role of the prosecutor, who must prove all charges, and the negative is assigned the role of the defense, who pleads the defendant not guilty and then waits for the prosecutor to meet the entire burden of proof. Another possible assumption is that a debate is like a lawsuit over ownership of land or property. Here the affirmative is assigned the role of claimant, and the negative is assigned the role of defense. In this assumption possession is nine-tenths of the law: The claimant must prove the case to remove the defendant from physical possession of the land or property in question. The defense does not have the opposite burden of proving that the claimant is *not* entitled to take the property away. A third possible assumption is that a debate resolution is a proposal to change an existing policy. In this instance the affirmative is assigned the responsibility of proving that the policy should be changed; the negative is given an initial advantage in that it is not required to prove that the resolution for changing the policy should be rejected.

These models of debate differ from one another in some respects, but they are similar in the common assumption that the affirmative has the greater burden of proof. This advantage for the negative is termed presumption. The present system is presumed to be adequate until and unless the affirmative fulfills its burden of proof by presenting a prima facie case for the adoption of the resolution. Presumption is an initial prejudgment that the resolution should not be adopted. Because that is the position upheld by the negative, this prejudgment favors that side of the debate.

Presumption is often left uncontested by debaters. Most of the time it does not play an important role in a debate. It can be crucial, however, in case of a tie. Suppose that neither team in a debate presents convicting reasons to adopt the resolution or to reject the resolution. Each reason for or against the proposition is refuted by the other side. How can the debate be decided? A judge may vote for the side that has presumption. Traditionally, the negative has presumption because, all things being equal, one should not change the status quo unless there is a good reason. The reason this rule is followed is that chaos would result if laws were made without sufficient reason.

Does presumption always reside with the negative (the team that is charged with defending the status quo)? Not always. In some situations there is no status quo policy, and the presumption resides with doing something, even if the proposed policy is of doubtful value. In addition, if a present policy contradicts a deeply held value, then arguably presumption may reside against the status quo. Since presumption need not necessarily reside with the negative, affirmative teams can argue that presumption should be given to the resolution. In case of a tie, the resolution is more representative of the course of prudent change than the status quo. Obviously, the negative will wish to contend the contrary.

Some other general principles of negative analysis should be explained before specific negative approaches to various affirmative case constructions are explored.

Topicality

It is the affirmative's privilege to define the resolution and to select the case area(s) to be debated. Provided the affirmative interpretation is deemed reasonable, the negative has the obligation to accept the affirmative interpretation for the purpose of the debate. But what is a *reasonable* interpretation?

Although the negative has the burden of refuting any reasonable affirmative case, the negative is not obliged to accept any affirmative interpretation as reasonable. Instead, it may challenge the affirmative interpretation of the resolution as the basis for the debate. If that challenge is successful, the judge will conclude that, even if the negative fails to refute the specific affirmative case, acceptance of that case would not be the same as accepting the debate resolution.

Such challenges are called *topicality* arguments. The basic idea is that both teams are invited to a tournament to debate a common resolution. The topic for debate is bound up in the statement of the resolution. If the affirmative interpretation strays too far from the stated resolution, the negative argues that the affirmative is off the topic and that the case therefore cannot be used by the judge as the basis for accepting the resolution.

A topicality argument contains four essential parts: (1) a *definition* of the word or phrase of the resolution that the negative claims has been violated by the affirmative proposal; (2) an explanation of how the plan violates this definition (commonly called the *violation*); (3) reasons the negative has provided a *superior interpretation* of the resolution; and (4) a reminder to the judge that topicality is an absolute *voting issue*, a crucial area of argument that must be addressed to support or reject the resolution, and on which the entire round may turn.

The most successful topicality arguments occur when the negative has presented good reasons that its interpretation of the resolution is more appropriate than the affirmative's. Three good types of superior interpretation arguments can be employed. First, the negative definition may simply come from a better source. Most judges would agree that, other considerations being equal, a definition from a legal dictionary is probably superior to one from *Webster's*, or that a definition from an expert in the field outranks one from a layperson.

Second, the negative interpretation may be more grammatical. If the resolution calls on the affirmative to "substantially change U.S. foreign policy," the negative might reasonably argue that it is the *change* that must be substantial, not the *policy*.

Third, the negative may argue that its interpretation is best because it provides a fairer division of ground between affirmative and negative. For instance, to define *change* as "alter" may seem to be a reasonable definition, yet it sets no real limit on the action that an affirmative team might take—and the negative will always want to argue that one function of a debate resolution is to *limit* the scope of discussion.

Variations of topicality argument include *extratopicality* and *effects topicality*. Extratopicality occurs when the affirmative plan meets the terms of the resolution and then goes beyond those terms to propose additional, non-topical action. Many judges think that extratopicality is every bit as illegitimate as non-topicality, and consider it a voting issue. Others are willing to ignore the extratopical part of the plan, and any advantages stemming from it, if the negative argues that the affirmative has gone beyond the bounds of the resolution.

Effects topicality occurs when topical action happens only as a remote result of the plan. A plan to replace Republicans in Congress with Democrats, for instance, would certainly *result in* a change in U.S. foreign policy toward China, but it would not in itself constitute that change. Most judges regard effects topicality as illegitimate, especially when there are many "steps" between the plan and its topical result.

Case Refutation

How does the negative go about attacking the affirmative case for change? The most direct way is simply to say that the affirmative reasons for change are wrong or lack proof. Thus, for every claim that the affirmative asserts is true, the negative offers a counterclaim asserting that what the affirmative says is false. Alternatively, the negative might say there is not enough proof to tell one way or another. The technique is known as *case refutation.* Case refutation says to the judge that the resolution should not be accepted because there is insufficient positive evidence to indicate that claims supporting the resolution are true. Case refutation leads the negative to make the following claims:

There is no problem in the status quo. This is often a difficult claim to prove. If the affirmative has done its homework, it will have isolated some problem. Remember, a resolution emerges from discussion of a topic such as poverty, crime, the environment, or foreign policy. Usually the status quo will be less than perfect in one of these major areas.

Instead of arguing that there is absolutely no problem, the negative may wish to modify its claim and say that *there is no significant problem in the status quo.* Significance is a quantitative and qualitative measurement.

To say that there is no *quantitative* significance to a problem means that even though a harm has been isolated, one cannot generalize to the conclusion that the entire status quo is jeopardized by the problem. For example, even if an affirmative is able to show an awful harm to the status quo policy, unless the harm is widespread, change cannot be said to be justified. Suppose the affirmative was able to show that the toxic chemicals at Love Canal were very harmful to the people there. Unless it can show that Love Canal is typical of the status quo, rather than the exceptional example, a national water policy might not be justified.

To say that there is no *qualitative* significance demands that the affirmative prove that the problem violates a significant value. Even if there are many instances of a harm, unless the harm can be shown to be something people care about, it does not constitute a reason for change. An affirmative may be alarmed about soft-drink machines that are broken and cheat people out of their money. However, given that the amount of change each person loses is small, there is no reason to worry about a national policy. Even if the affirmative claims a policy is important because it will resolve a number of individual harms, unless these harms are recognized as dangerous or deleterious to individual well-being, the case for change cannot be said to be significant.

Sometimes the negative finds cause to question the affirmative's evidence. The affirmative might have evidence that suggests that the magnitude and quality of the harm is bad, but the evidence itself may be suspicious. Sometimes a biased source is used to establish the truth of the argument. For instance, if the American Enterprise Institute, a business-related research institute, claims that strikes are jeopardizing U.S. productivity, one might request a less biased, more independent source. In addition, sources occasionally rely on out-of-date statistics. Although it is true that in the early 1970s many experts talked about a fuel shortage, since then fuel prices have risen and energy seems to be plentiful. The negative should check to see if the harm still pertains. Further, the evidence for establishing a harm may depend on theories that are subject to question. There has been a long-standing debate between meteorologists over the issue of climate. Some say the world will soon end in fire because the climate is getting hotter. Some say the world will end in ice because the climate is getting colder. There are signs both ways, and there are theories to support each conclusion. When consensus is not present in the expert community regarding the direction and nature of a harm, the negative has the right to request inaction on the grounds of significant uncertainty.

Another technique of refutation is to *deny that any problem that does exist will exist in the future*. Here the negative makes the claim that the affirmative's inherency position is untrue. There are essentially two lines of argument against inherency. The first reasons from a new causal factor that has appeared on the scene and will cause the problem of itself to diminish. For example, the recent problem in the stock market is said by some experts to have resulted from computer trading. Very large quantities of stocks are indexed by computers to market conditions and can be sold quickly, without human intervention. When stock prices fall, these programs can accelerate the decline and perhaps cause the whole market to crash. Hence, experts say that federal regulation of computer trading is desirable. A negative position against this kind of case might say that the very decline of the market will lead to self-regulation of computer trading by people involved in the market. Because brokers have an incentive not to see a crash, they will regulate computer use. Thus, the negative argues that a new factor has arisen in the status quo that will diminish the original cause of the problem.

Another inherency tactic is to argue that the present system could (if it wished to) channel more resources into existing programs and resolve the problem. This method of refutation is known as defending the efficacy of the present system. The logic behind this argument is the idea that quantitative increases of effort are not the same thing as a bona fide change in the status quo. Sometimes younger teams become confused by this argument. To challenge the affirmative team to prove that the status quo cannot adopt the affirmative plan is unreasonable. If the plan could never be adopted, then it could never work and the affirmative could not win. Similarly, to say simply that the status quo could change its mind and implement the affirmative plan if it wished is not to refute the fact that there is little likelihood for lawmakers to act differently, given inherent barriers to change. Rather than focusing on why the plan cannot be adopted or whether lawmakers might want to adopt the plan, a structural inherency argument simply says that putting more resources in the status quo programs would be just as good as the resolution, perhaps even better. Such an argument deprives the affirmative of its rationale for change.

Case refutation also covers plan issues. Most often, the case refutation on plan centers on the ability of a plan to solve problems or gain an advantage. These plan-meet-need or plan-meet-advantage arguments are frequently argued by the second negative, while inherency and problem arguments are introduced by the first negative. Ideally, the plan arguments would fit well with the inherency arguments, providing a complete rationale explaining why a problem can be solved only so much by the status quo and why any plan can go no further.

Defense of the Present System

As a line of argument, defense of the present system attempts to establish that the system as it exists is fully capable of dealing with the problem area. One way to defend the status quo is to offer a minor repair. A *minor repair* is an alteration of present policy that gains the affirmative advantage but involves substantially less change than that suggested by the resolutions.

In this line of argument, the negative proposes to compromise by admitting that it is possible for the present system to be deficient in some aspect of meeting its goals, but, if so, the existing mechanisms of the present system can be modified to achieve the same advantages the affirmative claims. In making this argument, the negative shows that the present system has sufficient policy foundations, including laws on the books and agencies in the field of concern, but what is needed is more extensive funding or personnel. It further charges that the affirmative policy change is unnecessarily radical, costly, or unwieldy.

Case refutation is often used in combination with defense of the present system. Notice that case refutation does not require the negative to give a consistent picture of the world. The negative makes a number of claims, not all of which are entirely consistent. The negative, arguing case refutation, claims that there is no problem; that the problem is not significant; that the status quo is taking care of significant problems; that nothing can be done to alleviate the problem further. Why can the status quo work if the affirmative plan cannot? Why is something being done to alleviate a problem if it is truly insignificant?

Case refutation always leaves these questions. Consequently, many negatives try to develop a consistent picture of the world. Rather than simply saying no to all affirmative claims, the negative tries to show how the present system is doing the best that can be done in a problem area. Whatever faults the status quo has can be easily repaired, but, beyond the parameters of present programs, no fruitful action can be taken. Thus, defense of the system uses case refutation to deny claims about the significance of harm or the degree to which it inheres in present policy. It adds to case refutation explanations about why present policy is working and cannot be improved. Case refutation does not require the negative to say that the status quo is very good or working at maximum capacity; it simply demands that the affirmative be rejected because its claims are not substantiated.

To summarize, case refutation can and often is used in combination with a defense of the status quo. The essence of this position is to claim that the opponent's claims about the inadequacy of the present system are wrong or that the present system can be made sufficient through minor repairs of existing mechanisms. These arguments tend to minimize or eliminate the significance of a claimed advantage. They also tend to show that the affirmative plan is not essential to cause the claimed effects. In other words, these lines of argument are used to attack the significance and the inherency of the affirmative case.

Solvency

Some laws that seem good on paper are unworkable in practice. Seat belt laws, for instance, undoubtedly save many lives, but they are difficult to enforce. It is nearly impossible to spot every driver who is not wearing a seatbelt. Moreover, given the shortage of policy in many areas, no one can expect that a large amount of time would be spent enforcing seatbelt laws.

Even the presence of adequate enforcement and funding may not be adequate to ensure that a plan will solve a problem if the negative can show that the affirmative provisions have holes in them, or that adverse circumstances will occur. The key to analysis of solvency arguments is to discover why, if the status quo cannot solve a problem, the affirmative thinks that it can. Perhaps there really is no good solution at present. For instance, the reason toxic poisons leak into the atmosphere is that there is no good way to contain them. If such is the case, despite the best intentions of the affirmative, in the long run toxins will harm as many people as if a program were never adopted.

In considering solvency, the negative should also be alert to the possibility of *case turns*, arguments that show that the affirmative actually worsens the problem that it has planned to correct. For instance, an affirmative team sets out to reduce human rights abuses by the Chinese government. It argues that if the United States offers certain trade and economic benefits contingent on good human rights behavior, the Chinese government will have an incentive to treat its political prisoners more humanely. The negative might argue that to insult a sovereign government with such a policy actually makes it more difficult for the United States to influence Chinese internal affairs, and that the plan will put more Chinese, rather than fewer, in prison.

Next, the plan may not meet the need or accrue the advantages claimed for it. There is a major distinction between this argument and the preceding one. This argument assumes that, although the plan itself may include all the necessary planks, the affirmative analysis has overlooked important factors in the present system that will continue to work against the effectiveness of the plan. The negative argument is that other causes exist for the problems noted in the present system instead of, or in addition to, those causal factors identified in the affirmative case. As a result, the plan will be hampered by those factors, just as the present system is, and the advantages will not accrue. Suppose the affirmative plan is to remove a certain amount from the military budget, arguing that excessive spending causes budgetary imbalance. If the reduction in government spending reduces overall demand, industries might produce less, and this could decrease the number of jobs, which in turn reduces the number of people paying taxes. Reduced taxpaying increases the deficit. The plan would not resolve the problem of deficits because of the chain of cause and effect it sets in motion. In general, the negative should look for the persistence of causal factors not addressed by the affirmative plan but still substantial enough to perpetuate a problem.

DISADVANTAGES

Disadvantages, reasons for not taking a course of action, are very important arguments for the negative. Offered in almost all rounds of debate, a disadvantage, in effect, asks the judge not to vote for the resolution on the grounds that it will probably cause substantial harm. To the extent that the harm brought about by the resolution is greater than the good that it does, common sense dictates that the resolution be rejected. Even if the advantages are slightly ahead of the disadvantages caused, the resolution may be rejected if its *residual benefit* (the total amount of good it does over and above the harm it brings about) is not great.

Disadvantages generally argue that the plan will bring about effects unanticipated by the affirmative. These effects are usually not directly related to the topic area. For instance, a comprehensive national water policy might clean up water pollution and save many lives but still be undesirable. Why? Controlling water pollution is expensive. Congress is in no mood to embark on new spending programs. Water pollution spending will detract from other programs that might be more cost-effective in protecting citizens' health. Especially at a time when Congress is talking seriously about deficit reduction and automatic spending cuts have been put into place at the federal level, additional funding may squeeze out important programs like health research or famine aid. Thus, even though a water pollution program will accomplish goals internal to the policy, its external consequences might make it undesirable.

No matter what kind of disadvantage is argued, the negative should compose disadvantages that contain the following components. First, the negative must identify how the plan causes the disadvantage; in other words, the *link* to the affirmative plan, the argument in a disadvantage that shows the plan will cause or aggravate a problem. Does the plan trigger additional spending? Does it cause a substantial increase in economic growth? Does it increase, or decrease, the display of U.S. military power in a crucial part of the world? In some cases these links will be quite obvious; they may even be claimed as advantages by the affirmative team. In other instances the negative will need to provide evidence to support its link. A clear and thorough understanding of the affirmative plan and advantages is always important in designing disadvantage links, especially since most affirmative teams will work hard to avoid triggering the negative's disadvantage.

Second, a disadvantage must be *unique*. This means that the disadvantage impact should result *only* from the implementation of the affirmative plan. If additional federal spending, economic growth, or military confrontation is likely to happen even if the plan is not adopted, the disadvantage cannot be a reason to reject the affirmative proposal. Specific, recent evidence indicating the uniqueness of the negative disadvantage is crucial.

Third, a disadvantage needs to have an *impact* that can outweigh the affirmative case advantages. There may be a number of internal links leading from the case action (new federal spending) to the ultimate impact (world depression, economic collapse). The quality of evidence for these internal links, as well as the ultimate impact, is crucial to the success of the disadvantage.

The relationship between the link to the plan and the ultimate impact of the disadvantage will vary, depending on the argument. Some negative disadvantages claim that even the slightest affirmative action will lead to a disastrous impact. These are called *brink disadvantages*, because the negative is arguing that the economic system or U.S.-Chinese relations, for example, are currently teetering on the brink of calamity—and one additional bit of federal spending, or one additional action that offends the Chinese government, will push us over the brink to world depression, or war. A brink disadvantage relies on the negative's ability to isolate a crisis that may or may not erupt in the future, depending on the direction government policy takes. It is difficult to find good evidence to support a brink disadvantage, and even more difficult to keep the disadvantage evidence timely. But when it is well supported, the brink disadvantage is a powerful weapon, since its full impact is likely to outweigh the case advantage.

Other negative disadvantages claim impacts proportional to the action taken by the plan. These are known as *linear disadvantages*. The negative might argue, for instance, that increased income will lead to increased consumption of fossil fuels, thereby increasing air pollution. Linear disadvantages are relatively easy to prove; the problem lies in establishing that they outweigh the affirmative case. It is not hard to find evidence to support such an argument, but it may be difficult to establish that the plan's action is sufficient to create a large disadvantage impact. Some negative teams argue *linear risk disadvantages*, in which the affirmative moves the world incrementally closer to a great disaster, such as massive climate change through global warming or species extinction. Here the disadvantage contends that there may be no way to predict the specific impact, but that the affirmative proposal definitely risks a disastrous consequence, and therefore should be rejected.

Since disadvantages are frequently contingent on many intermediate links, the quality of evidence used is crucial. Link evidence should be as specific to the affirmative proposal as possible, and the link and uniqueness evidence needs to be quite recent.

The different pieces of evidence supporting the internal links should come from authors who make essentially the same assumptions about the issue under discussion. Finally, the impact evidence should be powerfully worded.

For many years disadvantage arguments were introduced in the second negative constructive speech. Recently, disadvantages have begun to appear in the first negative constructive, usually in the form of a *shell*. The shell usually contains link, uniqueness, and impact arguments, supported by not more than four or five pieces of evidence. Additional arguments are reserved for the negative block, when the negative will have an opportunity to respond to the affirmative attacks on the disadvantage. As with many other arguments, it is important that the negative prepare for disadvantage debating by anticipating opposing arguments and organizing briefs that answer those objections with evidence.

THE COUNTERPLAN STRATEGY

Another avenue of negative argument is to present a *counterplan*, a proposed new policy for dealing with the problem area. It differs in major ways both from the present system and from the affirmative resolution. This strategy is used when the negative chooses not to defend the ability of the present system or minor repairs to the present system to measure up against the affirmative plan. It chooses, instead, to present its own alternative.

The negative should present the counterplan in the first negative constructive speech. It is considered inappropriate for the negative to withhold a major line of argument until after the affirmative constructive time periods have ended.

A counterplan carries essential burdens, just as an affirmative case does. The most important burden of a counterplan is that it must be *competitive*. Essentially, this means that for a counterplan to constitute a reason to reject the resolution, the judge must face a forced choice between the affirmative plan and the negative counterplan. It is not sufficient for the counterplan to be "more advantageous" than the plan; the judge could still adopt the affirmative proposal and do the counterplan as well, and the resolution would still be affirmed.

There are two ways in which a negative team might prove that its counterplan is competitive. First, it can prove that the counterplan is *mutually exclusive.* That is to say, the negative may be able to demonstrate that it would be physically impossible to do both the affirmative and negative proposals at the same time. If the affirmative plan bans arms sales and the negative counterplan increases arms sales, the two are obviously mutually exclusive.

More commonly, the negative will attempt to show that its counterplan is *net beneficial.* Simply put, a counterplan is net beneficial if a judge would not want to do the counterplan and the plan simultaneously, even if it would be possible to do so. A net beneficial counterplan accrues a greater advantage done alone than if it were done together with the affirmative proposal; therefore, it is a reason to reject the affirmative. For instance, on a resolution advocating increased federal action in the area of environmental policy, a negative team might argue a state action counterplan. The counterplan might be argued to be net beneficial because simultaneous state and federal action would waste resources on duplicative effort. It might also be net beneficial because federal action would cause a disadvantage—through increased federal government spending, perhaps—that a state action counterplan, done alone, would not cause. Of course, the competitiveness of the counterplan depends on the success or failure of the advantages or disadvantages that the negative chooses to argue.

In arguing counterplan competitiveness, negative teams should be prepared for affirmative permutation arguments. A *permutation* is a hypothetical response to counterplan competition. Generally, it contends that the parts of the counterplan that produce the counterplan advantage could be done along with the parts of the affirmative proposal that produce the affirmative advantage. Consider the example of state versus federal involvement in environmental protection. The negative might argue that its counterplan is superior because only state officials know the best way to solve water and air pollution in their areas. The affirmative might respond with a permutation: Execute its federal government pollution program, but incorporate the advice and consultation of state officials, thus gaining the advantages of both proposals. This permutation would demonstrate that the negative counterplan, while net beneficial on face, is not really competitive. The negative might then attempt to prove that there are other advantages to state action, or disadvantages to federal action, that the permutation does not account for.

Traditionally, debate theory has placed a second burden on the counterplan: it must be *non-topical.* For decades, most debate theorists have argued that the resolution is the fundamental division of ground between the affirmative and negative teams. If the affirmative advocates non-topical action, it has abandoned its duty to uphold the resolution, and it should lose the round. Similarly, if the negative advocates topical action, it has abandoned its duty to oppose the resolution, and it should lose the round. Judges forced to choose between two topical proposals, one advocated by the affirmative and one by the negative, may reasonably conclude that they are voting affirmative regardless of which proposal they accept. Accordingly, most counterplans include an observation explaining why they are not topical—often by defining one or more words of the resolution and explaining why the counterpart does not meet those terms.

While most high school judges still expect counterplans to be non-topical, there is growing acceptance of the legitimacy of topical counterplans. There are several reasons judges may find such counterplans acceptable. First, some judges regard the resolution as an initial directive to discussion of a problem area, rather than as a stone wall separating the two teams. According to this point of view, if teams are well prepared to argue the issues of the debate, no particular harm is done if one team or another wanders onto the other's "ground."

Second, it can be argued that the wording of some resolutions makes it difficult for the negative to develop non-topical counterplans. This is particularly true when a resolution is *bidirectional*; in other words, when the topic does not specify the direction in which policy change should go. An example would be the 1995–96 high school resolution, "Resolved: That the U.S. government should substantially change its foreign policy toward the People's Republic of China." Under this resolution almost any reasonable alternative to an affirmative proposal is likely to be topical.

Third, many judges believe that the requirement that a counterplan be competitive constitutes a sufficient limit on negative ground; therefore, the non-topicality requirement is unnecessary. Beginning debaters will want to consult their coach and colleagues concerning the attitudes of local judges toward topical counterplans.

Does the negative forfeit presumption when it runs a counterplan? Can a negative team argue a counterplan and still make arguments attacking the affirmative harm or solvency? For many years there was a consensus among coaches and judges that in a counterplan round, the negative team must essentially concede the affirmative case and devote its speaking time entirely to the counterplan. In recent years, however, judges have become more accepting of "if-then" or conditional arguments. Consequently, negative teams sometimes do argue that there is no real harm in the present system—but that if harm did exist, the counterplan would be a better solution. Some judges will even permit a negative team to abandon a counterplan midway through the debate round if it believes that a different issue—topicality or a disadvantage, for instance—is more likely to win the team the ballot. Again, debaters should carefully consider the preferences of judges on their local and regional circuit before deciding their counterplan strategy.

NEGATIVE REBUTTALS

Chapter 6 discusses the division of labor between the second negative constructive and the first negative rebuttal. Essentially, the first negative rebuttal extends issues not developed by the second negative constructive. Frequently, these are negative arguments against the case, or topicality arguments.

The second negative rebuttal is arguably the most difficult speech in the debate. These rebuttalists must select the issues that they think they have the strongest chance of winning—two or three at most. Often debaters are tempted to address too many issues in the second negative rebuttal, perhaps in an attempt to overwhelm the last affirmative rebuttalist. This is almost always an error in strategy. Because this is the last negative speech, it is important to leave time not only for a line-by-line review of arguments, but also for explaining why the negative wins each issue, and why winning that particular issue means that it should win the round. In a stock issues round, for instance, it is particularly important to explain why the negative wins its solvency arguments, but also why those arguments, when taken together, are so compelling that the affirmative must lose on solvency. If the strategy focuses on outweighing the case advantage with a disadvantage, the last rebuttalist should focus on a comparison of impacts. If the negative can show that the disadvantage impact will happen first, is supported by stronger evidence, or is more certain than the advantage impact, he or she will stand a good chance of winning the round even if the affirmative still carries some advantage.

Since the negative cannot answer the affirmative's last speech, the second negative rebuttalist must also try to anticipate what the second affirmative rebuttalist will say. The second affirmative, for example, will almost always try to maximize and perhaps overclaim the importance of certain case arguments. Consequently, the second negative rebuttal should try to minimize their importance. The second affirmative may also attempt to introduce new arguments, particularly if the first affirmative rebuttal's coverage of the flow was less than perfect. The second negative rebuttalist, then, must remember to warn the judge against accepting these new arguments.

SUMMARY

In this chapter negative approaches to topicality, case issues, disadvantages, and counterplans have been discussed. The mix of negative arguments used by a debater in a given round will depend on the style of the affirmative case (need-plan or comparative advantage), the types of harms it addresses, the preferences of judges in his or her region, and the resolution itself. In any style of debate, negative teams are successful if their rebuttals focus on a limited number of winning issues. Any strategy that has the effect of minimizing the affirmative case advantage and maximizing the impact of a disadvantage speaks to the heart of what any judge looks for: Does the world become a better place if I vote affirmative? If the judge cannot answer yes to that question, the negative has done its job in the round.

QUESTIONS FOR DISCUSSION

1. Define *presumption*.
2. Explain the role presumption plays in debate.
3. Does presumption always reside with the negative position?
4. Why are topicality arguments important?
5. What difference could it make to a judge if an affirmative plan plank is proven to be extratopical?

6. What difference could it make to a judge if an affirmative advantage is proven to be extratopical?

7. Give some examples of quantitative and qualitative measures of significance and distinguish between them.

8. What is the relationship of the affirmative advantages to the negative disadvantages in terms of the judge's assessment of the debate?

9. What are the requirements of a counterplan?

10. What is a permutation?

ACTIVITIES

1. Write a short paragraph that introduces a negative position for a debate. Use either affirmative cases developed for previous chapters or reconstruct an actual round of debate and develop a position other than the one that was employed in the debate.

2. Develop a list of the most common challenges you have observed in case refutation. Which challenges are most useful? Which are least useful?

3. Write a disadvantage to any affirmative plan that spends a significant amount of federal tax dollars.

4. Deliver a speech that compares a disadvantage to an advantage. This short speech should be given once comparing disadvantages that are in the same area as the affirmative advantage.

5. Discuss the strengths and weaknesses of disadvantages you have heard pertaining to different cases on the current national topic.

6. Write a counterplan and practice delivering it. What cases would the counterplan be used for refuting?

7. Conduct a practice round of debate in which a counterplan is used as a negative strategy.

8. Make a list of possible permutations you could use on the affirmative against common counterplans. Discuss how you would word each one, and how you might defend it against negative objections.

9. Consult a flow of a second negative rebuttal from a tournament or practice round. Write out notes for a new overview that "tells the story" of why you will win the round. Deliver this rebuttal to your coach or teammates.

PRINCIPLES OF CROSS-EXAMINATION DEBATE

OBJECTIVES AND KEY TERMS

After studying Chapter 9, you should be able to

1. Explain the obligations of each speaker in a round of cross-examination,
2. Explain and demonstrate the objectives of the cross-examination period in debate, both as the examiner and the respondent, and
3. Participate effectively in a round of cross-examination debate on both the affirmative and negative sides.

After reading this chapter, you should understand the following terms:

clarification of points

exposing errors

obtaining admissions

preparing for cross-examination

role of questioner

role of respondent

setting up arguments

When it comes to learning the skills of argument, cross-examination debate provides excellent training. The cross-examination period is a time during which there is direct confrontation between opposing members of the two teams. A public question-and-answer exchange takes place for the purpose of influencing a judge.

First used in academic debate during the 1930s, the cross-examination format has become the most common form of debate at the high school level.

CONVENTIONS OF CROSS-EXAMINATION

Certain conventions are observed during the cross-examination period. First, one speaker asks questions and an opponent answers them. Neither the questioner nor the person being questioned should attempt to abuse that time by extended speech making. If, however, the questioner does not control the period, that is likely to happen.

Second, this period is a time to establish the judge's and the opposition's attitude toward you. Sarcasm, evasiveness, browbeating, or generally obstructive behavior does not advance your status in the round. Although there will be many occasions when the opposition will give you ample reason to retaliate with behavior of this sort, remember that doing so makes you seem immature. No one finds it easy to pass up the opportunity to be clever with words or to make the other person look inadequate. However, blatant bad manners are no more in order in the cross-examination period of a debate than in any other formal setting.

Because the cross-examination period is essentially a question-and-answer exchange for the purpose of influencing the judge, the two debaters should not face each other; rather, they should stand side by side and face the judge. Both the questioner and the respondent should be prepared to function independently of their partners. Many judges do not approve of conference between debaters and their partners during the cross-examination period. In some regions it has become common for respondents to seek help from their partner on an answer, or for questioners to permit an interruption from their partner, who may have his or her own question. Even if you know that your judge may tolerate such "tag-team" or "open cross-ex" practices, it is best to minimize them. A debater who is regularly interrupted by a partner runs the risk of being perceived as inadequate or overdependent. In addition, frequent interruptions may make the cross-examination period chaotic and difficult for the judge to follow.

The cross-examination period is not meant to give an opportunity for direct argument between the two debaters involved. To argue with each other is not only juvenile, it is counterproductive. Both the person questioning and the one responding should always remember that cross-examination is the time when you can look really good. It is the time in which you can establish your control of the situation and demonstrate poise and a sense of being in command. But it is also a time when you can erase all those positive impressions by losing your temper and getting upset. Try to avoid such negative behavior.

OBJECTIVES OF CROSS-EXAMINATION

There are essentially four objectives in a cross-examination: (1) to clarify points of the opposition's position, (2) to expose factual error or unsupported assertions made by the opposition, (3) to obtain damaging admissions from the opposition, and (4) to set up arguments for use in subsequent speeches by you or your partner. All of these objectives must be pursued in a civil manner.

To Clarify Points

Clarification is an important objective. Probes that begin with such phrases as "Would you explain the use...," "State briefly the ultimate goal of...," "Did you mean that...," or "Restate the...." are valuable in the course of the debate. They allow the opposition to clarify, and they keep you from wasting time and appearing to be foolish by arguing a point that you have misinterpreted. Probes such as these serve to clarify the thinking process by which the opposition arrived at a given position. You cannot attack arguments you do not understand; they must be clarified first and then attacked.

To Expose Errors

A second kind of clarification that cross-examination can provide is a clarification of evidence. This clarification process, however, should be utilized to expose factual error or lack of substantiation by the opposition. Evidence can be attacked in many different ways. In standard debate you can criticize evidence, call for clarification and repetition of certain pieces of key evidence, and challenge interpretation of evidence, but you have no guarantee that the opposition will respond. In cross-examination there is no way for the other team to avoid response without impeaching the team's evidence through silence. Remember in the cross-examination period that since evidence is the cornerstone of support for any argument, undermining evidence is a key way to attack an issue. There are four basic attacks against evidence that you can set up through skillful cross-examination questions.

1. The source of the evidence itself may need to be questioned. For example, you might question your opponent in the following manner: "You read evidence from Dr. John Smith in support of the point that solar energy is a viable source of energy for home and industry. What was the date on the piece of evidence?" "Are you aware that six months after that date, Dr. Smith testified before the House Energy Committee that it would be ten years before solar energy would be cost-beneficial on a mass production basis?" Such a line of questioning creates doubt about source credibility. Similarly, if you are aware that the source of the evidence is biased or has traditionally taken the opposite view from the one in evidence, then your questions should move in that direction. The date of the source, the reputation, or direct qualification may also be questioned.

2. You can aim your questions at the content of the evidence. If the evidence is an empirical study, a series of questions on method, the existence of counterstudies, and the size of the sample should be employed. When the evidence is conclusionary, beware of qualifiers in the body of the quotation. The affirmative, for example, could advance an argument on regulation of health care that the present system forms an industry-wide cartel precluding the development of prepaid group practices. Listen to the evidence, and question as follows: "In the evidence on an industrywide cartel, please reread the first sentence. Does that sentence use the words 'cartel *may* exist'?" Be aware in this line of questioning of any kind of language in the body of the evidence itself that qualifies its impact: words such as "some," "few," "indications are," and "seem to be." Your attack is stronger, of course, if

you can point out such words by calling for a rereading of the specific point in the evidence where the qualifier occurs, rather than by asking for a general rereading.

3. Another form of questioning is to pinpoint issues in the case that were not evidenced during the initial presentation. Your approach here is to repeat the opposition's contention and then ask for the repetition of the specific piece of evidence used on that point. You might also ask during cross-examination for additional evidence. For example, "You claim that the United States will be severely energy-deficient in several years. You give us a projection by Senator B. Since that one contention constitutes the basis for the entire affirmative plan, do you intend to read statistical evidence to support it?"

4. A final line of questioning is to ask about the link between data and claim. Too frequently people have a tendency to assume that the evidence read by the opposition says what they indicate it says. You must listen to the evidence and pursue questions in cross-examination. For example, in a debate on a policy for energy self-sufficiency, the affirmative argues that current federal programs should develop alternate energy sources but are inherently incapable of solving the problem. They then read evidence from a congressional hearing stating that the administrators of the existing programs are inefficient. Your obvious line of questioning in cross-examination would be to establish that the piece of evidence does *not* establish the point advanced by the affirmative. With this line of questioning, you are not attacking the point the evidence *does* make; you are establishing the failure of that piece of evidence to prove what the affirmative has asserted.

To Obtain Admissions

A third goal of cross-examination is to find answers that will change the opponent's case or plan. This particular objective is difficult to achieve, for no opponent is going to confess to the truth of an attack. Don't expect the other team to give up. Also, don't get frustrated when an opposing speaker does not respond directly to a damaging line of questioning. Do not belabor a line of questioning. Simply make your point and then move on.

Consider a sample cross-examination on the topic of medical care. The affirmative advocates a national system of health maintenance organizations. It establishes the justification for preventive or group care: Shorter hospital stays reduce iatrogenic, or hospital-borne, diseases. A line of questioning to employ might be similar to this:

Q: Iatrogenic diseases are the result of exposure to germs that thrive in the hospital environment, right?

A: That is right.

Q: You tell us that a significant number of people are the victims of iatrogenic diseases each year, right?

A: Yes.

Q: It is your contention that these diseases are contracted because the person is in the hospital?

A: Yes.

Q: And you claim a significant reduction in this type of disease because you reduce the number of days a person will be in the hospital? I believe you said three days would be average under your plan.

A: Yes.

Q: Will you please read the piece of evidence in which it is specified that iatrogenic diseases are only contracted after the third day of hospitalization?

A: Uh...I didn't read such a piece of evidence.

Q: Oh, I see. Well, read the piece of evidence that showed an empirical study demonstrating that people who stay in hospitals for more than three days are more likely to contract iatrogenic diseases than those who stay only three days or less.

A: I didn't read that, either.

At this point, you have the admission you want. No causal link is established by the initial presentation. You may invite the affirmative to bring up such evidence later, or you may simply go on to other things. You have established a strong beginning point for an attack on the causality of the affirmative advantage.

Similar lines of questioning can be designed to show appeals to emotions, begging the question, shifting ground, exaggeration of claims, and internal dilemmas or contradictions. A particularly strong line of questions might be developed for the second negative speaker on plan attacks. An affirmative cross-examination that skill-fully takes the negative speaker through reestablishing the inherency argument and then quickly pushes back to disadvantages will expose a contradiction or at least a dilemma that the negative will then have to deal with.

To Set Up Arguments

Underlying each of the first three objectives of cross-examination is the fourth and most vital one. Regardless of what you establish in the questioning period, it must set up a line of argumentation that can and will be used in subsequent speeches. Surprisingly enough, many debaters fail to use the results of what they establish in cross-examination. If you gain an admission, it may certainly speak for itself at the time, but you must review it and tie it in with a specific argument. Its significance must be demonstrated—you must help the judge see that the admission is as damaging as a piece of expert testimony would have been. In other words, the results of cross-examination must be used as material evidence in the debate itself. Use statements such as "The negative speaker herself admitted under direct cross-examination that she had no counterstudy to submit"; or "The affirmative speaker admitted to you in cross-examination that he could not tell us how many people are harmed by the conditions he described"; or "Remember that first cross-examination period in which the affirmative admitted that there were no structural barriers to adopting such a system right now. I believe you will agree with me that this is the most important thing the affirmative has said, for in this statement the affirmative forfeits the burden of proof that is its obligation in today's debate." These statements give the judge a direct relationship between what was said in the cross-examination and what was established in the debate. They get the cross-examination period into the mainstream of the debate.

To employ cross-examination responses in later speeches, debaters should form the habit of writing down important answers. Not only should the person questioning take notes, but so should a colleague of the person being questioned. It may become crucial later in the debate to have an accurate record of what was said.

CROSS-EXAMINATION TECHNIQUES

Preparation

Preparation is important for good cross-examination debating. There are few debaters who would approach debate without researching their own case carefully and attempting to anticipate the kind of cases they might meet. Rarely does a debater go to a tournament without practice rounds, yet it is not infrequent for debaters to enter into a cross-examination debate without specific preparation for the cross-examination period.

Once you establish an affirmative case, you and your partner should think about possible opposing negative positions. This practice should suggest possible cross-examination questions that the negative might ask after hearing your case. Once you identify some questions that might be encountered, then design appropriate answers. By the same process, you should think of possible questions that might be used in the second examination period and design answers for them. It is not enough to prepare a series of questions; you should anticipate the questions that might be asked and practice answers.

At one NFL National Tournament, a first negative speaker developed a very strong topicality argument without thinking it through to cross-examination. The first question from the affirmative was for the negative to identify an affirmative case that would meet the definitions provided by the negative in the topicality argument. Because the negative had not thought this through, the first negative could not provide an example that could withstand challenges by the affirmative questioner. The second affirmative speaker used this exchange to argue that the definition offered by the negative was unreasonable and that the topicality argument should not be accepted. All the negative needed was one example to win the argument.

Role of Questioner

There are a number of guidelines that should be remembered for the role of questioner.

1. Begin the cross-examination period with a question that will capture the judge's attention.

2. Conclude the cross-examination period on a high note. Do not keep questioning about trivia just because you have time left. If you have established a psychological advantage and still have time left, stop.

3. Employ a line of questioning leading to your point. That is, ask for a series of small bits of information that will, when accumulated, lead to your conclusion about an argument. The concluding question of each line of questions may serve as a summary of what you have accomplished, such as "In view of these facts, is it still your position that…?" Do not expect your opponent to admit that your conclusion is correct, but lead her or him to the point that your judge will accept it.

4. Remember that you are in control of the questioning period. Do not allow your opponent to take control by asking questions, conferring with a colleague, or practicing evasion. When such ploys are used, interrupt the speaker with firm courtesy. Remember, do not lose your poise, but do not lose control of the questioning, either.

5. Confine yourself to asking questions. Phrase your questions simply and concisely. Do not ask open-ended questions that impart an opportunity to filibuster. Phrase your questions in such a way as to call for short and specific answers, preferably yes and no.

6. Ask only one question at a time, and get an answer to each question before asking the next one.

7. Use a quiet, moderate style to encourage the witness to relax and enter into a fair exchange about arguments in the debate. If you come on too strong, you will set up an adversary atmosphere that might lead to hostility.

8. Avoid questions to which you do not know the answer, with the exception of questions to clarify points in the actual plan or case of the opposition. One questioner gave an opponent an excellent opportunity by asking, "You claim that P.S.R.O.'s unfairly limit the expansion of health maintenance organizations. Can you give even one example of an HMO that was limited by a P.S.R.O.?" The respondent advanced the affirmative case by replying, "Yes, I can. I have the records to the HMO in a midwestern city that

was kept from...." The point here is that if your own knowledge is inadequate, you may open an opportunity for the opposition with a question to which you do not know the answer.

9. Do not attempt to establish your reputation as the budding Perry Mason. Strutting about, pointing accusing fingers, ridiculing the witness, and putting on a performance may make a good scene in a movie, but it has no place in an academic debate.

Role of Respondent

Another aspect of cross-examination debate is the role of the person being questioned. The respondent in the cross-examination period has a viable part to play and should be prepared to perform in such a fashion as to win the period. This can be better ensured if you prepare in advance by anticipating questions.

1. The respondent should stand tall, look directly at the judge and audience, and speak loudly enough to be heard clearly. Every nonverbal message sent should indicate a relaxed, yet alert, individual. A hanging head, evasive eye contact, and soft voice all indicate a person who is unsure or untruthful. Either position does nothing to advance your position.

2. The role of respondent is one of answering questions. You are not free to ask questions during this time. There is an exception, however, that should be remembered. If the question was phrased in a confusing manner, if it asked for several items of information, or if in any other way it was difficult to respond to, then you not only may, but you should ask for clarification.

3. Any fair and reasonable question should be answered. When you are the respondent, employing deliberately vague or evasive tactics will only weaken your position eventually. Do not hedge. If you know the answer, give it. If you don't know the answer, say so.

4. It is permissible to qualify an answer, but this should be done briefly. Don't give these qualifications unless they are necessary for clarification. A good technique to use is to state the qualification ahead of the answer. For example, the question

"Do you believe that the federal government should control private enterprise?" might best be answered, "To the extent that the federal government is responsible for the safety and well-being of the nation's citizens who are being endangered by a lack of energy, I think the federal government should have a role in the regulation of that private industry."

5. The respondent should never underestimate the result of an answer nor lose sight of the fact that every question is designed to weaken her or his own case or help the case of the opposition. Be on guard.

6. When you are the respondent, you may decline to answer questions that are ambiguous or loaded. The old technique of posing questions of the "Have you stopped beating your wife yet?" variety is a trap, and you do not have to respond to them. However, you should decline to answer by explaining that the question is not clear or is leading and ask for it to be rephrased.

7. Do not volunteer information. Answer only the questions that are asked and do so briefly and concisely as possible. Do not anticipate the next question by answering it ahead of time; you may put arguments into the hands of the opposition that way. Remember, even if the question gets close to a weakness you know your case has, there is no guarantee the opposition will see it. Just wait; don't point the way for them.

The cross-examination period in a debate can be a time of enjoyment and excitement. It is also a time designed to accomplish a valid set of objectives. When the examiner and the respondent both understand these objectives, the result is a better debate.

SUMMARY

Cross-examination debate is an excellent format for learning the skills of argument. It enables debaters to question one another and thereby learn the skills of public defense and attack. Like any other debate activity, if it is not handled well it can result in unfortunate exchanges that mar the intellectual excitement of argument. Also, as with other debate activity, strategies and methods are always evolving, so the debater has to "keep up." With experience and maturity, you should be able to handle even the most tense situation with style and class. For an example of a ballot used during the judging of cross-examination debate, see the NFL ballot in Appendix D.

QUESTIONS FOR DISCUSSION

1. What is the value of cross-examination in debate?
2. Outline the four objectives of a cross-examination period.
3. When trying to clarify evidence in a cross-examination period, what are four attacks that can be set up? Provide an example of each.
4. Because the negative gains a tremendous advantage during the negative block, how can the cross-examination of the second negative speaker be used to help the first affirmative rebuttalist? Provide an example.
5. When you question an opponent, why is it important not to ask open-ended questions?
6. It is said that the questioner should not ask questions for which the answer is not already known. What would be the harm of asking a question just to gain more information or to explore an argument?
7. As the respondent, you are advised not to volunteer information unless it is asked for specifically. Why?

ACTIVITIES

1. Using the articles you collected for Activity 4 in Chapter 6, prepare a list of questions you would ask in a cross-examination period.
2. Using your affirmative speech from Activity 4 in Chapter 7 and your negative speech from Activity 4 in Chapter 8, outline questions you feel an opponent might ask. Now outline your answers.

3. Referring to your flow (sheets) from previous affirmative speeches, outline cross-examination questions. Write down what you anticipate the answers to be. How would you use these in your next rebuttal speech?

4. After having participated in a cross-examination debate, go back and review the debate. What questions or answers served you well in the cross-examination periods? Where you had problems, rework your questions or answers.

LINCOLN-DOUGLAS DEBATE

OBJECTIVES AND KEY TERMS

After studying Chapter 10, you should be able to

1. Distinguish value propositions from fact and policy propositions,
2. Distinguish constructive speeches from rebuttal speeches,
3. Explain why defining terms is uniquely important to Lincoln-Douglas debate,
4. Explain the burdens of proof and rejoinder unique to Lincoln-Douglas debate,
5. Explain and provide examples of clash in Lincoln-Douglas debate,
6. List the fundamental parts of a Lincoln-Douglas affirmative or negative case, and
7. Write a case for acceptance or rejection of a particular value proposition.

After reading this chapter, you should understand the following terms:

> **burden of proof and rejoinder**
> **core value and value criteria**
> **cross-examination**
> **judging criteria**

Lincoln-Douglas debate is an academic debate event that features the clash of two speakers over the truth or falsity of a value proposition. It is different from team debate or policy debate in many ways. To gain an understanding of Lincoln-Douglas debate, it is important to examine its origins.

THE NATURE OF LINCOLN-DOUGLAS DEBATE

History

Lincoln-Douglas debate can be traced directly to the famous debates between Stephen A. Douglas and Abraham Lincoln in their race for the United States Senate during the summer and fall of 1858. In these debates, which would often last more than three hours, the affirmative gave the first speech and was allowed one hour. The negative spoke next for an hour and a half. Then the affirmative would return to speak for a final half hour.

After those historic debates, the Lincoln-Douglas format continued to be used by political candidates. Televised debates between presidential candidates or debates between candidates for local office often follow a similar format, which has long served to communicate the clash of ideas on important issues of the day. But when Douglas agreed to that series of joint appearances with Lincoln so long ago he set in motion not only a part of our political process, but also a debate format that would inspire academics to establish an interscholastic competitive event that grows more popular every year. In 1980 the National Forensic League established Lincoln-Douglas debate as an event at its national high school speech and debate tournament, and the Lincoln-Douglas format moved from the political arena to American classrooms.

Since that time, more than 100,000 students have competed at local, state, and national levels. At first, comparisons to two-person team debate, oratory, and extemporaneous speaking were the most understandable and meaningful preparation methods for a Lincoln-Douglas debate. But in the time since 1980 there has evolved a body of knowledge unique to debating value propositions in general and using the Lincoln-Douglas format in particular. Introducing that body of knowledge *basic* to Lincoln-Douglas debate is the purpose of this chapter.

One of the reasons for the creation of the Lincoln-Douglas format was to offer an alternative to academic two-person team debate. Because of this, several distinguishing features were established. Let's begin by looking at the fundamental differences.

As Distinct from Policy Debate

Lincoln-Douglas debate differs from two-person team debate in three basic ways.

Policy Propositions versus Value Propositions

First, the propositions for Lincoln-Douglas debate are value propositions, while the propositions for two-person team debate are policy propositions. As a result, two-person team debate is often referred to simply as *policy debate*. The type of proposition places (or relinquishes) particular burdens on the persons debating. Understanding the different demands of different proposition types is key to understanding how to debate.

Annual Propositions versus Bimonthly Propositions

Policy debate at the high school and collegiate levels establishes policy propositions that are debated interscholastically for an entire academic year. On the other hand, Lincoln-Douglas debate establishes value propositions that are debated for merely a couple of months before changing to a new proposition. And individual states, regions, and leagues have agreed to debate Lincoln-Douglas topics that differ from topics debated nationally. As a result, policy debate has grown to be much more labor-intensive: The research possible in a year's time causes policy debate to rely upon files and files of evidence. Changing topics more frequently in Lincoln-Douglas makes such files impossible if not unnecessary. Therefore, Lincoln-Douglas has been an attractive debate alternative for students who cannot give as much time to debate. It also means that if you do not like this month's topic, maybe you will find next month's more attractive! Of course, this comparison applies only to interscholastic competition. In the classroom, changing topics frequently can apply to any type of proposition.

Two-Person Teams versus Single-Person Entries

A third fundamental difference is that policy debate competitions take the form of a two-person team opposing another two-person team. Lincoln-Douglas debate is one-on-one: one person opposing another. Teamwork and cooperation are very much a part of policy debate, while individual initiative and self-reliance are very much a part of Lincoln-Douglas. Lincoln-Douglas debate is a great alternative for the debater who cannot find a partner (or simply prefers working solo). The Lincoln-Douglas debater can take greater personal pleasure in success, but has fewer people to blame for failure.

Other Features

Lincoln-Douglas debate has several other distinguishing features. The time frame for this format is much shorter than the traditional one for policy. (The Lincoln-Douglas format for debate is featured on page 166 of this chapter. Compare it with the policy debate format on pages 87–88.) There are other important differences as well. Value propositions invite argument that is more philosophical; the foundation of the debate is often some moral or ethical premise. Lincoln-Douglas is more conceptual as a result. Its anecdotal (or narrative) evidence is often persuasive but hardly conclusive, and real-life examples may illustrate some philosophical truth, but do not prove it. Policy debate tends to be more pragmatic and realistic. It depends upon and accepts as conclusive any expert testimony and "hard" facts, arguing probabilities of real results, causal connections, actual events as analogous, current institutions as important, real time as a parameter. Lincoln-Douglas may seek perpetual truths, whereas policy wants to predict specific outcomes that result from particular initiatives.

A Lincoln-Douglas proposition might declare, "It is more important that justice seem to be done than that justice actually happen," or "Machiavelli was right." A policy proposition might contend, "The United States should significantly change the jury system," or "The United States should establish, finance, and administer a national system to select presidential and vice presidential candidates."

DISTINGUISHING TYPES OF PROPOSITIONS

Propositions are statements or declarations that something is so. There are three proposition types: fact, value, and policy, and each type makes a different sort of declaration. To advocate the truth of each type places different demands upon the advocate. Debating values (as in Lincoln-Douglas debate) is different from debating facts or policy. Therefore, it is important that a debater should know how each proposition type differs from the others.

Fact Propositions

A *proposition of fact* is a proposition that declares some material truth. A *material truth* is some reality that can be objectively determined and supported to the satisfaction of most. For example, "The temperature is seventy-two degrees in this room" is a proposition of fact. The temperature can be determined by using an objective tool such as a thermometer; the reliability of the thermometer can be tested as well. After some investigation, the seventy-two-degree declaration will be affirmed or denied to the satisfaction of most people.

Fact propositions do not make for good debating unless the debaters agree to argue over the meaning of terms. A classroom debate can occur over the fact proposition "The grass is green," but the debaters must agree to approach the proposition creatively. What is meant by "grass," what is meant by "is," and what is meant by "green"? If color is a perception, then does that mean things only "appear" to be green rather that actually "being" green? You can imagine that such a topic might be challenging, not to mention entertaining. The debate can still be an insightful classroom exercise, but the proposition would not keep one's interest for months or an entire year, as is the case with value and policy propositions.

Value Propositions

A *proposition of value* is a proposition that declares some judgment about some reality. You should realize immediately that this proposition demands more of the advocate than the proposition of fact. The value declaration requires that the debater can determine and support the reality as well as determine and support the reasonableness of the judgment. For example, "The temperature is too hot in this room" is a proposition of value. It should be obvious that everyone debating this proposition must agree upon the temperature and the room—and that in and of itself may be open to debate as a question of fact. But the debate does not end there. It must also pursue the correctness of the judgment declared by the proposition. What is "too hot"? That judgment cannot be debated until a standard of judgment is established. The question must be asked, "Too hot for what?" The moment that question is answered, there is a standard of judgment against which to argue the declaration in the proposition: "Too hot to boil water?" "Too hot to freeze water?" "Too hot for school?"

The value judgment is not just a matter of personal opinion. Argument can be made as to appropriate standards of judgment. And comparing the actual temperature (say, seventy-two degrees) to the argued standard may result in a strong case for or against the judgment declared in the proposition. Notice most importantly that propositions of value cause the debaters to argue both facts (material truths) and values (appropriate standards of judgment). And the debate does not end there—the debaters must also argue how the facts measure up against the standards of judgment.

Policy Propositions

A *proposition of policy* is a proposition declaring that some plan or course of action should occur. Implicit in this type of proposition is the assumption that the declared course of action is possible and that the course of action can be justified. Consider this policy proposition: "The temperature regulating system at our school should be changed." It should be immediately clear that this type of proposition has all sorts of demands. Some of those are fact considerations (what is the current system of heating and cooling, what has been the history of temperatures in school, are there legal requirements for minimum and maximum temperatures, how much has it cost, how much money do we have to spend, what are the alternatives, how much will a new system cost) and some are value considerations (has it been too hot or cold, are we spending too much, will a new system hurt spending on other programs that are more important, are books more important than temperature). The debaters will argue an array of facts and values, propose or reject a new system, and seek to justify or reject the reasons for change.

Because policy propositions are by their very nature *inclusive of* facts and values but *go beyond* facts and values, their demands upon advocates are great, calling for analytic and research skills in addition to being very labor-intensive. That is why policy propositions make for good debate when the purpose is to select a proposition that will hold debaters' interest for long periods of time (the national interscholastic policy topic is debated for a year). In contrast, a value proposition can be very challenging, but the debate ends with advocacy of the value judgment itself. Neither the affirmative nor the negative has to propose change or offer some course of action to secure the value.

DEBATING PROPOSITIONS OF VALUE

In the previous section, the burdens of debating propositions of value were contrasted with those of debating propositions of fact or policy. One of the inherent characteristics of debating propositions of value is that the truth of the proposition depends upon some acceptable standard of judgment.

Standards of Judgment

When arguing the value of an entity, one immediately notices the need for some appropriate standard of judgment. Let us consider a simple example: You cannot decide that your wristwatch is worth more than my watch until you agree upon the standard with which to establish its worth. Let us assume for the moment that the standard of judgment is dollar value. My watch is plastic, and it was included free of charge when I purchased athletic shoes. Your watch is an antique solid-gold Rolex. Your watch is worth more than my watch if we agree that the appropriate standard of judgment is monetary value. My watch is nearly worthless; your watch may be virtually priceless. But what if we both need to be at the airport on time? My watch keeps great time, while your Rolex has not kept time for the past fifty years. My watch is worth more than yours if the standard of judgment is telling time.

But if we cannot agree upon the appropriate standard, then we will have to argue over what standard is the more appropriate for deciding the worth of wristwatches. That may be an argument more difficult to decide. I may have to argue that the essential nature of watches is as timepieces, and that telling time is the best standard for judging value. I may argue that the monetary value of a watch may be secondary to the essential purpose of the watch. You may argue that both watches have the same purpose, yours can be repaired, and that the ultimate worth of something is the accumulation of all of its potential values. Your watch may not tell time today, but that does not deny that it could someday. That potential value added to its monetary value makes your watch ultimately the most valuable because it has more total value. How would an objective judge decide this debate? It would depend upon which of us seemed most reasonable in arguing the appropriate standard of judgment.

Similarly, in Lincoln-Douglas debate there is a declaration of worth. The word *worth* may not actually occur in the proposition, but some value term does. It may occur as a declaration of *importance*, as a matter of being *better*, or as a matter of something that *should be valued*. However the proposition appears, it is clear that the statement is making some declaration of judgment. The connotation if not the denotation is one of judgment. You as a debater will need to decide what should be the appropriate standard of judgment. Advocating the proposition may require a different standard of judgment than rejecting the proposition. In Lincoln-Douglas debate the selected standard of judgment has come to be known as the *core value*.

The Core Value

To defend or reject a proposition of policy requires a standard of judgment against which the "facts" of the proposition can be compared. The standard of judgment in value debate is the *core value*. The core value is often implicit within the context of the proposition; for example, "Individual rights are more important than social order." Implicit in this topic are such core values as freedom, liberty, safety, stability, and so on. A debater upholding the importance of individual rights might argue that liberty would be secured by the value judgment, and that liberty is of utmost importance. A debater rejecting the proposition might argue that the upholding liberty above all else would be an endorsement of anarchy and chaos. The case for rejection might argue that stability is essential to the survival of society, and therefore social order is of greater importance than individual rights. The rejection might argue further that unless stability can be guaranteed, liberty is meaningless if not impossible. Social order may be necessary for liberty to be meaningful. In fact, you might notice that liberty could be the core value for either side. One side might argue that individual rights are necessary for liberty, while the other side might argue that social order may be more important to securing liberty. In any case, the core value is the standard argued to be of utmost importance when trying to decide the truth of the value judgment. Since you are trying to advocate your side of the proposition, you choose a core value that you think most people would accept as an assumed value to society and one that your side of the proposition uniquely upholds.

Value Criteria
When you are arguing that liberty is being met by upholding the proposition that individual rights are more important than social order, you find yourself explaining what constitutes liberty, its elements, and its conditions. This explanation is important because anyone listening to the debate needs to understand how one knows that liberty exists or has occurred. If liberty, as a core value, demands that there is some continuity to the liberty, continuity then becomes a criterion for deciding where liberty meaningfully exists. Individual rights may be important to continuity because individual rights guarantee that some freedom not only exists once, but continues to exist. Individual rights, then, give continuity, and continuity is important to liberty being meaningful. Therefore, individual rights contribute to and may even be necessary for liberty.

In this proposition, value criteria are the measures by which the facts of individual rights are compared to the standard of judgment, which is liberty. Generally speaking, *value criteria* are the measures by which the facts of the value proposition are said to uphold the core value. Different types of value propositions demand different considerations for both core values and value criteria.

Types of Value Propositions

Two fundamental types of value propositions will be introduced here: propositions that make some declaration of value or importance about a *single* entity, and propositions that declare some comparative worth held by *two* entities.

Judgment about a Single Entity
Consider the 1995 national proposition, "Laws which protect citizens from themselves are justified." After defining terms (definitions are very important and will be discussed later), the debate over this topic will center upon the values of society that are upheld

by such laws. A case to reject this resolution will focus on precious values that are compromised, limited, or denied by such laws.

To support the resolution, an appropriate core value might be social contract, justice, or protection of the public welfare. Value criteria might include duty, fairness, or safety. The appropriate value criterion will depend upon the core value: Safety may be important for measuring the protection of the public welfare; fair administration of laws may be the test for justice, and duties fulfilled may be the criterion for determining whether social contract is met by government. The case upholding the resolution could argue that laws that protect citizens from themselves—for example, seat belt laws or Federal Department of Agriculture standards for food—are justified because they promote safety (the value criterion), which is necessary for gaining the protection of the public welfare (the core value). Such laws may prevent discrimination; less discrimination is more fair (the value criterion) and is necessary for justice (the core value). A third case might argue that laws protecting citizens from themselves are justified because such laws are a duty (the value criterion) held by a government to preserve the social contract (the core value).

Rejecting the resolution will require thinking from the opposite perspective. It will require arguing that liberty, autonomy, self-esteem, or progress are core values. Appropriate value criteria will depend upon the core value selected: Freedom from restriction may be an important value criterion for liberty or autonomy; individual responsibility may be an important measure of self-esteem; and risk may be a necessary part of progress. The case for rejection will argue that laws that protect citizens from themselves deny liberty, autonomy, self-esteem, or progress (the core values) because they restrict freedom, invite irresponsibility, and are detrimental to risk (the value criteria).

Sometimes the proposition that makes a judgment about a single entity can make advocacy interestingly complicated. A 1995 national proposition declared, "The pursuit of feminist ideals is detrimental to the achievement of gender equality." This proposition seems to assume that gender equality is good. While you might want to argue or disagree with that assumption, it seems to be implicit in the statement. Interestingly, the value term in the proposition is not a positive value. The term of worth, "detrimental," is a *negative* judgment. The case upholding the proposition actually has to support a core value and value criteria for determining that which is detrimental. Rather than upholding positive values, the case upholding the resolution has to show a danger that is being supported by the pursuit of feminist ideals, or the case has to argue that a positive value is being denied. The opponent to this proposition has to do just the opposite. Because the language of the debate can become complicated and even seem to be contradictory, debating a proposition that makes a negative judgment about a single entity requires special care.

Judgments of Comparison between Entities

A value proposition that declares a judgment of comparison between two entities requires a different approach from the one discussed above. First you need to be able to recognize such a proposition. For example, the 1996 national Lincoln-Douglas debate proposition, "An oppressive government is more desirable than no government," declares that between two separate conditions, items, or ideas, one is to be preferred over the other. Such a comparison of entities proposition can make the declaration of comparative preference in many different ways: of higher priority, more desirable, more important, of greater value, and so on. The proposition makes it clear what is being compared, and it uses the value term (desirability, priority, importance) to declare a judgment about the comparison.

When beginning work on the above comparative statement, definitions will again be of first importance: What is meant by "oppressive," and what is meant by "no government" in particular? How harsh or cruel does a government need to be to qualify as "oppressive"? Does anarchy equal "no government," or is anarchy a type of government? Then you need to decide upon core values. When supporting the proposition, it seems that order and stability or continuity may be important core values. When rejecting the proposition, justice and liberty will be central to the debate.

Now you need to decide the value criteria that are appropriate. Laws and rules may be important criteria for determining order and stability. The proposition advocate might argue that while laws and rules are often restrictive and even oppressive, such laws and rules are necessary for stability and continuity, both of which are essential values of civilized society. On the other hand, the case to reject the proposition might argue that fairness and dissent are essential to justice and liberty. No government would mean no organized restrictions upon fairness and dissent, and while chaos might flourish with no government, fairness and free expression would be worth the cost of avoiding the cruelty and harshness that can come with organized tyranny and oppression. The case against might admit that society without government could be cruel, but no more cruel than government that is oppressive, and it has the potential of not being cruel at all.

The value proposition of comparison has a more direct indication of what the foundations of the debate will be about. The "sides" to the debate (not affirmative and negative, but rather the *responsibility* of the affirmative and the negative) are more obvious because they are stated within the proposition.

Burdens

Previous chapters have discussed that the position of supporting the proposition is termed the *affirmative*, and the position of rejecting the proposition is termed the *negative*. You have also learned that in policy or two-person team debate, each side has assigned burdens of proof and burdens of refutation, or rejoinder, expectations that have evolved in academic debate. Remember that *burdens* are duties, obligations, or expectations that are held by affirmative and negative debaters when faced with the judge of the debate. How these burdens either do or do not apply to Lincoln-Douglas debate will be discussed here.

Burden of Proof

In policy debate, *burden of proof* means those obligations held by the debater initiating an argument. In other words, whoever initiates a particular argument has the burden of proving the truth of the premises and the validity of the argument. This debater must show a weight of evidence that supports the contentions of the argument because in academic debate, it is not enough to assert something as true and demand that the opponent prove the assertion false.

The debater who initiates the argument has the responsibility of providing proof in support of the argument. If no proof is provided, the opponent can defeat the argument by labeling it a mere assertion or unsupported statement without merit in the debate. The judge of the debate is free then to reject the argument from the debate. Whichever debater depended upon that argument may lose the debate because he or she has lost the argument. Each argument in the debate carries with it this same obligation of support.

You learned in policy or two-person team debate that the burden of proof falls initially upon the affirmative because the affirmative initiates the debate. You also learned that this burden falls initially upon the affirmative because the policy proposition calls for some change in the present system. Therefore, since the affirmative is calling for change, and it is assumed to be unreasonable to change for the sake of change, the affirmative has the burden of proof in policy debate.

Lincoln-Douglas debate does not make any special assumptions about burden of proof for the affirmative. The value proposition is not assumed to be a judgment that is different or the same as accepted values in the present society. The affirmative may simply be affirming what *everyone* believes, or the affirmative may be affirming what *no one* believes. This debater has the job of arguing that the proposition is reasonable for *anyone* to believe. Therefore, the affirmative has the burden of proving the reasonableness of the proposition regardless of contemporary belief. And since the affirmative initiates the debate, this person has the initial burden of proof.

In Lincoln-Douglas debate, since contemporary belief does not assign burden of proof, the negative has the burden of proving the proposition false or unreasonable. If the affirmative has *not* met his or her burden of proof, the negative can argue victory by default. But that argument will not decide the debate because neither side of the proposition is assumed to be true at the beginning of the debate. Therefore, each side has an obligation to support their side of the proposition.

Burden of Rejoinder

The *burden of rejoinder* or refutation simply means the obligation to respond. Once an argument is made by one side in the debate, the argument demands response from the other side. If the opposing side does not respond, the initiator of the argument in question can claim victory for the argument by default.

Since both sides have burdens of proof, both sides have burdens of rejoinder. The affirmative has an obligation to respond to the negative case and argument. If the affirmative does not respond, the negative can claim victory for the argument.

Since the affirmative initiates the debate, the negative has the initial burden of rejoinder. Here *burden of rejoinder* simply means that in addition to presenting a case against the proposition, the negative also has an obligation to respond specifically to what the affirmative has presented. If each side presents his or her own case but does not respond to the opponent's case, there is said to be a lack of clash.

Clash

Clash is the name given to specific interactive argument that happens during the debate: If the negative specifically attacks a point made by the affirmative, and next the affirmative responds specifically to the attack, after which the negative attacks the response, and finally the affirmative repairs the damage done by the negative to the affirmative's effort to respond, there is said to be clash!

The essence of debate, clash defines the interaction of the two sides. It causes the two sides to attack and defend the arguments of the debate, and it causes arguments to be exposed as weak or to shine as strong. Clash requires debaters to be able to think on their feet, so it is spontaneous, exciting, sometimes informative, and other times devastating. It bears repeating: Clash is the essence of debate; otherwise, the activity is just an individual speaking event. Because it determines who does the better job of debating, judges look for clash.

FORMAT FOR LINCOLN-DOUGLAS DEBATE

As you may recall, academic interscholastic debate does not happen randomly or even haphazardly. The debate occurs within a particular time frame referred to as the *format for debate*. A number of formats may be experimented with in the classroom but the format established by the National Forensic League in 1980 has received wide acceptance and is likely to be the format you face in interscholastic competition:

Affirmative Constructive Speech	6 minutes
Cross-Examination of Affirmative Speaker by the Negative Speaker	3 minutes
Negative Constructive Speech	7 minutes
Cross-Examination of Negative Speaker by the Affirmative Speaker	3 minutes
Initial Affirmative Rebuttal	4 minutes

| Negative Rebuttal | 6 minutes |
| Final Affirmative Rebuttal | 3 minutes |

The judge will usually keep time and signal each speaker to indicate the time remaining. Each speaker is usually given preparation time to use as he or she chooses during the debate. The amount of preparation time may vary, but three minutes for each speaker has become standard. The judge will also note the use of preparation time and announce to the next speaker how much preparation time has elapsed or remains. The debater whose turn it is to speak next is the speaker against whom the time is charged for preparation. There is no requirement that the debaters use all of their preparation time. It is a good idea for you to ask the judge how time will be indicated, signaled, or announced so that you can make efficient use of time available.

SPEAKER DUTIES

Speaker duties for each item of responsibility below are similar in many ways to the speaker duties for policy debate. In fact, if you are knowledgeable of policy debate speaker duties and understand what this chapter has already introduced about Lincoln-Douglas debate and debating value propositions, you already have a good idea of judges' expectations of you in Lincoln-Douglas tournaments.

Constructives

Given a value proposition for debate, just as in policy debate, *constructives* are those speeches during which debaters present those arguments upon which they hope to win the debate. This presentation of position, or constructive, is usually referred to as the *case for acceptance* or the *case for rejection* of the proposition. Any argument is considered legitimate to present during a constructive speech, with time being the only limit. Of course, some arguments may be better than others. In Lincoln-Douglas debate, each side will present the core value and value criteria that it hopes is the most supportive to the position of advocacy or rejection of the value proposition. The rest of the constructive *case* will be filled with reasons and evidence defending the advocacy or rejection of the proposition as related to the core value and value criteria.

Affirmative

Because the affirmative has the job of defending the truth of the proposition, in Lincoln-Douglas debate this debater advocates the judgment that is declared in the value proposition. After an introduction the affirmative will define the terms in the proposition. As you can guess, the affirmative has the duty of arguing an appropriate core value with which to examine the judgment made in the proposition. Further, this debater argues appropriate value criteria to measure the importance of the value proposition in reaching the core value. The affirmative will usually give two or three primary reasons for the judgment held in the proposition being critical to society maintaining the core value. All six minutes of the constructive speech are typically used to present the affirmative case.

Negative

The negative constructive is longer by one minute. It tries to accomplish two separate purposes in seven minutes of constructive: present the negative case and respond to the affirmative case. The negative's duties grow out of the fact that there is no presumption of truth or falsity of the proposition in relation to the present value system of society. As a result the negative has just as much duty to show that the proposition should be rejected as does the affirmative to show a compelling case for acceptance. But the negative cannot spend all seven minutes presenting a case, because it would limit opportunity for clash!

Remember that because the affirmative initiates the debate, that puts several initial burdens of proof upon that side. If the affirmative case is filled with assertions, the negative will want to argue that the affirmative has not met his or her burdens. Most negatives will design a case that can be presented in four minutes so that in the three minutes that remain, the debater can launch particular attacks against the specifics (or lack of specifics!) of the affirmative case. The negative case will also seek to define the terms of the proposition, often in direct contrast to the definitions declared by the affirmative. Sometimes these definitions literally determine the direction of the debate. If the affirmative takes advantage of an unusual interpretation of the proposition, the negative will want to argue that the definitions beg the question. Of course, two can play at that game, and the affirmative will want to listen carefully to the negative's interpretation as well. A famous lawyer once said, "Pass any law you want as long as I get to define the terms." Definitions can be critical to the direction and meaning of the debate.

Cross-Examination

After each constructive speech a time for cross-examination will occur. Since the affirmative speaks first, the first cross examination will be the questioning of the affirmative.

When the affirmative has finished presenting his or her six-minute speech, the affirmative is open to cross-examination. This debater remains standing in the front of the room, and the negative stands and approaches the affirmative. During the three-minute examination period, the negative has control of the time to ask questions. Questions will usually be of two types: (1) those designed to clarify by asking for explanation or repetition; and (2) those designed to expose weaknesses by asking for support where there was mere assertion or explanation. Questions should be direct, concise, clear, and polite. This is not a time for the negative to argue or make speeches, just to ask questions. When time has elapsed, both debaters return to their seats, and the preparation time for the negative constructive begins.

When the negative constructive speech has finished, the affirmative debater approaches the negative. The affirmative's questioning has a purpose similar to that of the negative speaker's earlier. Since the negative may have presented case *and* attacked the affirmative, the affirmative's questioning may pertain to both. When time has elapsed, the preparation time for the initial affirmative rebuttal will begin.

Rebuttals

It is very important to understand the difference between constructive speeches and rebuttals. Constructive speeches are those presentations during which it is permissible to present any and all arguments upon which either side hopes to win the debate. In rebuttals, however, no new argument is permitted. To the beginning debater, this expectation may seem to end the debate. If you cannot present new arguments, does each side just summarize that which has already been said? No, because the purpose of rebuttals is to attack or defend. It is not only permitted but expected that you *attack* your opponent's arguments and *defend* your side's arguments that were established during constructives. You simply may not present *new* arguments.

For example, let us say that the affirmative argued justice as the core value necessary to affirm the proposition. The negative constructive argues that in the proposition, great disparities and more injustice will occur than justice. It is a violation of the rules for the affirmative to declare a new core value during rebuttal, say, "variety is good, and this is not disparity, just variety." All the negative would have to do then in the negative rebuttal is to reject the new core value as "new argument in rebuttal" and also to stress that the original core value had been defeated.

It is during rebuttals that the debate will be won or lost depending upon the success and failure of the attacks and the defense. It is here that clash occurs. The debater who merely repeats what has gone on before will be vulnerable to the opponent who is launching attacks, because mere repetition allows the opponent to win arguments simply by pointing out that no response (often referred to as *extension of argument*) is happening. The opponent doing the attacking can claim to win by default. A judge expecting clash to be a duty of each side will reward the side that defends and attacks in rebuttal. When *both* sides defend and attack in rebuttal, then the judge applauds the debate as a superior contest that he or she was happy to have judged. And as we know, it is important to make the judge happy!

Affirmative
The affirmative has the initial rebuttal, and during that four-minute period, this debater has two challenging tasks. He or she must respond to the negative case, which probably lasted four minutes, and defend against the negative's constructive attacks, which may have lasted another three. Seven minutes of negative positioning must be answered within four minutes of rebuttal. The affirmative will do two things here: (1) be sure to speak first specifically in response to the negative case; and (2) return to the fundamental structure of the affirmative case. As a general rule, the affirmative should budget about two minutes for each task, though adjustments will be necessary depending on where the negative did the most damage. Deciding which task to emphasize is the key to a successful debate.

When this speech is finished, the remaining preparation time for the negative begins. Since the next speech will be the last negative speech, the negative may choose to use all of his or her remaining preparation time.

Negative

During its final speech, the negative has three fundamental duties: (1) defend against the attacks that the affirmative chose to bring into rebuttal; (2) extend the attacks against the affirmative that the affirmative did or did not respond to in rebuttal; and (3) summarize the most important reasons the negative has won the debate (these could be arguments won by the negative, arguments lost by the affirmative, or both).

When the negative rebuttal time has elapsed, the judge begins to record the remaining preparation time for the affirmative. Since the next speech is the last affirmative speech, the affirmative may choose to use all of his or her remaining preparation time. An important note should be made here: Many debaters try to use as little preparation time as possible early in the debate so that sufficient time is left to prepare the crucial final speeches.

Affirmative

The affirmative initiates the debate and gives the last speech. This format can be an advantage simply because the affirmative gets the final word. In this final rebuttal, the affirmative has the same three duties listed earlier for the negative: (1) defend against the attacks extended by the negative and notice the constructive attacks that were dropped in rebuttal; (2) extend the attacks against the negative that the negative did or did not respond to in rebuttal; and (3) summarize the most important reasons the affirmative has won the debate (affirmative's successes, negative's failures, or both).

At the end of the final affirmative rebuttal, the two debaters shake hands, thank the judge, politely wait a moment to give the judge an opportunity to comment, and then quietly leave the room so that the judge has time alone to decide the debate.

GETTING STARTED

By the time you reach this point in studying Lincoln-Douglas debate, you are ready to get started, which often seems to be the most difficult step. You have received the proposition, and you have reacted to and thought about it, but a written case for or against the proposition seems far away. Establishing a process for approaching any value proposition is truly useful. Once the process or system of approach becomes familiar, any new proposition can simply be "plugged into" it. A valuable element to this system of approach is brainstorming.

Brainstorming

A synonym for brainstorming is creative ideation. *Ideation* means to generate ideas; *creative*, of course, suggests that which is original, new, or different. *Brainstorming* is the process whereby new, different, or original ideas are generated. When starting work on a new value proposition for debate, generating ideas is very important. To brainstorm, let your mind wander to consider all the possible topics, issues, principles, and especially values that might be relevant to the proposition. Key to effective brainstorming, though, is interaction. Do not brainstorm by yourself, but join teammates, friends, or relatives in the process. The creative energy caused by this interaction will generate more ideas.

A second key to brainstorming is to establish few rules. Do not rule out ideas as silly, wrong, or weak, for a silly or unrealistic idea often leads to other ideas that may be legitimate and truly important. Allow one idea to lead to more; allow others and yourself to "branch out" from what has been said. The brainstorming process is not intended to be efficient. Rather, it is intended to be thorough—the more ideas the better. When ideas seem to be exhausted, group them into common categories. Decide which ideas seem to have the most merit or hold the most promise. Explore these ideas further. With ideas in mind, if not in hand, you are ready for another important step to getting started in Lincoln-Douglas debate. You next need to define the terms in the proposition.

Defining Terms in the Proposition

One of the most important, yet frequently neglected parts of the debate preparation process is defining terms in the proposition. In fact, some would contend that this step should be taken before brainstorming or as a part of brainstorming. Defining terms means literally to research (consult dictionaries) and to decide what each term in the proposition means or may mean. Some of the terms may be open to a good deal of interpretation, so the debate over the proposition may be taking many different directions. To be truly prepared to debate means to prepare to debate all of the different interpretations.

Some debate coaches contend that the terms in a proposition have some obvious intent, but those coaches are naive. Lawmakers and court justices in the "real world" know only too well how important vocabulary is to the administration and execution of laws. Consider the 1996 national high school resolution, "An oppressive government is more desirable than no government." Some authoritative sources would define *anarchy* as a particular type of government, so "no government" cannot be about anarchy. Another source might define *anarchy* as the name given to a society without government, so anarchy (no government) is certainly within the proposition. There seems to be an important difference between these two definitions.

Being prepared to argue that one definition is to be preferred over another is necessary if you are going to be ready to face both definitions. For example, you might argue that "no government" must be possible for the debate to be meaningful. Furthermore, "no government" needs a name. You might argue that it is reasonable to believe that *anarchy* is the name given to "no government." And you might argue that "no government" is in fact a type of government; it is merely the type of governance that occurs when no formally agreed-upon rules have been established. In other words, what seemed to have been a big difference can be argued away.

Learning the meaning of terms is essential to understanding what the debate might be about. What's more, thinking about these definitions is essential to your convincing response when faced with a particular interpretation. *Black's Law Dictionary* is an excellent place to begin your research of terms, but do not stop there. Consider dictionaries of philosophy, political science, sociology, psychology, and all social sciences. The reason for this approach is simple: Arguing the definitions, the principles, the issues, and the topics within the proposition does not depend upon your own thinking or collective brainstorming. Instead, it depends to a great extent upon principles discovered, theorized, and established by the great thinkers of the past and present. Debating values is not just a matter of personal opinion. Arguing values successfully rests upon good reasoning and the use of persuasive ideas from respected sources. While evidence in values debate may be more open to interpretation than evidence in policy debate, supporting the premises to your arguments is still critical to your success. As the ideas to support or reject the proposition grow both in number and in quality, you need evidence to support the ideas.

Gathering Evidence

What constitutes proof when debating values? Actually, "proof" may be impossible to determine. Proof is impossible if it means evidence that is not open to interpretation and evidence that has some sort of objective, tangible existence. The stumbling block here is proving in some objective way the appropriate standard of judgment. While we might agree on the value of your gold wristwatch based upon the current price of gold, we may not agree that the entire value of your wristwatch lies in its weight in gold. And there may be no objective way to prove that the total value of a wristwatch comes from some set of characteristics that can be measured by some objective standard.

As another example, how does one weigh the value of time-keeping? If you are late for dinner, what is that worth? If the dinner is one that you are preparing for yourself before watching a movie on television, the fact that you are late may prove inconsequential. But if you are late for a dinner hosted by your boss as he or she is contemplating your promotion, the lateness may be worth thousands of dollars and your professional future. And how do we judge the value of your future?

Proof—that is, objective proof—may be impossible to determine. But that does not mean that evidence is irrelevant to value debate. Great thinkers, past and present, may offer convincing reasons for measuring the value of some idea (liberty, oppression, order, stability) in some particular way. The convincing reason is persuasive, and the fact that the convincing reason came from some credible source adds to the persuasiveness. So where do you conduct your research? Become familiar with political, theological, and social philosophers. Authors that might prove helpful include Aristotle, Cicero, René Descartes, John Dewey, Sigmund Freud, Erich Fromm, Alexander Hamilton, James Madison, John Jay, Georg Hegel, David Hume, Immanuel Kant, John Locke, Niccolo Machiavelli, John Stuart Mill, Plato, David Riesman, Jean-Jacques Rousseau, Socrates, Henry David Thoreau, Alexis de Tocqueville, Paul Tillich, and Sun Tzu, to name a few. Some are classic thinkers, and others are more modern. Do not confine your reading to Western thought, but do keep in mind that you are choosing ideas from sources that you believe your audience (the judge) will respect. A mid-1990s talk-radio personality like Howard Stern or Rush Limbaugh may have a lot to say, but will not necessarily be viewed by your audience in a positive way. A good source to start your thinking is the basic text on Western civilization used by your nearest university. The authors and schools of thought presented in such a text will be familiar to and/or respected by most of your judges.

What are you looking for when gathering evidence? You are looking for ideas that support the thinking necessary to accept or reject the proposition. Your brainstorming and your definitions of terms will help to guide your research.

WRITING CASES

At this point in the debate preparation process, you will want to begin work on what is called a *case*. Whether affirmative or negative, the *case* is the written composition containing the arguments with which you hope to win the debate. The affirmative case is the composition of arguments that calls for acceptance of the value proposition. On the other hand, the *negative case* is the composition of arguments that calls for the rejection of the value proposition. While the arguments will change from proposition to proposition, the judges' organizational and content expectations of the case will remain the same. Remember that the case will be presented orally to the judge, and as a public speech, it must meet important organizational expectations.

Basic Case Organization

The case, whether affirmative or negative, should have a similar outline:

I. Opening the Case
   A. Introduction
   B. Preview
      1. Presentation of Proposition
         a. Statement of Proposition
         b. Definition of Terms

  2. Presentation and Explanation of Standards of
   Judgment
    a. Core Value   .
    b. Value Criteria
  3. Forecast of Contentions
 II. Developing the Case
  A. Contention #1
  B. Contention #2
  C. Contention #3
 III. Closing the Case
  A. Postview
   1. Summary of Contentions
   2. Restatement of Standards of Judgment
   3. Restatement of Proposition
  B. Conclusion

Remember, the affirmative case needs to fit within six minutes of speaking time; the negative case, within approximately four minutes (according to the format, pages 166–167). While the negative constructive speaking time totals seven minutes, the negative case needs to be finished within approximately four minutes so that the remaining time can be used to attack the affirmative case. Each element of the case needs to be given careful attention, and the case itself is written as a script that will be read aloud to the judge and audience.

Opening the Case
Neither the affirmative nor the negative script should jump immediately to the arguments for or against the proposition. Lincoln-Douglas debate is a public speaking event as well as a debate event. In fact, this debate format was first created as an interscholastic co-curricular activity to develop speaking skills as well as purely logical and analytic skills. The opening of the case determines the audience's first impression of the speaker, and any good speech should begin with an introduction.

The introduction is what the case script says first to gain the audience's attention and establish interest before moving to a more formal position in the debate. It may be a story or analogy to relate the audience's thinking to the rationale of the value judgment in the proposition. The introduction ends with a transition that leads the audience to a formal statement of the proposition, which opens the preview section of the speech.

The preview section of the script does three fundamental things: presents the proposition and defines terms; presents the core value and value criteria and explains how they are fundamental to the speaker's stand on the proposition; and lists the arguments that will be developed in the case. Preview components are as follows:

- *Presentation of proposition*: First, the value proposition for the debate is scripted exactly as it has been decided for the debate.
- *Statement of proposition*: Do not paraphrase the proposition—script it exactly as it appears.
- *Definition of terms*: Present the definition of each term essential to understanding your interpretation of the proposition.
- *Presentation and explanation of standards of judgment:* Here is where you explain how you plan to defend the judgment made by the proposition.
- *Core value*: This is the fundamental value that you think is upheld (affirmative) or denied (negative) by the proposition. Present the core value in simple terms and explain its general connection to the proposition.
- *Value criteria*: These are the characteristics that are evidence of the core value being met. Declare the general connection between these characteristics and the judgment that is in the proposition.
- *Forecast of contentions*: Simply list the arguments that the case will develop. This helps the judge to know what is ahead and makes it easier for the judge to follow the development which will follow.

Developing the Case

Case development forms the body of the case. It is here that the reasons for acceptance or rejection are developed. Each separate argument has a point to make, which is often referred to as a *contention*.

Contention No. 1 is the first argument of the case. It usually contains premises that are supported by evidence. These premises lead to some larger point that is a reason for accepting or rejecting the value judgment held in the proposition.

Contention No. 2 is the next argument. Many cases will have just two main arguments because time is limited, and it is often difficult to develop more than two good arguments.

Contention No. 3 is argued only if it seems logical, there is time in the case for three arguments, and the other two arguments have been sufficiently developed. Most cases will not have more than three arguments.

Closing the Case

Don't just quit after finishing the script of the last argument; the speech needs a finish as much as it needs an opening. The closing of the case is important because it determines the final impression the audience has of the case. As such, it should begin with a postview of the case and end with a solid conclusion.

The postview contains three elements: a summary of the arguments developed in the case, a restatement of the core value and value criteria, and a restatement of the proposition.

- *Summary of contentions*: Clearly and concisely present a list of the arguments developed in the case.
- *Restatement of standards of judgment*: Restate both the core value and the value criteria. Declare how your arguments tied the judgment made in the proposition to the core value and the value criteria.
- *Restatement of proposition*: Remind everyone of the exact wording of the proposition. Restate it.

However, don't stop with the postview. Next, in the conclusion, refer to the introduction of your case. Tie the position of your case to the point made by the analogy or story that started your side in the debate.

Basic Case Content

While the organizational structure of every case is similar for every debate, content must be tailored to the particular proposition. However, there are some general truths about case content regardless of the proposition.

Affirmative

Since the affirmative launches the debate, the affirmative case sets its tone. This gives the affirmative the responsibility of articulating the foundations important to the proposition. The affirmative cannot assume that the audience is thinking anything in particular about the topic. Instead, this debater needs to be rather objective in leading the audience to the judgment that is declared by the proposition. While the affirmative bears no more or less of a burden of proof than the negative, the affirmative has the initial burden simply because he or she speaks first. An affirmative case should seem thoughtful, thorough, insightful, and, especially, fair-minded. Each side will try to seem the more reasonable. The affirmative that is not clearly reasonable from the start is an affirmative that may be devastatingly open to attack.

Negative

The negative case cannot assume that the affirmative is going to take a particular approach, so this debater's position has to be written in a more universal sense. The negative needs to be written as a rejection of the proposition in general. Then, during the final few minutes of the negative constructive, the negative can argue specific applications of the negative case to the affirmative case. The negative also must remember that although the burden of proof rests upon both sides in the debate, he or she needs to keep the burden of proof on the opponent as much as possible. For example, if the affirmative has argued a position without support, the negative should focus on this lack of support. If the negative chooses instead to merely claim that the opposite of the affirmative is true, then that countertruth becomes the negative's burden to prove.

The negative also needs to remember that in the constructive time, as much effort should be made attacking the specifics of the affirmative as is made presenting the negative case. Some negatives make the mistake of concentrating the most effort on presenting a fluent and persuasive case and then commenting on the affirmative almost as an afterthought. A balanced negative spends as much effort on attack as on presentation and defense of his or her own case. The case should be scripted so that it invites comparison or application to the analysis of the affirmative. Some of that comparison and application must be extemporaneous, so the script needs to be concise enough to allow for such commentary on the opponent.

Affirmative and Negative

Finally, it is essential for both the affirmative and the negative to appreciate the importance of persuasively scripted cases. Using descriptive language is highly important. For example, much philosophical and ethical commentary is very conceptual. As a result, it is very easy for these subjects to fly beyond the understanding of a judge or audience. Using imagery is essential to making concepts meaningful and memorable. Case content should be made as "visual" as possible with vivid description and dramatic use of example.

As soon as cases are written, even if they are rough drafts in need of refinement, it is important to get on your feet, experience the format for Lincoln-Douglas debate, and PRACTICE! Actual debating will tell you more about what to do next with the development of your case content than will any other step in your writing. Get a first draft of your case completed as soon as possible so that you can begin debate. Experience will eventually be the most important teacher in your development as a debater and writer of cases, and practice debates will provide your first real experience with a particular proposition. The sooner you get to practice, the faster your cases will develop.

PLANNING, PREPARATION, AND PRACTICE

It is very important for the beginning Lincoln-Douglas debater to realize the value of actual practice. Lincoln-Douglas debate is not an essay contest, nor is it a competition in writing cases. It is a form of actual debate competition. The debating happens on your feet, facing an opponent, attacking his or her case, asking and answering questions, responding to attacks upon your case, extending the argument, and being persuasive. Success in debate is not found in some book (notwithstanding the excellent introduction that you are receiving in *Basic Debate*!) or quietly contained in your written cases. Success in debate comes from debating. One of the most critical mistakes made by beginning debaters is not budgeting enough time for a practice debate before a tournament or before a graded classroom event happens. Instead, the debater stays up the entire night before the big event finishing the writing of cases with no time left for testing the cases against an opponent. Then at the tournament or graded classroom event, simple mistakes are made, concentration is not focused, questions are answered incorrectly, thinking is superficial, weaknesses that could have been easily corrected are exposed in the worst possible light, the debate is lost, and the debater decides that Lincoln-Douglas debate is not for him or her.

You cannot become successful at basketball by just reading, writing, and thinking about playing. You have to pick up the ball! You have to dribble it, pass it, and shoot it. And it takes practice to get good at the game. By the same token, one does not become a good debater without practice, and practice takes time. You will not have time for practice unless you *plan* for it. You will not learn from practice unless you *prepare* for it. And without *practice*, you will never be a success in debate. Planning, preparation, and practice are the real keys to success in debate.

STRATEGIES FOR REFUTATION OF VALUES

As you gain experience from practice, you will notice that competing against an opponent who is using the same core value as you are is not the same as competing against an opponent whose core value is different from yours. In rebuttal it can become confusing to extend the debate over values in a way that best serves your interest. The checklist below is a handy reference to use during rebuttals when you are trying to resolve the comparison of values.

Identical or Same Values

Vote for me—value more likely

Vote for them—value less likely

Therefore, vote for me because more likely

Different Values but of Agreed-upon Equal Worth

Vote for me—more likely to get and just as good

Vote for them—less likely to get and no better

Therefore, vote for me because no loss of value and a greater probability of likelihood

Different and Competing Values

Mine wins a comparison
 Mine (while not necessarily better) is more likely
  Vote for me—more likely to get and just as good
  Vote for them—less likely to get and no better
  Therefore, vote for me because no loss of value and a greater probability of likelihood
 Mine better than theirs
  Vote for me—get mine
  Vote for them—get theirs
  Therefore, vote for me because mine is better
 Mine better and more likely
  Vote for me—get mine for sure
  Vote for them—get theirs maybe
  Therefore, vote for me because mine is not only better but more likely
Doesn't make any difference which is better
 The values are mutually exclusive from my opponent
  Vote for me—get both
  Vote for them—get neither
  Therefore, vote for me to get either and both
 The values are causally related
  My value is the necessary or sufficient condition for their value
  Mine must happen first to cause theirs
  Therefore, vote for me to get either and both

INTERSCHOLASTIC COMPETITION

With well-written cases and lots of practice, you will be ready to compete against debaters from other schools. Remember, one of the key differences between policy debate and Lincoln-Douglas debate is that in competition you are on your own. At a tournament you usually have the opportunity to face several opponents, and in each debate, you will uphold one side of the proposition while your opponent will uphold the other. A judge will be assigned to listen to the debate, take careful notes, and decide a winner when the debate is completed. Tournaments vary in length. Some tournaments will run for two or three days, while others will be complete in an afternoon and evening. The following aspects are the same at every tournament.

Tournament Structure

You will know the proposition in advance and will be expected to debate both the affirmative and negative sides. You will have some identification code (letter or number) or you may be identified by name, school, or both. A schedule for the debates will be distributed. This schedule (often referred to as the *schematic*) will indicate the room in which you are to debate, the time at which the debate is to begin, the side you are to uphold, your opponent, and the judge. For example, let's say Catherine Spector is a debater from New Trier Township High School. Among the schools in the tournament are Apple Valley High School, Glenbrook South High School, Wheeling High School, Chesterton High School, and George Washington High School A portion of the schematic might look like this:

Round 1—8:00 a.m.—The Greater Detroit Lincoln-Douglas
Debate Championships—January 26, 1996

Room	Affirmative	Negative	Judge
219	NTcs	GBSbr	Tantillo
270	AVpc	GWjl	McClain
259	WHkb	NTns	Whipple

The capital letters code the identity of the schools involved in each debate, and the lower-case letters are the initials of the individual debaters. Some tournaments establish a coded system to mask the identity of schools and individuals.

In the example above, at 8:00 a.m., Catherine Spector from New Trier needs to be in room 219 to face an opponent from Glenbrook South High School. The format of the debate will be the format we discussed earlier. Judge Tantillo will keep time, listen carefully to the two debaters, take notes, fill out a ballot similar to the one included in the Appendix, and render a decision as to who won and who lost. The judge will deliver the completed ballot to the tournament headquarters, where the results of all the debates will be carefully recorded. Then debaters and judges alike will move to the location where schematics are distributed and pick a schedule for Round II.

The host of the tournament will decide the schedule and determine the system whereby debates will be established as the tournament continues. Larger tournaments may continue to pair those debaters having the best records to eventually determine a tournament champion. Smaller tournaments may simply set the rounds randomly, with the best record at the end winning the tournament. Ties are usually broken by considering the speaker rating points that judges assign to each debater in each round of debate.

Some tournaments are *double-flighted*. Since Lincoln-Douglas debates are much shorter than policy debates, it is possible to have two Lincoln-Douglas debates finished in about the same amount of time as one policy debate. Some tournaments schedule two debates to occur in the same room to be heard by the same judge. The first debate is termed *the first flight* and the second *the second flight*. Thus, Round I might have a first flight of debate occur at 8:00 a.m. and a second flight of debate occur at about 8:45 a.m. The schematic for a double-flighted tournament indicates which four debaters are to be heard by a particular judge and which two debaters will debate first:

First Flight (A)—8:00 a.m.   Second Flight (B)—8:45 a.m.

Room	Affirmative	Negative	Flight	Judge
219	UIjw	BUtd	A	Wykoff
	CHbk	AVpc	B	"
270	GBNtb	FWsr	A	Oddo
	RMww	StIgsd	B	"

You want to make sure that you are on time to your debate. Even if you are scheduled to debate the second flight, you should be nearby at 8:00 a.m., because someone from the first flight may be absent, and you may be asked to debate ahead of schedule.

Rules

In addition to standard format and judges' expectations about cases, several rules apply to Lincoln-Douglas debate. Individual tournaments may have their own rules, so it is important that you read a copy of the tournament invitation or of the terms and conditions established for the tournament so that you can comply with them.

Written Rules

Written rules are those that have been established as a code of conduct for a particular tournament. For example, it is usually a rule that the debater whose turn it is to ask questions has control of cross-examination. If the debater answering the questions persists in talking against the questioner's wishes, the questioner has the authority to interrupt and continue with a new question. Such conduct is not just acceptable, it is written in the rules for most tournaments.

Written rules may be open to interpretation, but they should not be ignored nor intentionally violated. Violating them may result in forfeiture of a round or even disqualification from the entire tournament.

Unwritten Rules

Unwritten rules are more subtle but no less important. Your deportment at a tournament may be critical to your competitive success. If you are loud and obnoxious; if you complain loudly about judges, opponents, or other schools; if you seem to show a lack of respect for the judge or the opponent, you may pay a high price in an event that can be subjectively judged. While judges do not seek to punish or reward your behavior in any obvious way, in a very close round your credibility and ethical appeal may be an important ingredient in the final decision.

Your appearance is also important. The impression that you make as you enter a round of debate is the first argument you make, so dress as if the round of debate is a job interview. For men, that means dress shirts, ties, and suits or jackets with dress trousers; women should wear suits, dresses, or skirts with jackets. Dress as if you are preparing to present your case in court. Remember that you are defending moral, ethical, and value judgments, and your appearance says a great deal about how seriously you take the debate. Your ethical character, credibility, and image may be among the most important arguments of the debate.

Judging

Each school entering a tournament in Lincoln-Douglas debate is obligated to provide officials to judge the debates. These judges may be members of the school's debate coaching staff, faculty, or community, or the officials may be hired from outside the school. Each official should be assigned to judge debates that do not involve students affiliated with the official in any way. For example, a coach judge will not judge students from his or her own school.

Judging Criteria
The judging of Lincoln-Douglas debate is a bit more subjective than policy debate because value propositions contain judgments that many of us hold near and dear. We often find ourselves predisposed toward a particular proposition simply because we agree with the principles represented in the value judgment. Thus, competent judges of Lincoln-Douglas debate should be on their guard to keep their own value systems out of the judging. But some values are nearly universal, and as a debater you need to recognize that the assumptions that come with particular propositions should be exploited when writing cases. Do not ignore core values that you think most people accept as worthwhile, and do not take positions that run counter to what most people believe. If the value proposition declares that individuals with physical limitations ought to have the same opportunities to compete in sports as other athletes, it will not serve you well to make sarcastic remarks about disabled people. Most people believe that we have some obligation either privately or publicly to help those less fortunate than ourselves. As a debater, you need to notice such assumptions and make them work for you.

Types of Judges
The more you compete, the more adept you become at adapting to particular sorts of judges. Generally, you will encounter three types of judges in Lincoln-Douglas debate: lay judges, coach judges, and undergraduate student debate judges.

Lay judges are any judges who do not have an extensive background in current debate theory. Lay judges may be professionals related to debate—for example, attorneys or courtroom judges—or they may have little experience in debate, such as community leaders or booster club parents. It is most important when facing such a judge that you avoid jargon that is either debate- or proposition-related. It is also important to expect such a judge to listen more and to write less. These judges may not keep an extensive written record of the debate (the flow sheet), but they may be very perceptive and thorough in their understanding of the principles and issues involved. Be particularly careful not to speak too quickly in front of such a judge.

Coach judges will certainly be aware of the proposition and current debate theory. Be thorough, efficient, and particularly logical in front of such a judge. They listen to countless debates per week and may have heard literally thousands of debates during their career. Do everything you can to make this a debate worth judging.

A large number of judges may be ex-debaters who are currently undergraduates at a nearby university. Tournaments require large numbers of judges, and such students often make a ready resource when tournament officials must be hired. These judges will usually be a bit more liberal than coach judges and often study philosophy or ethics in college, making them eager to hear you debate values. College student judges will often be more tolerant of a more rapid rate of delivery, but be careful not to speak so quickly that you generate more heat than light.

A sample ballot for Lincoln-Douglas debate is included in Appendix D, courtesy of the American Forensic League Association.

SUMMARY

Freeport, Illinois, was the site of the second and historically most significant debate between Abraham Lincoln and Stephen A. Douglas. Edward F. Finch, a seasoned debate coach from Freeport, Illinois, sums up the goal of Lincoln-Douglas debate as an academic interscholastic competitive event: "Lincoln-Douglas Debate (must) retain the values base that was originated in 1858. Not merely an exercise in political rhetoric, the original debates were soundly rooted in a clash of values. Lincoln repeatedly argued that the value of individual freedom as set forth in the Declaration of Independence for 'all men' was of such importance that it should override state or local preferences. Douglas, on the other hand, firmly believed that the closer government was to the people, the better guarantor of liberty it was, even if this 'local control' produced such immoral institutions as slavery. Thus the debates clashed not only on the issue of popular sovereignty, but also on the issue of which members of society were entitled to liberty. This clash of values permeated the original debates, and so the modern competitive event should also be firmly grounded in the clash of values."

You as a student of value debate have the power to advance the legacy of the event.

QUESTIONS FOR DISCUSSION

1. What are some reasons debating value propositions may be much more subjective than debating policy propositions?

2. Why is the judging of Lincoln-Douglas debate more subjective than the judging of policy debate?

3. What is the relationship among propositions of fact, value, and policy? Compare and contrast.

4. Why is establishing the standard of judgment so important in debating propositions of value?

5. How can core values be distinguished from value criteria? What are some of the relationships?

6. Why is extending the argument in rebuttals so much more difficult than repeating arguments?

7. Why can it be said that most of the real debating in any given round happens during rebuttals?

8. Why is practice so important to learning about debate?

9. Why are unwritten rules often as important as written ones?

10. Why do judges look most for clash when deciding who did the better job of debating?

ACTIVITIES

1. Conduct a brainstorming session using the resolution provided by your instructor. List all of the ideas for both the affirmative and the negative that can be generated within an hour.

2. Research the definitions of terms in the current Lincoln-Douglas debate topic; then brainstorm the topic for both affirmative and negative ideas. Notice how having definitions before brainstorming changes the brainstorming process.

3. Outline contentions for both an affirmative case and a negative case on the current topic.

4. Write first-draft cases for both the affirmative and the negative on the current topic.

5. Conduct practice debates using your first-draft cases. Discuss what you learned from the practice and how it will help your revisions of both the affirmative and negative cases.

6. Practice "flowing" the arguments of one of the practice debates in which you are not participating.

7. Conduct a classroom cross-examination of an affirmative speaker. Notice the answers that are particularly good, those that are weak, and how the questioning suggests developments in the case.

8. Conduct a classroom cross-examination of a negative speaker following the same guidelines as in Activity 7.

9. Invite other classes to observe your practice debates. Ask for comments.

10. Invite neighboring schools to send students to observe your practice debates and plan, prepare, and practice against your cases.

PART THREE

STUDENT CONGRESS

LEGISLATIVE DEBATE

The democratic tradition of government values the individual. It is built on the importance of collective action by informed individuals interested in solving problems they could not deal with alone. In our society, when we wish to enact policy for the larger group, we have chosen to do so through representatives in legislative groups. Student congress is an event that gives to you, the forensic student, an opportunity to work, speak, and function in that deliberative decision-making environment. This section is designed to introduce you to the principles, structures, and organization of student congress. Further, you will be shown how to prepare for student congress and how to utilize some strategies for success in that activity.

THE NATURE AND PURPOSE OF STUDENT CONGRESS

OBJECTIVES AND KEY TERMS

After studying Chapter 11, you should be able to

1. Discuss the nature of student congress debate, especially as it differs from conventional debate,
2. Understand the purpose of parliamentary procedure and its three main principles,
3. Appreciate the skills needed to become a member of a student congress assembly, and
4. Discuss various student congress events held throughout the country, especially those authorized by the National Forensic League.

After reading this chapter, you should understand the following terms:

chamber

house

legislative debate

parliamentary law

parliamentary procedure

practice congresses

senate

Super Session

The application of persuasion in the legislative setting differs from any other situation in one major way. Speaking in legislative debate, or in student congress, is done within a structured environment of specific procedural rules known as *parliamentary law*. These rules or principles evolved out of the experiences of individuals, action groups, and law-making bodies as rules of order to permit groups to work together efficiently and successfully. In a democratic society, the foundation of parliamentary procedure is rooted in three principles: (1) the will of the majority ultimately decides action and policy; (2) the rights of the minority to speak and otherwise participate must always be protected; and (3) the rules exist to serve the organization and are equally applicable to all of the membership. If you wish to persuade in student congress, you must not only invent the argument and find the data to support it, you must also understand parliamentary rules and the application of those rules in the student congress. In addition, you must be sensitive to the shifting weight of opinion within the group and be prepared to offset arguments that are given in opposition to your position. Finally, you must develop the skill of disagreeing with ideas without being disagreeable. Student congress also enables you to extend your skills of extemporaneous speaking, debate, and interpersonal communication.

THE VALUE OF STUDENT CONGRESS

A librarian once contended that out of all students who used the school library for research—forensic students or otherwise—the ones most astute, most politically aware, and most knowledgeable about the techniques of research were the student congress competitors. The attributes necessary to be a competent student congress member are also attributes necessary for survival in the "real world" of politics, political science, and persuasion. In addition to practicing a variety of public speaking events, from oratory to extemporaneous speaking to impromptu speaking, student congress calls on skills crucial for successful participation in discussions, debates, and parliamentary situations. An added dimension is provided by the fact that student congress mimics real-life legislative assemblies and presents its participants with an insight into some of the issues and problems that actually confront our lawmakers. What better choice for a learning experience and competitive event than student congress?

THE TYPES OF STUDENT CONGRESSES

The *National Forensic League*, a national honorary society that promotes high school speech competition, recognizes three types of student congresses. *Practice congresses* can be held by any school and may be organized in conjunction with a regular speech or debate tournament or as a separate event. Schools that are not affiliated in any way with NFL may attend and participate in such congresses. However, if NFL points are to be awarded to NFL members, a minimum of four schools must attend. Such practice congresses are very important to the training of student congress members, and if they are available to you, you are fortunate. Every NFL District should try to have at least one practice congress during the year. Coaches who wish to host competitive activity but who think that they cannot handle a full forensic tournament should certainly consider hosting a practice student congress.

A second type of student congress is held once each year for the express purpose of sending students to the NFL National Student Congress. Each NFL District may hold a *District Student Congress* and may send as many as two Senators and two Representatives to the National Student Congress, if there are at least twelve schools or 50 students in attendance at the District Congress.

The third type of student congress promoted by NFL is the *NFL National Student Congress*. The student congress was first held in 1937, and although procedural alterations have been made from time to time, the basic format has remained much the same in the intervening years. The National Student Congress, which meets during the National NFL Tournament, is held in high esteem by students and coaches alike. With more than 250 participants each year at the National Congress, the contest is organized into seven Senates and seven Houses. There are special rules for the National Student Congress, but most of them have to do with the awarding of points and the selection of Superior Congress award winners who advance to a final session. The final session has become known as the *Super Session*. The legislative deliberation in any of these types of student congress is essentially the same. Specific NFL rules are listed in two booklets entitled *Preparing for Student Congress* and *Student Congress Manual*. Both are published by the National Forensic League and are available from the NFL National Office in Ripon, Wisconsin. The National Catholic Forensic League hosts a national congress at its annual Grand National Tournament. The league publishes its own specific rules in the NCFL *Student Congress Manual*.

Besides the National Forensic League and the National Catholic Forensic League, a number of other organizations sponsor congressional events. Many of these are parliamentary procedure events. Others are geared toward teaching principles of citizenship and government through direct practice. To participate in most of these activities, a student must apply for acceptance. However, some are available to any student who is a member of the particular organization. Some of the most notable are the Model United Nations, Youth-in-Government (sponsored by the YMCA), state activity league congresses, and Boys State and Girls State, which are sponsored by the American Legion. Students who are chosen to participate in these latter programs organize their own city, county, and state governments. They choose their own officials and introduce and argue their own bills in the legislature.

The 4-H Clubs of America, the Future Farmers of America, and other clubs emphasizing a knowledge of parliamentary procedure have competitive events that make use of teams trained in parliamentary procedure. In addition, their national conventions are organized to give legislative experience to students in attendance.

The types of student congresses in which you may participate and compete are many and varied. However, they all share the common goal of giving experience to students in the use of legislative debate. Because this book is aimed at students who are interested in building skills in the competitive areas, the discussion and examples used here will be drawn primarily from materials supplied by the National Forensic League and the National Catholic Forensic League and from experiences of the authors and their students in NFL and NCFL Student Congresses. However, all student congress events have common elements. If you are involved in other groups besides the NFL and NCFL, you can apply the basic principles discussed here within the framework of rules and regulations specified by other groups.

STUDENT CONGRESS HINTS

You are now well on your way to becoming an informed member of a student congress assembly. There are only three goals you need to achieve to become a proficient and effective participant: Prepare better on each bill (on one or both sides) than other members do; know how to prepare briefs correctly and how to use them in your debating; and study the Table of Most Frequently Used Parliamentary Motions (presented in Chapter 12) and know how to use it better than even the Presiding Officer does! Are you up to the task? Each of these three key elements will be covered in-depth in the chapters that follow.

The area that seems to cause the most concern to students at the beginning phase of learning student congress is having to use parliamentary procedure. You need not be clever in using involved motions, but you should know how to put common motions into the proper form and when to make such motions. You will be provided with a table of frequently used motions and suggestions on when and how to make correct motions. If you hope to chair an assembly as its Presiding Officer, then you must have special interest in and understanding of parliamentary procedure and know why and how it is used. You should know how to state a question in correct parliamentary language, how to take a vote properly, which types of votes to use, and how to announce the result and effect of the vote. For this reason you should carefully study the role of the Presiding Officer found in Chapter 14. If this commentary about parliamentary procedure intimidates you a bit at this point, please don't worry; just remember that the purpose of student congress is to *debate*, not show off knowledge of parliamentary procedure.

SUMMARY

Student congress offers you a chance to practice most of the skills used in political discussion and public speaking. The National Forensic League promotes a variety of congresses at all levels of competition. As a participant, you will need to be familiar with the mechanics of student congress, including bill preparation and parliamentary procedure.

QUESTIONS FOR DISCUSSION

1. What is parliamentary procedure? What are its three main principles?

2. What are the three types of student congresses sanctioned by the National Forensic League?

3. How would you answer a novice student congressmember who asked you what it takes to become an effective congress participant?

4. In general, what is the purpose of congressional debate as a part of our legislative system?

ACTIVITIES

1. Read, as a minimum, the Preface and section on Definitions in *Robert's Rules of Order*. As an added challenge, read *Robert's* Introduction on Parliamentary Law and Article I, "How Business Is Conducted."

2. Identify the two U.S. senators from your home state. Compose a biographical sketch of each, including political party, length of Senate service, prior political experience, and noteworthy congressional accomplishments.

3. Pinpoint your own congressional district by number and name your congressional representative. Compose a biographical sketch similar to the sketches you wrote for your senators.

STUDENT CONGRESS PROCEDURES

OBJECTIVES AND KEY TERMS

After studying Chapter 12, you should be able to

1. Understand the purpose of various motions and how to use them in the course of a legislative debate,
2. Understand the purpose of bills and resolutions and be able to compose an example of each that will meet the standards outlined in the text,
3. Use the rules of parliamentary procedure to participate in a smooth-running discussion group or assembly, and
4. List the basic procedural rules that govern a session of student congress.

After reading this chapter, you should understand the following terms:

amendment	precedence
authorship speech	preference vote
bill	resolution
Division of the House	second
floor	standing vote
joint (resolution)	voice vote
motion	

Certain procedural rules have been worked out by the National Forensic League to ensure equity in floor debate. Observing these rules will ultimately benefit all student congress members. To participate in student congress, you should be familiar with the rules. You should obey them to avoid embarrassment during debate.

DEBATE

Procedural Rules

All speeches are strictly timed. No speech, including an authorship speech, may be longer than the specified time, which is usually three minutes. The timekeeper will be instructed to inform the speaker and the Presiding Officer when that limit is reached. (In many congresses the P.O. will also serve as the timekeeper.) During a speech, congress members may ask for recognition by the Presiding Officer and ask the speaker if he or she will yield to a question. Because the time for both the question and the answer is taken from a speaker's allotted time, the speaker may preface the speech by stating that he or she will not yield to questions until the conclusion of the speech. If a speaker specifies this, then questions are answered as time allows after the speech. It is currently a common practice to establish a standing rule at the start of a legislative session that no one is to interrupt a speaker. A special rule can be created by an assembly using the motion to suspend the rules. This rule establishes an automatic cross-examination period following every speech. However, it is not an NFL rule. NFC and NCFL Congresses have a mandatory two minutes of questions after *authorship speeches*, appeals made by the legislation author for justification for the bill's passage, based on conditions that the bill will be correct.

The author of a bill or resolution is privileged to speak first. But once the debate has opened, the legislation belongs to the group and not to the author. Thus, it is not necessary to get permission from the author to offer an amendment, nor is it correct to ask the author what the bill means. A bill means what it says to the assembly. It is not open for interpretation from the author, and the group is not obligated to interpret the bill in the same way the author intended.

Following the authorship speech, each member who wishes to speak may ask for recognition only if he or she assumes a position opposing that of the preceding speaker. Observation of this rule accomplishes several things. First, it ensures that the debate is truly a debate and not a long series of "me, too" speeches that do not advance the cause of anything but point-gathering by members. Second, it ensures that both sides will have an equal opportunity to present their position openly and fairly. It also safeguards the Presiding Officer against charges of loading the debate for one side or the other. Third, it maximizes the number of issues on each side that will be aired.

Because a member's success hinges on getting recognition and being able to speak to the student congress, another set of procedures is enforced. First, Presiding Officers call on speakers in the inverse order of the number of speeches they have delivered— that is, they recognize those who have not spoken or have spoken less often before those who have spoken more frequently. In addition, a member may speak only five times a day. When a member has reached this limit, the Official Scorer will mark his or her name off the seating chart, and that member may be recognized only if no other member of the assembly wishes to speak. Finally, toward the end of the session, the Presiding Officer may announce that until further notice recognition will go only to those who have not spoken more than once. If, however, debate begins to lag, indicating that those who have not spoken more than once do not desire to do so, the Presiding Officer can return to general recognition.

Etiquette

In addition to the restrictions and limitations placed on the length and substance of floor speeches, you need to be familiar with the etiquette of student congress. There is a right and a wrong way to speak in a legislative session. When referring to another participant, use the terminology "Representative Green" or "the Representative from West Texas." Such forms of address help keep the entire group aware that their positions are ones of dignity and seriousness, and also underscore the fact that each competitor is playing the role of a legislator. The Presiding Officer should always be addressed as "Mister or Madame Speaker." If the house has been designated as a Senate, then the term for the Presiding Officer is "Mr. or Mme. President." Another commonly used term is "Mr. or Mme. Chairman."

The proper way to gain the *floor*—the right to address an assembly—in order to make a motion or participate in debate is to rise as soon as the preceding speaker has finished and at the same time say, "Mr. President" (or "Mme. Speaker"). If the Presiding Officer recognizes you, he or she will state, "The chair recognizes Representative Green." You may then make your motion or give a speech on the pending legislation. If, however, another member of the assembly is recognized, resume your seat until he or she has finished. To interrupt a speaker for questioning, use the following language: "Mr. Speaker (or Mme. President), will the speaker yield for a question?" The chair will then ask the speaker if he or she wishes to yield. If so, you may ask one question; if not, you resume your seat and do not interrupt again. The Presiding Officer should discourage frequent interruptions of the same speaker. If the speaker has prefaced his or her remarks by saying he or she will not yield until the speech is finished, then no one will be recognized during the speech.

Under no circumstances are you or any other member of the student congress allowed to argue with the Presiding Officer. He or she has been elected to that position, and his or her decisions are final. The decisions are only discussed if there is a failure to follow parliamentary procedure that causes a violation of the rights of the assembly. Even then, there are two recourses. First, the Parliamentarian should intervene without any remonstrance from the membership. If this does not occur, however, you may "rise to a point of order" or "appeal the decision of the Chair." Use these motions only if you have a sound parliamentary reason, not a personal one. (These motions are addressed in the Table of Most Frequently Used Parliamentary Motions on page 207.)

PARLIAMENTARY PROCEDURE

Parliamentary procedure is a useful tool that must be respected and used for the purposes for which it was designed. The basic principles of parliamentary law, once understood and accepted, make its many rules easy to understand. First and foremost, parliamentary rules exist to make it easier to transact business. They exist to promote cooperation, not to create discord. All groups that operate under parliamentary law are dedicated to the precept that the majority will decide the action of the group. However, they are also equally committed to the concept that all members have rights and privileges that must be safeguarded. Furthermore, particularly in a legislative assembly, parliamentary rules are intended to ensure that full and free debate of every proposition will be allowed.

Parliamentary law is built on the idea that time and effort should be utilized and decisions reached by the simplest and most direct procedure. Specific rules of parliamentary procedure allow for a definite and logical order or priority for business. They also ensure that every member has the right at all times to know what is being done by the assembly. These basic concepts of democratic procedure are accomplished by the judicious and fair application of parliamentary procedure. The most important thing for you to remember is that the ultimate purpose of parliamentary procedure is to ensure the rule of the majority and guard the rights of the minority. Used properly, it will keep debate going and will allow for full discussion. The Parliamentarian, the Presiding Officer, and each individual member should be dedicated to this principle and should strive to guarantee its fulfillment in the student congress.

On the other hand, being a "parliamentary card shark" is a waste of everyone's time. In fact, if you attempt to use the floor of student congress to show off long and involved or clever motions, you will be quickly spotted as an obstructionist and will have difficulty getting the floor thereafter. As stated earlier, the purpose of the student congress is to debate, not to show off expertise in parliamentary procedure. A good working knowledge of parliamentary procedure allows freedom of debate and gives you the assurance that the proper language is employed.

A *motion* is a proposal or suggestion made by a member of a group that he or she wishes the entire group to consider and ultimately adopt. Most motions require a *Second*, or a second person who believes that the motion is worth discussing and considering. The proper form for common motions is "I move that...." rather than "I make a motion to...." You should have a thorough enough knowledge of the chart of *precedence* that you will not introduce motions that are out of order. Simply stated, if the motion you wish to present in order to accomplish your purpose is higher on the table of motions than the motion currently being considered, then your motion has a higher priority; it has precedence. It is in order at that specific time to introduce the motion to the group for its consideration. If you wish to move with poise and assurance through congressional debate, you will carefully study the parliamentary procedure necessary. In a student congress, certain adaptations of the parliamentary procedure as outlined in *Robert's Rules of Order* have been made. A careful look at the following table of motions will indicate where some of those changes have been made. Notice how the motions are grouped by type into four distinct classes. Try to understand the purpose listed for each of the twenty-four commonly used motions, and notice the technical information presented about voting requirements for each. You need not memorize such a chart, but you should have a copy handy for easy reference during a congress session.

For a more in-depth discussion of parliamentary procedure, please refer to Chapter 17.

VOTING

Voting procedures serve their purpose best when they are carried out in a particular fashion for student congress. For example, voting on legislation and amendments should always be done by a *standing vote* unless a roll call is demanded by one-fifth of the members. *Preference votes*—and votes requiring a two-thirds majority—should be conducted by either a standing vote or a show of hands. At the discretion of the Presiding Officer, some motions may be disposed of by a *voice vote*; this can be used to simplify and speed proceedings. A *Division of the House* may be demanded by any two members on any question on which such a voice vote was taken. This call for a division to verify a voice vote must be made before another motion is placed on the floor. Votes for Presiding Officers and Superior members are by secret ballot.

BILLS, RESOLUTIONS, AND AMENDMENTS

Aside from elections, all business conducted in a student congress centers around either a bill or a resolution. A *bill* is an enumeration of specific provisions that, if enacted, will have the force of law. Put more simply, a bill is a proposed law that is intended to solve some problem. Once debated and passed by congress (and signed by the President), a bill becomes a new law. A bill must be definite; state exactly what is to be done or what is to be discontinued; include

Table of Most Frequently Used Parliamentary Motions
Adapted for use in NFL Student Congresses

Type	Motion	Purpose	Second Required?	Debatable?	Amendable?	Required Vote	May Interrupt a Speaker
Privileged	24. Fix Time for Reassembling	To arrange time of next meeting	Yes	Yes-T	Yes-T	Majority	Yes
	23. Adjourn	To dismiss the meeting	Yes	No	Yes-T	Majority	No
	22. To Recess	To dismiss the meeting for a specific length of time	Yes	Yes	Yes-T	Majority	No
	21. Rise to a Question of Privilege	To make a personal request during debate	No	No	No	Decision of Chair	Yes
	20. Call for the Orders of the Day	To force consideration of a postponed motion	No	No	No	Decision of Chair	Yes
Incidental	19. Appeal a Decision of the Chair	To reverse the decision of the chairman	Yes	No	No	Majority	Yes
	18. Rise to a Point of Order or Parliamentary Procedure	To correct a parliamentary error or ask a question	No	No	No	Decision of Chair	Yes
	17. To Call for a Roll Call Vote	To verify a voice vote	Yes	No	No	$\frac{1}{5}$	No
	16. Object to the Consideration of a Question	To suppress action	No	No	No	$\frac{2}{3}$	Yes
	15. To Divide a Motion	To consider its parts separately	Yes	No	Yes	Majority	No
	14. Leave to Modify or Withdraw a Motion	To modify or withdraw a motion	No	No	No	Majority	No
	13. To Suspend the Rules	To take action contrary to standing rules	Yes	No	No	$\frac{2}{3}$	No
Subsidiary	12. To Rescind	To repeal previous action	Yes	Yes	Yes	$\frac{2}{3}$	No
	11. To Reconsider	To consider a defeated motion again	Yes	Yes	No	Majority	No
	10. To Take from the Table	To consider tabled motions	Yes	No	No	Majority	No
	9. To Lay on the Table	To defer action	Yes	No	No	Majority	No
	8. Previous Question	To force an immediate vote	Yes	No	No	$\frac{2}{3}$	No
	7. To Limit or Extend Debate	To modify freedom of debate	Yes	Yes	Yes-T	$\frac{2}{3}$	No
	6. To Postpone to a Certain Time	To defer action	Yes	Yes	Yes	Majority	Yes
	5. To Refer to a Committee*	For further study	Yes	Yes	Yes	Majority	Yes
	4. To Amend an Amendment*	To modify an amendment	$\frac{1}{3}$	Yes	No	Majority	No
	3. To Amend*	To modify a motion	$\frac{1}{3}$	Yes	Yes	Majority	No
	2. To Postpone Indefinitely	To suppress action	Yes	Yes	No	Majority	No
Main	1. Main Motion	To introduce a business	Yes	Yes	Yes	Majority	No

*No. 5 should include:
1. How Appointed?
2. The Number
3. Report When?
    or
To What Standing Committee

T — Time

*Nos. 3 and 4 by:
1. Adding (Inserting)
2. Striking Out (Deleting)
3. Substituting

Courtesy of the National Forensic League

some enforcement procedure; and specify a method of implementation. Specific items, such as phase-in time and financing, may also be a part of the bill. A penalty should be stipulated if appropriate, or the law will not have any force. There should also be a date for enactment, or when the law will take effect.

A *resolution*, on the other hand, is usually a generalized statement expressing the belief of the group, and it does not carry the force of law. A resolution is, in other words, a proposition of value or fact. It may be preceded by "whereas" clauses stating the principle reasons for adopting the resolution, although such clauses are not mandatory. A clear understanding of the differences in the form and substance of bills and resolutions is important. Participation in some student congress events is predicated on your submitting either a bill or a resolution, and the thrust of the debate could differ depending on whether a new policy or a value judgment is being debated. A resolution will generally center the debate on the broad principles of the concept; a bill is more likely to focus the debate on the merits of the specific provisions it contains.

As you prepare to write your own bill or resolution, you need to start either with a problem area that the congress might attempt to solve by proposing a new law, or with a condition that the group thinks should be addressed within a resolution. Consider some of the following types of problems that face our country: military, energy, foreign trade, legal and judicial affairs, education, economy, welfare, crime, national security, and technology. As you finalize your choice of topic, remember that your sentiment or proposed solution must be debatable. That is, it must have two sides to it, a pro and a con, or it will not serve the purpose of an item for legislative debate. Also, it must have information available on both sides, and it should be timely and of current interest.

Both the form and substance of these documents are important. The National Forensic League (NFL) has particular rules concerning the form of a bill and of a resolution. Other groups may have different rules, but those from NFL are useful as a model:

1. The bill or resolution must be in camera-ready form for printing.
2. The bill or resolution must be typed.
3. The typing must be doublespaced, and the bill or resolution may not be longer than one page.

4. The first words of a bill are "Be It Enacted...." Following any "whereas" clauses, the first words of a resolution are "Be It Resolved...."

5. Each line of a bill or resolution, including the "whereas" clauses, must be numbered.

6. A resolution may be preceded by one or more "whereas" clauses, but bills and *joint resolutions* (bills introduced into both houses of the legislature at about the same time, such as to amend the Constitution) never have them.

7. All facts and statistics contained in the bill or resolution must be correct, and the bill or resolution must be clear and complete.

8. The language of a bill must always be in the imperative mood. That is, it must state exactly what is to be done, how it is to be done, and who is to do it.

The following examples highlight the difference in format between a bill and a resolution and show how a variety of solutions might be offered. (In actual practice this material would be prepared using doublespacing according to NFL rules.)

Simple Resolution

1. Whereas, few definitive ethical principles have been
2. promulgated by either the medical or legal professions
3. concerning the subject of human organ transplants and/or
4. artificial organ replacements, and
5. Whereas, not all patients with organ failures have equal
6. access to organ transplantation, and
7. Whereas, the selection criteria to determine which patients
8. are suitable candidates for organ transplantation surgery are
9. arbitrary at best and discriminatory at worst, and
10. Whereas, a disparity exists between the number of patients
11. in need of transplantation surgery and the number of readily
12. available organs, and
13. Whereas, the investment of time, money, personnel, and
14. facilities for transplant surgery is a grossly inefficient allocation
15. of medical resources, therefore
16. Be It Resolved by the House of Representatives in Student
17. Congress assembled that it is the sense of this legislative body

18. that the proliferation of human organ transplants and artificial
19. organ replacements cannot be justified.

A Bill

1.   Be It Enacted by the Senate in Student Congress
2. assembled that
3.   Section 1. A human organ donor organization, titled the
4. National Organ Donor Program, shall be established under the
5. auspices of the Federal Department of Health and Human
6. Services and a universal donor card shall be created to replace
7. the widely varied state donor cards.
8.   Section 2. A national educational program shall be
9. instituted using public service announcements on radio and
10. television and within the print media, encouraging people to
11. join the National Organ Donor Program. Said educational
12. program will be funded from the approved budget of the
13. Health and Human Services Department.
14.   Section 3. All state health departments and appropriate
15. private agencies shall be invited to join this national donor
16. system and "pool" their available organs, thus establishing a
17. national donor bank. All agencies and states that do join said
18. system shall be linked via a central computer system that will
19. keep records of available organs.
20.   Section 4. The current system of financing and maintaining
21. organ banks shall be transferred to the control of the
22. Department of Health and Human Services and organ
23. recipients shall reimburse the national donor bank through
24. regular hospital charges and insurance payments.
25.   Section 5. Establishment of said National Organ Donor
26. Program shall begin immediately upon passage of this bill, and
27. all necessary operational needs shall be completed on or before
28. the beginning of the next fiscal year following ratification of
29. this legislation.

If you read these examples carefully, you can see what bills and resolutions should include. Note the use of very specific language and the inclusion of monetary conditions. When writing a bill, you should be certain of what the law is at the present time. Preparing a bill for student congress is much like preparing an affirmative case, and the bill itself is comparable to an affirmative plan. The authorship speech is similar to the affirmative need. If you approach that task without adequate research and knowledge, you will probably get a lukewarm reception!

A special category is reserved for constitutional amendments. They are classified as resolutions because they must be submitted to the states after they are passed by congress. Although they are only a suggestion to the states, they must be as specific as a bill in their wording. A proposed constitutional amendment should indicate the part of the Constitution being changed and also specify the desired outcome of the amendment.

Bills and resolutions introduced on the floor for legislative debate may generate another kind of consideration: the *amendment*. In student congress, because the delegates have had the bills and resolutions well ahead of time, there are certain kinds of restrictions put on amendment procedures. First of all, an amendment must be submitted in written form. The written amendment must indicate (by line number) the exact portion of the bill that is being changed. It must indicate the method of change being employed, whether by addition, substitution, or deletion. An example of a properly worded amendment for the preceding sample bill would be as follows:

> I move that the bill under consideration before this house be amended by altering Section 4 as follows: On lines 22 to 24, delete all words following "Health and Human Services" and substitute with the following: "and all ongoing costs for maintaining these banks and for transporting human organs for use in transplant operations shall be borne by the federal government."

To submit an amendment, you must first send it in written form to the clerk. Then you must get recognition from the Presiding Officer; no special consideration will be given because you have an amendment to offer. Once you have the recognition of the chair, you should stand and say, "I move to amend the motion by...." and then state the amendment exactly as it is in writing. An alternative method would be to say, "Mr. or Mme. Speaker, I have an amendment to offer and would like permission for the clerk to read it." In either event, it is necessary for one-third of the assembly to second the amendment before discussion is in order. This rule is a departure from the rules as promulgated in *Robert's Rules of*

Order, but it is used in student congress to ensure that an endless stream of amendments is not presented as a delaying tactic, as is sometimes the case in the U.S. Senate. Once the amendment is on the floor, then all debate must relate to the amendment until it is either passed or defeated. At that point, debate resumes on the bill or resolution in either its original or amended form.

SUMMARY

The procedural rules governing student congress debate are designed to enable all members to participate. Parliamentary procedure is your key to contributing to student congress. By knowing the rules concerning voting, and the introduction of bills, resolutions, and amendments, you can be sure that you are moving the business forward effectively.

QUESTIONS FOR DISCUSSION

1. What is a motion? What are the four classes or types of motions?
2. What is a Second? What is its purpose?
3. How is parliamentary precedence (or priority) determined when you are dealing with motions?
4. Why do debate speeches on a bill alternate from affirmative to negative to affirmative and so on?
5. A member proposes an amendment that you think is insignificant and would be a waste of debate time. What alternatives are available to you?

ACTIVITIES

1. Using the four methods employed for conducting votes in a congress session, determine when each could or should be used and list at least one advantage and disadvantage of each method.

2. Make a list of ten current issues or subject matters that you think could be the basis for a good bill or resolution. The issues could be national, state, or local in scope.

3. Write both a bill and a resolution using two different issues listed in Activity 2 and turn them in to your class student congress hopper.

4. In *Robert's Rules of Order* read Article II, "General Classifications of Motions."

THE MECHANICS OF STUDENT CONGRESS

OBJECTIVES AND KEY TERMS

After studying Chapter 13, you should be able to

1. Discuss the theory and practice of congressional apportionment,
2. Explain how legislative sessions are scheduled and how an agenda can be developed for a standard congressional meeting, and
3. Understand how a variety of elections are conducted.

After reading this chapter, you should understand the following terms:

agenda

apportionment

bicameral

legislative session

majority

Novice House

Outstanding Member

preferential balloting

Superior Member

unicameral

For every student there is a first-time experience in student congress. Although participation in student congress draws heavily on speech skills acquired in other areas and events, there are many characteristics unique to the student congress event. A complete understanding of the mechanics and structure of student congress will help to ensure that your experience is meaningful and successful.

HOUSES AND APPORTIONMENT

The student congress is organized to replicate, when possible, the actual legislative bodies of our national government. The number of houses a student congress will have depends on the number of schools and students participating. Consequently, a student congress may be *unicameral* (one legislative chamber), *bicameral* (two legislative chambers), or multihouse in its organization. Some local practice congresses have become so popular and so well attended that they are organized with numerous houses, each simulating a group of representatives formed into legislative committees considering a variety of legislation. Some multihouse congresses extend the analogy of the U.S. Congress by being composed of a Senate and a House. Therefore, the use of the titles *Senator*, *Representative*, or simply *Congressmember* will be considered as equivalents in this text.

National Forensic League experience has shown that a house containing too many members will be unwieldy and will not give enough students the opportunity to participate. By the same token, a house containing too few students will not offer sufficient interaction to make the experience worthwhile. Consequently, NFL advises that the optimum membership in a house of a student congress is between twenty and thirty.

To govern the number of students participating, the individual NFL District will set a particular *apportionment*—a proportionate distribution—for each chapter in the District Congress. If at least twelve schools or fifty students are participating, the NFL District may send four members to the National Student Congress and would need a bicameral student congress. The apportionment is usually different for Senate and the House. The NFL District Committee may designate anywhere from one to three senators per chapter. In keeping with the principle exercised in our U.S.

Congress, the apportionment of senators would be the same for each NFL chapter, no matter what the size, while that of the House of Representatives is based on population. The population of an NFL chapter is the total number of members and degrees held by that chapter. A typical apportionment might be two senators from each chapter and one member in each house for each thirty members and degrees held by that chapter. Practice congresses and State Activity League Congresses can follow similar guidelines for apportionment. Whatever the formula, the official responsible for it will notify the participating schools prior to the student congress.

When participation in the district or state is large enough, it is a good idea to run a tricameral congress and to designate the house that will not be sending representatives to the National Student Congress as the "Novice House." The *Novice House* provides students who have not previously participated in student congress with an opportunity to learn and experiment with the event without competition from experienced participants. Some NFL Districts restrict such a house to freshmen and sophomores, and some even eliminate participation by students who have debate experience. The idea is to provide a training ground for students and, in effect, to enhance the quality of future student congress participation.

If the student congress is set up as bicameral, it can parallel the actual relationships between the Senate and the House of Representatives in the U.S. Congress. This parallel can be accomplished by following the suggestions made by NFL. For example, when a bill is passed by one house, it can be sent to the other house with the request that the other house concur. If agreement is not reached, or if amendments are offered and not accepted by the initiating house, then a conference committee can be formed to reach consensus. A report from a conference committee or from one house to another shall be privileged, but may not interrupt a speaker. This kind of relationship between the houses helps to ensure good debate and keeps student congressmembers aware of the larger group. Most NFL and National Catholic Forensic League Congresses have grown too large to allow for relations between Chambers.

SESSIONS

The length of a legislative session depends on the desires and facilities of the general director of the student congress, more commonly known as the Clerk of the Congress. Most practice and district congresses hold a one-day session; many others, such as statewide or invitational congresses, hold two-day sessions. NFL rules specify that each legislative day of a District or National Congress must contain a minimum of four hours of floor debate in addition to the time used for committee meetings or elections. For a one-day congress, it is possible to have a morning and an afternoon session, each of about three hours' duration. When an *agenda*, or order of business, for a congress session calls for committee meetings, these may be accomplished either formally or informally. Committees frequently are asked to review proposed bills and resolutions, choose appropriate legislation for later congresses, or choose the order of debate at the current congress. They may rewrite clumsy legislation or recommend amendments for the entire house to consider. A final purpose might be to write commendatory resolutions. The sample time schedules that follow contrast various organizational structures.

Sample Time Schedule for a One-Day Student Congress
8:00 a.m.–8:30 a.m. Registration and verification of entries
8:30 a.m.–11:30 a.m. Morning session
11:30 a.m.–12:30 p.m. Lunch break
12:30 p.m.–2:30 p.m. Afternoon session
2:30 p.m.–3:30 p.m. Elections and awards

Sample Time Schedule for a Two-Day Session
3:00 p.m.–3:30 p.m. Registration and verification of entries
3:30 p.m.–7:30 p.m. Session I

Second Day
8:30 a.m.–11:30 a.m. Session II
11:30 a.m.–12:45 p.m. Lunch break
12:45 p.m.–3:00 p.m. Session III
3:30 p.m. Joint meeting, elections, and awards

At the National Student Congress, each house is in session for the length of the National NFL Tournament. This will usually be three full legislative days (in addition to committee meetings and election time) for the preliminary sessions and one additional legislative day for the final session.

ORGANIZATION

The mechanics of student congress are much simpler than those of a debate tournament. However, because of its unique nature, careful attention to details will determine whether the student congress will be exciting and successful or disappointing to all.

Prior to the actual student congress, bills and resolutions should be distributed to all participating schools. NFL specifies that all schools should receive copies of the bills and resolutions that will be on the agenda at least thirty days prior to the student congress. This amount of time allows for adequate preparation by competing students and enhances the quality of floor debate.

As students report to the congressional session, certain organizational details must be taken care of. Prior to the session a seating chart should have been prepared that accurately represents the seating arrangement and the number of delegates. Each seat should be numbered, with a corresponding set of numbers for delegates to draw as they register. The number drawn determines where the delegate will sit. Some student congresses arbitrarily assign seats ahead of time, but in the interest of fairness, seating should be determined by a random drawing even in this case. Sometimes local congresses alphabetize the seating chart to assist judges and pages.

A suggested Order of Business is printed in the *NFL Student Congress Manual*. Although certain legislative bodies may follow a different agenda, this one is suitable for any such group. An *agenda*, or order of business, is vital to ensuring that all items are handled in an orderly and timely manner.

Order of Business for Student Congress

1. Invocation
2. Call to order
3. Roll call of members and confirmation of seating charts
4. Special orders
   a. Review of special rules
   b. Review of congress procedures
   c. Special announcements and questions
5. Consideration of the calendar
6. Election of Presiding Officer
7. Committee meetings (optional) may be held at a time prearranged by the District Chairperson

8. Floor debate on bills/resolutions
9. Selection of Outstanding and Most-Outstanding congress participants
10. Award of congress gavel and plaques
11. Fixing time for next meeting
12. Adjournment

Elections

Presiding Officer

The Presiding Officer conducts the assembly as efficiently and fairly as possible to accomplish the purpose of the congress and give each member a full chance to demonstrate his or her ability to speak and subsequently to improve. Because of this responsibility, it is important that this person is chosen with care. It is also important that the student chosen have a real desire to serve in that capacity and take pride in her or his ability to keep the group running smoothly and fairly. To ensure this, students at the District Student Congress are asked to submit their names in advance for consideration as Presiding Officer. If a very large number of names are submitted, the district committee or the General Director will have to select three for each house. Each nominee for Presiding Officer will be allowed to preside for twenty to thirty minutes in rotation. Then the members of the Chamber will select by ballot the one who will preside for the duration of the student congress. At practice congresses, the same selection process can be used.

The procedure for selecting the Presiding Officer of the National Student Congress is somewhat different. At the first session, the General Director will appoint a temporary Presiding Officer. This person will open the session, introduce the Parliamentarian and scorer, and will then accept nominations for Presiding Officer. In most cases there will be a nominating speech in which each candidate may present pertinent qualifications and experience. After all nominees have been heard, there will be an election by ballot. Each member, including the temporary Presiding Officer, writes the name of one nominee on a slip of paper. When one nominee receives a *majority* of the vote—a number of voters greater than half of the total—the voting ceases, and the winner is announced. However, until that time, the following procedure is used: After each ballot, the person (or persons, if there is a tie) receiving the fewest number of votes is dropped from the list, and the members vote again. Sometimes a runoff ballot is needed if the two tied for last place have a total combined vote of more than the person that is third from last. This procedure is used until one person receives a majority and is declared the Presiding Officer for the session. Because the first half day at the National Student Congress is used for committee meetings, the term of office for each Presiding Officer will be one afternoon and one morning, making up a full legislative day. There will be a total of three different Presiding Officers for each of the houses of the National Student Congress. This procedure could be used by practice congresses as well.

Although the Presiding Officer cannot be nominated for the Superior Representative during the session at which he or she presides, an official congress gavel is awarded to the student for that session. Traditionally, the Presiding Officer will be on the ballot for the session he or she presided over, due to the adding fact that any students having the most NFL points are added to the list of nominees. The Presiding Officer usually receives credit for five hours of presiding.

Superior Members

Each Chamber of the student congress selects outstanding students for awards. The nomination and election procedures that NFL outlines for practice and NFL District Congresses differ somewhat in duration and complexity from those used at the National Student Congress. However, the basic principle of selection is the same in all situations. The nomination for outstanding students is done by the official scorer and the Parliamentarian of each Chamber, each of whom nominates a designated number of students as superior participants. The Clerk of the Congress determines and adds the top NFL point recipients to those nominated, and the final selection of the most outstanding student from among the nominees is done by balloting all the student members of the Chamber. The standard terminology that has developed for student congress award winners recognizes the first-place competitor as Most Outstanding, the runner-up as Outstanding, and others nominated as superior participants.

In NFL District and practice congresses, after the nominations have been made without consultation between the two officials, there is a vote at the conclusion of the congress. Preferential balloting is used to select the top two legislators in the Chamber and also list third- and fourth-place recipients as possible alternates to nationals if it is the NFL District Congress. The Parliamentarian also ranks all nominated legislators, as this ballot is used to break any ties. If the student congress is the NFL District Congress, the students receiving the plaques also qualify for the National Student Congress.

At the National Student Congress, the Parliamentarian and the scorer nominate, without consultation, two students for each legislative session. In addition, the three top point earners of the session are added to the list of nominees if they were not nominated by either official. The officials may not nominate the Presiding Officer, but he or she could be among the top three NFL point earners for the session. At the end of each legislative day, the names of all nominated students are placed on a ballot, and preferential balloting is used to determine for each Senate or House the Superior Representatives. These students qualify to participate in the fourth, or final, session, from which come the final award winners for the National Student Congress.

In *preferential balloting*, each member marks all names on the ballot with numbers—for example, first through sixth place for a ballot with six candidates. Only one ballot is used to determine preferential winners. The ballots are first separated according to the first choice that is shown on each. The person receiving the lowest number of first-place votes is temporarily set aside, and his or her votes are then distributed according to the second choice expressed on those ballots. The person then having the lowest number of votes is set aside, and his or her votes are redistributed. This process continues until one candidate has received a majority of the votes and is declared the winner of the balloting. The same ballots may then be used in a similar manner to determine the second-most-preferred candidate once the winner's name has been removed as a further contender. The use of this method of voting ensures secrecy of the results until the conclusion of the third session or, in the case of the final session, until the National Tournament Awards Session. Understanding how preferential balloting functions should make a student more aware of the importance of marking the candidates' places below first. To break any ties, the Parliamentarian also marks a ballot.

SUMMARY

The rules of student congress are similar to those of the U.S. Congress, although the student congress may have more or less than two houses. The houses meet in sessions with a specific order of business. As a member, you will be responsible for knowing the bills and resolutions on the agenda prior to the session. You will also vote to elect the Presiding Officer and Superior Members of your house.

QUESTIONS FOR DISCUSSION

1. In the U.S. Congress, what is the difference in apportionment between the Senate and the House? Why is there such a distinction?
2. What is the difference between a unicameral and a bicameral congress?
3. What are the purposes of committee meetings?
4. Why are student congress award winners nominated by official scorers and Parliamentarians but actually elected by the congress members themselves?

ACTIVITIES

1. Using a local organization, such as a service club or school council, compose what you think would be a suitable agenda for a typical group meeting.
2. Using your own state's population in relation to our national population, determine how your state's congressional apportionment was computed in the U.S. House of Representatives.
3. Put together an outline for a short self-nomination speech that you could deliver to your class to highlight the qualities that would make you a suitable Presiding Officer candidate for a session of congress.

RESPONSIBILITIES OF STUDENT CONGRESS OFFICIALS

OBJECTIVES AND KEY TERMS

After studying Chapter 14, you should be able to

1. Identify the officials of a student congress and their responsibilities,
2. Serve as a Presiding Officer for a practice session of congress, and
3. Understand the criteria used to judge student congress presentations.

After reading this chapter, you should understand the following terms:

Clerk of the Congress	**speaking points**
gavel	**timekeeper**
General Director	
official scorer	
page	
Parliamentarian	
Presiding Officer	
recess	

E very student congress must have a General Director, more commonly called the *Clerk of the Congress*, who will make arrangements and give general supervision to the entire event. Within each house of the student congress, certain officials are necessary for smooth operation of the event. National Forensic League rules specify that each house must have a Parliamentarian, a Chief Clerk, or both. At the national level, these are always two different persons, but at lower-level student congresses, the duties may be performed by one person. An official scorer is also appointed for each half day of legislative session. In addition, the host school or district should provide two students to act as pages for each house. A person serving as timekeeper is also necessary if that responsibility is not being handled by the Presiding Officer. In addition to these officials, who are appointed by the Clerk of the Congress, each house of the student congress elects a Presiding Officer for each session. Current practice has the Presiding officer rap his or her gavel once after two and one-half minutes have expired and twice at the end of the three minutes typically allotted to a speaker.

Clerk of the Congress

The responsibilities of the Clerk of the Congress (General Director) are, for the most part, supervisory in nature. If the student congress is an NFL District or National Congress, then the arrangements that the Clerk must make are outlined by the rules of that organization.

The Clerk of the Congress of a practice student congress or any student congress patterned after the NFL model needs to be aware of the many responsibilities that position carries with it. For one, this official is responsible for securing a suitable location for the congressional sessions. Ideally, the meeting area is not a classroom or an auditorium, but an environment that resembles a congressional meeting place: a board room, the city council chambers, a library, or a courtroom. Experience has shown that an appropriate student congress location helps produce the frame of mind in each competitor that will lead to outstanding performance.

All other student congress officials—the Parliamentarian, Chief Clerk, scorer, pages, and timekeeper—are selected by the Clerk of

Congress. Because these persons greatly influence the success of the congress, the Clerk of the Congress should select them carefully according to the guidelines of their positions. After selecting them, the Clerk of the Congress should meet with them, give them written instructions, and make sure that they fully understand their responsibilities and the overall activity of student congress.

Another responsibility of the Clerk of the Congress is securing awards. Each Presiding Officer must have a gavel during the session he or she leads; at the conclusion of congress, the Clerk of the Congress presents a gavel to these officials. In addition, there should be a plaque for the first- and second-place competitors from each house, with possible awards for all those nominated as superior participants.

OFFICIAL SCORER

The official scorer judges student congress performances. This official carries the major responsibility for determining the relative merit of each speech and awarding points to it. In NFL and practice student congresses, there is a maximum of six points awarded for each speech, with five or six points given for a superb presentation, three or four points given for an average speech, and one or two points reserved to indicate that the presentation was deficient in major areas. These point restrictions are different at the National Student Congress.

The scorer must have a firm idea of the standards to be used in scoring, and a clear knowledge of the rules that govern speaking in student congress. Such factors as persuasiveness, communicative delivery, innovative and effective arguments, sound reasoning and logical analysis, and incisive and knowledgeable answers to questions should weigh heavily in an official scorer's criteria for judging speeches. The speaker's ability to follow the flow of the debate and respond to previous speakers is also important, as is the speaker's ability to support and document assertions. In all, an official scorer is asked to evaluate both the content and the delivery of each speech.

The scorer must know, in addition, that no student may speak more than five times in a legislative day unless no other delegate is asking for the floor. Further, he or she should realize that no points can be awarded for clerical duties. The scorer must also award points to the Presiding Officer at the end of each hour that reflect the quality of his or her performance—a maximum of six points per hour. Because the scorer's job is difficult and demanding, it should not be accepted without careful consideration of what is involved. Each legislative session has a different scorer.

At the end of the session, the scorer nominates an agreed-upon number of members (usually two or three) for student congress honors. These nominations, along with those submitted by the Parliamentarian, are voted on by the students. Nominees should be those students who have done the most outstanding job during that session. Although the scorer awards points only for speeches that were given, every facet of the students' congress performance should be considered when making nominations.

PARLIAMENTARIAN

Although the Parliamentarian's role is also supervisory, the position requires a great deal of responsibility. The person who serves in this capacity must not only know parliamentary procedure, but also be very familiar with the special rules of student congress and be willing to see that procedural errors are remedied immediately. As a consequence, the Parliamentarian must be someone whose authority will not be questioned, but also someone who will not assert that authority until it is necessary to do so.

The Parliamentarian must have a clear understanding of the nature of student congress and must be dedicated to advancing it in the most efficient way possible. It is the Parliamentarian's primary duty to back up and reinforce the Presiding Officer's leadership. Further, because the purpose of student congress is to debate legislation, the Parliamentarian sees to it that time is not wasted on other matters. The Parliamentarian also nominates students for honors at the conclusion of each session, taking into account total contributions made to the student congress by members during that session.

An accurate record should be kept of all proceedings and, consequently, of any parliamentary problems that arise. Often the Parliamentarian is responsible for such a record, either keeping it or delegating the responsibility to someone else. A preferred system is a dual one in which either a clerk or a page and the Parliamentarian both keep a written record of legislation and motions and their disposal. The Parliamentarian will also rank all nominated speakers and his or her ballot is used in breaking ties. An example of a voting record form is included in Appendix D.

PAGE

The page for a house in student congress is a bearer of messages, facilitating communication among the members of the house, between the Presiding Officer and members, and among the officials. He or she should be seated in an area that is easily accessible to the Presiding Officer, scorer, and Parliamentarian. The location should also provide a clear view of the assembly so that the page can respond to a summons from a member.

Excessive message sending is not to be encouraged, but notes can often allow for better working relationships and offset poor debating conditions. In addition, the page should assist with clerical duties, such as point recording at the end of each session, passing and collecting ballots, recording motions and their disposal, and giving any other assistance to student congress officials.

TIMEKEEPER

Because each speech is restricted to only three minutes and because accurate adherence to time limits ensures fairness, a timekeeper is an essential official in the student congress. He or she should be equipped with a stopwatch and should be instructed in the use of time cards. The time cards allow a speaker to see the number of minutes remaining in the speech and alert the Presiding Officer that the speaker's time is expiring. For this reason, the timekeeper should be seated in a place that is clearly visible to the Presiding Officer, Parliamentarian, scorer, and speaker. Strict enforcement of time limits is necessary. If a timekeeper is not available, the Presiding Officer should be prepared to assume this duty.

PRESIDING OFFICER

The Presiding Officer for each session of student congress is elected from the membership of that group. It is absolutely essential to place a person in that position who can exert leadership. The person who is presiding must also know parliamentary procedure, be willing to use it, and be able to use it with authority. This does not mean that the ideal Presiding Officer is a martinet who has no interpersonal skills. It *does* mean that the Presiding Officer is "boss" and should be obeyed within the structure of parliamentary law. A weak Presiding Officer can wreck a student congress and waste everyone's time.

The Presiding Officer must be aware of the restrictions placed on the recognition of speakers and must apply the rules regardless of school and personal loyalties. A Presiding Officer who is not fair in giving recognition will quickly have a group of enemies in the student congress who will become an obstructive force. Although the Presiding Officer is in charge, it is much better to be in charge of cooperative individuals.

In addition to the recognition of speakers, the Presiding Officer is also responsible for ensuring the rotation of speakers from affirmative to negative. This procedure is usually achieved by announcing clearly each time, "The chair will now entertain a speech for the affirmative (or negative) side." Furthermore, the Presiding Officer must establish a consistent leadership method that is clearly understood by all. For example, following each speech the chair can announce, "Procedural motions are now in order." Of no one asks for recognition, the Presiding Officer can then call for the next speech, thereby eliminating misunderstandings of the reason a member seeks recognition. The Presiding Officer must also control time limits for speeches and have a clear, consistent policy on stopping speakers at the conclusion of their allotted time. One of the functions of the chair's gavel comes into play at this point in the proceedings.

The Presiding Officer must make sure that a member yields only to a question and not to allow another member to speak. The main goal of the Presiding Officer should be to ensure fairness and equity set out in the rules of student congress, such as the procedural rule specifying that no one shall be recognized to speak a second time if anyone asking for recognition has not spoken for the first time.

To allow a person who receives recognition under that rule to yield speaking time to one who has already spoken would obviously circumvent the established equity. If a Presiding Officer fails to enforce such rules, he or she is subject to parliamentary moves from the assembly or to a ruling from the Parliamentarian.

In addition to performing a leadership and a procedural role, the Presiding Officer must also fulfill a political role. Unfortunately in our society, the label of "politics" or "politician" has come to carry negative connotations. However, we use the term here in the context of the interpersonal roles that are a necessary part of the student congress environment. The Presiding Officer must work constantly with assembly members to cement and solidify relationships. He or she should be aware, for example, of the pressures under which members of the assembly are working. The Presiding Officer should be sensitive to their desire to be treated fairly but should also sensitize them to the difficulty of the Presiding Officer's roles. Very minor yet highly effective strategies can make such a relationship possible. For example, the Presiding Officer may become aware of a person who has asked for recognition but has not received it and is angry. A quick note explaining that others will have to be recognized first but that the Presiding Officer will get to that member in due time may certainly alleviate the anxiety. Such an act by the Presiding Officer can take the edge off the member's frustration and keep that person from turning the frustration into a negative element in the debate ahead.

The Presiding Officer should also recognize those in the assembly who make the job smoother and easier. The member who makes a helpful procedural motion or the one who handles a problem by suggestion rather than by challenging the Presiding Officer's authority should be acknowledged by the Presiding Officer. In addition, the member who gives a particularly outstanding speech or the one who uses valuable speaking time to clarify a rather muddled debate has made an important contribution to the assembly. The Presiding Officer who is alert to these positive elements in the student congress should send notes or make a point of speaking to these persons during a *recess*. Each kind of positive move made by assembly members makes the performance of the Presiding Officer easier and more impressive to observers.

Interdependency is the key to a successful term as Presiding Officer of student congress. The Presiding Officer should certainly be prepared to deal with intransigent or stalemating members by using parliamentary rules properly and decisively. However, to fulfill an obligation to the entire assembly, school, regional, or personal loyalties should be firmly set aside when the Presiding Officer picks up the gavel.

Each official of the student congress, whether appointed or elected, has very specific and important obligations for making the student congress successful. Even so, these officials function within an environment governed by certain mechanics of procedure that must be clearly understood by all. Review Chapters 11 and 12 for a discussion of parliamentary and student congress procedures.

SUMMARY

Although every member plays an important part in student congress business, officials have special roles. The Clerk of the Congress (General Director), scorer, Parliamentarian, page, timekeeper, and Presiding Officer all function to keep debate running smoothly and fairly. Serving in one of these offices can enhance your student congress experience.

QUESTIONS FOR DISCUSSION

1. Why is the job of the Clerk of the Congress (General Director) so important?
2. What are the roles of the official scorer in a competitive student congress session?
3. What is the purpose of the Parliamentarian in a student congress session?
4. How might the use of time cards assist all participants in a student congress session?

ACTIVITIES

1. Research the background and historical origins of the gavel.
2. Determine a satisfactory method by which a Presiding Officer could set up a priority system to help recognize both

speakers and questioners fairly throughout an entire session of congress.

3. In groups of about five students, take turns serving as Presiding Officer. Recognize a member of the small group to make a motion and then respond to the motion using correct terminology, putting the motion to a vote, if appropriate.

PREPARATION FOR STUDENT CONGRESS

OBJECTIVES AND KEY TERMS

After studying Chapter 15, you should be able to

1. Make use of such speech preparation tools as research, library skills, briefing, organization, and outlining,
2. Research and analyze a bill or resolution and set up an "issues file" on the topic,
3. Prepare an authorship speech for a chosen piece of legislation, and
4. Prepare a congress brief for a prospective bill or resolution.

After reading this chapter, you should understand the following terms:

    authorship speech
    briefs
    evidence files
    squad preparation

Once you have a sound understanding of the principles of student congress and have mastered the mechanics of the event, you are ready to prepare for participation. Although most students who are part of a National Forensic League chapter will be preparing along with the whole squad, there are a number of things you should do for yourself.

INDIVIDUAL PREPARATION

Analysis

The first step in student congress preparation is to carefully and thoughtfully read the legislation under consideration. Chapter 2, which covers analysis, contains all the elements you will need to utilize in this process. Remember that in student congress, however, some differences in outlook must be considered. For one, a more global point of view is necessary for student congress analysis than for interscholastic debate analysis. The analysis of bills and resolutions for student congress must fall into the realm of what is good and best for the nation, not just what will win a debate round. A long-range view and a national perspective are important in congress debates. In your analysis you should strive to get beyond local, partisan, or regional outlooks. This is especially important in preparation for the NFL or NCFL National Student Congress, but it can be equally important in other levels of student congress.

The student congress representative from the Deep South whose only perception is a regional one may find her or his views rejected outright and may suffer from a credibility gap difficult to overcome. Similarly, the Texan who sees the energy crisis from the perspective of "Let the Yankees freeze to death in the dark" may alienate a large number of people quickly. And so would a student congress senator from New York who asserts that the energy situation is a fraud perpetrated by the major oil companies to hike up profits. This is not to say that these viewpoints are invalid. However, they are not the *only* valid viewpoints. You must attempt to discover many points of view prior to entry into floor debate. You may choose not to espouse them, but you must know that they exist. A purely provincial analysis will not serve you well.

Another area in which your analysis for student congress differs somewhat from that for debate is in the historical perspective. In recent years it has become the fashion for college and high school teams to indicate in the affirmative plan that "Affirmative speeches will constitute the legislative history of this proposal." What this does, in effect, is erase the entire history of any other attempts to adopt or reject such a proposal. Consequently, the negative's charge that the "U.S. Congress just last year voted not to fund a proposal to develop solar energy" would have no validity in the debate. Such a practice is not in vogue in student congress, however. Since this congress attempts to function within the framework of reality, the legislative, political, and judicial history of any proposal is not only relevant, but vital to legislative consideration. If the bill to come before the assembly concerns a moratorium on research and development spending for the Strategic Defense Initiative, a student who attempts to speak about that bill without an understanding of past arms treaties and without an understanding of the military and political relations between the United States and the former Soviet Union on the issue of "Star Wars" has done a poor job of analysis of the bill.

Finally, analysis for student congress must also involve an understanding of the vested interests that are represented by the proposal. It must reflect an awareness of the ultimate effect of the adoption or rejection of the bill and of the possible compromises that may be needed to gain adoption. Having gained this understanding and awareness, you will then know what alliances will be necessary to achieve your goal. In short, the analysis of legislation for debate in student congress involves not only the proposition itself but also the interaction between advocates and opponents. It should be apparent that if there weren't these partisan positions and competing arguments, there would be no clash created and the legislation would be adopted without debate.

Research

As you analyze the bills and resolutions for student congress, you are laying the groundwork for the research process: Read everything you can find on the subjects covered; collect as much information as you would in preparing a research paper; and talk with people whose ideas might be particularly valuable.

Begin your research by investigating generalities on the subject matter. Find out the present problem that the bill attempts to solve or that the resolution addresses. Be sure to research both sides of the question, for you ultimately might decide to give a speech either for or against the legislation. Be aware of the subject matter in the news; approach the situation as if you were an actual legislator dealing with actual legislation. Although you will not accumulate the bulk of files and evidence cards that the average debate team collects, you must begin with the notion that special research is necessary for thorough preparation. For this purpose you will need to consult some sources not traditionally used by debaters. To gain a historical perspective on each bill, a good place to begin is an encyclopedia or a government textbook. Books that would probably not be quoted in a debate round hold a great deal of value for the student congress deliberation.

You must be able to speak with authority about the present as well as the past. Current magazines should be utilized (keep the *Readers' Guide to Periodical Literature* handy), with special emphasis on such publications as *Vital Speeches, Congressional Quarterly, Congressional Digest, The Congressional Record, The Congressional Quarterly Weekly Report*, and *Current History*. The value of these particular publications is their regular inclusion of actual legislative debate on issues similar to those considered by the student congress. *Facts on File* for the current year, as well as for the past several years, is an important source of specific examples and statistical data. The current issue of an almanac such as *Information Please Almanac* will give up-to-date materials. If your squad maintains extemporaneous speaking files, it will have a wealth of current information on many of the bills. In addition to these sources, you may want to write to your own U.S. congressional representatives for materials. Personal letters, telephone conversations, newscasts, and personal interviews are admissible as evidence in student congress as long as they are accurately and carefully cited. Evidence in student congress is necessary just as it is in debate, and a great variety of sources is useful. The same attention to accuracy and ethics in evidence usage must be taken in student congress as in debate.

A final note on research: After you have researched the subject matter on each bill and resolution, another area of general research will prove very valuable. Gather facts and statistics on the decision-making process as it relates to government spending. How much money is being spent and how much the national debt is growing are important facts and should be readily available to use in floor debate. Beyond these obvious facts, you need to know more about how the specific bills considered by the student congress fit into an overall budget picture in the current economic and fiscal situation in the nation. Be creative. Find out how much money is going into "pork barrel" projects, congressional junkets, strange research subjects such as the mating habits of the three-toed sloth, and other areas in which government money might be said to be wasted. Investigate government bureaucracy and departmental organization. These facts might seem trivial, but they can frequently serve you well as you are pressed to demonstrate priorities. Such material injected into the floor debate can also alleviate tension through the judicious use of humor.

Organization

Once you have gathered the evidence you need for each bill and resolution, you must put it into a form that will make it easily retrievable and usable. Many students have used various methods of organizing their congress files. Two methods used with a high degree of success by students of the authors are offered here as examples.

A *vertical file* organization is flexible and easy to set up. Secure one legal-sized manila file folder for each bill or resolution. On the outside of the folder, draw a vertical line that divides the front into two equal parts. On one side list all the arguments in favor of the bill, on the other side list all the points against the bill. Devise a simple numerical designation to place beside each argument, such as A-1, A-2, and so on. Place inside the folder all the evidence you have collected to support each of the points listed on the front. Each piece of evidence should be given a numerical designation corresponding to the point it supports. Laminate or glue the actual bill or resolution to the inside front cover of the file so that all the pertinent materials about each bill are easily accessible for quick reference during floor debate.

A second method of evidence organization is the use of a *loose-leaf notebook*. A section is set aside for each bill or resolution by means of a divider labeled with the name of the item. Plastic "slick sheets" are used to hold the bill at the front of each section.

Next, a section for all arguments in favor of the bill is set up. On a sheet of paper outline all of these arguments. Immediately behind that page, enter all evidence supporting those points. After the section in favor of the bill, a page of outlined arguments against the bill is placed, followed by evidence to support those points. In this kind of organization, photocopies of articles with pertinent sections underlined or highlighted can be number coded in the margin to match the section on the outlined arguments.

You can also put together a series of congress briefs for each bill or resolution. *Briefs* contain a multitude or arguments in outline form, including interspersed evidence taken from a variety of sources. Such a brief becomes a "living document" that could be used during the floor debate. If a few of your own arguments happen to be used by one or more speakers, you could cross off those points from your brief. As new issues or challenges arise, add arguments or responses to your brief. As you seek recognition for your speech, it is easy enough to order the major points remaining on your brief and add an introduction, transitions, and a conclusion to round out the speech. The ability to speak from an outline is indispensable to this style of organization. Regardless of which method you use, remember that in congress just as in debate, citations should be given for all evidence.

A third organization method being used is creating a *hanging file* for each bill or resolution. This system makes it easy to collect magazines, newspaper tear sheets, and even material from the Internet.

Additional ways to organize evidence may occur to you. Students frequently group bills by broad categories, such as Foreign Aid, Energy, or Defense. General information is then collected and filed in the appropriate categories. Other students prefer to take extemporaneous speaking files into the congress meeting room. Whatever method works well for you is the one you should use, the point being that you must impose some organization on your material. The student congress competitor who arrives with a group of loose papers, a randomly selected magazine or two, and no clear idea of what to say is at a severe disadvantage. On the other hand, the student who comes with organized and well-supported positions will be able to get into the debate quickly and give a good accounting of herself or himself in the bargain.

Preparing Speeches

After analyzing, gathering, and organizing evidence, carefully examine each bill and resolution to determine whether you would like to offer any amendments. If so, they should be written out, and evidence should be gathered for each one and filed according to the organizational scheme you are using. Of course, amendments may emerge from the debate, in which case they cannot be prepared in advance. However, giving careful thought to each bill may reveal several possible amendments that can be prepared and researched ahead of time.

If you have submitted a bill or resolution to the student congress, you will need to prepare your *authorship speech* carefully. This speech will be the first one given on the bill and will serve to introduce it to the assembly. Because the speech can be prepared ahead of time, it can and should have the careful construction and audience appeal of an oration. The authorship speech could be used to spike out the major objections that the opposition might try to voice. Anticipating and preempting arguments will make the position of the bill stronger initially and will make it more difficult for the opposition to find a valid argument. As with all congress speeches, the authorship speech should begin with an arresting introduction to challenge the audience, contain a well-organized body, and close with a thoughtful summary and conclusion.

Remember that during this individual preparation you will be collecting far more than you will be able to utilize in actual speaking situations in student congress. The problem is that you will not be able to anticipate just what you will get to say or the circumstances under which you will be able to say it. If you plan only one specific issue to cover only one side of a bill, you may find yourself unable to use it for a variety of reasons. The first person to get recognition may say precisely what you had planned to say, neutralizing your impact if you should get a chance to speak. Or it may be that a great many students wish to speak on the same side you had originally planned for, making it difficult for you to get the floor. However, no one may have been prepared to speak on the opposite side, leaving the floor wide open for you if you are suitably prepared on that side as well. Clearly, since participation is the door to success in student congress, broad and careful preparation is the key to that door.

SQUAD PREPARATION

Ideally, a speech and debate squad will have several opportunities during the year to participate in practice student congresses. Sometimes, however, the only student congress of the year is the NFL District Congress. Whether student congress is a continuous event throughout the year or a once-a-year occasion, a squad working together can do much to prepare its members to participate. Squad participation in the preparation process is important even if only a few are allowed to attend, because experience needs to be gained for future participation.

Attitude

The most important part of a squad's preparation for student congress is the proper attitude toward the event. A coach should talk about and help the squad prepare for student congress to grant it the importance that it is due. The squad should see student congress as a respected and valuable activity. A clear understanding of the principles of student congress and of the place such experience has in the forensic progression can help build those attitudes that will foster success for the individual as well as the group.

Bills and Resolutions

Each member of the squad should already have written at least one bill or resolution. There are several reasons for this. First, each member will gain a great deal of understanding about analysis of a bill from doing the research necessary to produce one. He or she will then be better able to evaluate the merits of the legislation actually used in the student congress and detect a weak or improperly worded bill. There is also the pragmatic need for practice bills for the squad practice sessions. Requiring everyone on the squad to write at least one bill will produce an ample supply for that purpose. Finally, the school will usually be required to submit at least one bill or resolution for use in the debate at student congress. The more bills the squad has to choose from, the better the quality of the bill it eventually sends to the student congress General Director.

Once the bills have been written, it is useful for the squad to read them carefully, evaluate them on form and substance, and make suggestions for revision. Then the squad should make some initial analysis of the bills as a group. This squad analysis gives each member practice in preparation for the time when he or she will have to analyze the bills that will be used in the student congress.

Research

Squad research is another important tool. This is not to say that individuals will be excused from their own research. Quite to the contrary, each person must conduct independent analysis and research in any given area. But a certain amount of background for particular bills can be assigned to squad members who can then share the information and save time for the group. The specific arguments that you will bring up for or against a bill must be researched by you, but the overall background of the topic will be common to all, regardless of your position on the bill. Files can be kept from year to year, as many of the crucial issues will carry over from one season to the next. Some squads have students do extensive research on the Internet. They begin by collecting a large database of information and abstracts.

Parliamentary Procedure

Individual students can read the parliamentary rules and review a precedence chart. But the way to achieve a working knowledge of parliamentary procedure is through practice and use. This requires a group effort, and it is one of the most important things a squad can do to prepare for student congress. After an initial review and discussion of motions, precedence, and rules, the coach should appoint a Presiding Officer, hand out a bill that has been researched, and begin a series of practice sessions in class. The coach can prescribe motions to be made at given points or can simply encourage students to experiment with all the motions. The Presiding Officer should be rotated with each new bill so that all members of the squad can learn the rudiments of presiding. In this fashion you can find out in the relative safety of the classroom which motions can be used and what their effect on an assembly will be. A word of caution here is appropriate: Expect the first several sessions to be somewhat chaotic and confusing. This is not the fault of parliamentary procedure but rather the result of inexperience. That in itself should encourage a lot of practice sessions before competing in student congress. You might consider inviting a current or former member of your forensic squad having some congress experience to serve as Presiding Officer for your first practice session.

During these parliamentary practice sessions, it would be a good idea for the coach or an outside observer to score the speeches given. This will give the squad members an idea of how well their speeches were structured and what each one needs to do to improve. A clerk should also keep records of the parliamentary procedures used during these sessions so that the coach can check for motions that may not have been used before the end of the session. Through practice, the group will get a great deal of experience in the use of parliamentary rules and legislative debate. Make sure there is time and a method for debriefing after each practice session so that the experience constitutes learning, not just the repetition of mistakes. The old adage that "practice makes perfect" might, without such a process, be restated as "practice makes perfectly awful!"

Rules and Regulations

In addition to practicing parliamentary procedure, the practice sessions conducted by the squad should familiarize everyone with the rules and regulations governing the congress that will be attended. Rules on speaking, time limits, methods of addressing the chair, and other procedures should be strictly enforced during practice sessions. If the squad uses these rules enough, it will learn them thoroughly and will feel more secure in the student congress as a result. What's more, the squad members will have time during the debates to think more about what they are going to say than about the form in which they should be speaking or other procedural considerations.

SUMMARY

You prepare for student congress both by yourself and with your squad. On your own, you analyze and research the bills and resolutions and then organize your information. You also prepare your authorship speech or any amendments you wish to propose. As a member of a squad, you develop bills and resolutions for an upcoming congress and practice parliamentary procedure.

QUESTIONS FOR DISCUSSION

1. What are the differences in style and method of research between conventional debate and student congress debate?

2. How would you respond to the statement, "Student congress is the easiest style of debate because you don't really have to worry about extensive research and a plethora of evidence"?

3. Why is knowing the status quo of a bill's subject matter useful in preparing student congress arguments?

4. How is squad preparation an important supplement to individual preparation?

ACTIVITIES

1. Walk through the reference section of your school or community library, making a list of the variety of political, legal, historical, and statistical reference books and specialized encyclopedias that could be used for student congress research.

2. Using a piece of legislation written for Chapter 12, prepare a file of notes, articles, reproductions, and other pertinent materials that could be used later to prepare a congress brief for use in an actual legislative debate.

3. Using an additional piece of legislation written for Chapter 12, use the squad preparation technique for brainstorming a series of pro and con arguments relating to the bill. Work from the class's knowledge of the background and current situation as it applies to the bill in question.

4. Plan to devote a future week of your class to a five-day congress session. This will require utilizing the principles and procedures presented in Chapters 13, 14, and 16 of this textbook, including writing bills and resolutions and researching the legislation to prepare congress briefs. Classmates will serve as Presiding Officers, and your teacher should fill the role of Parliamentarian. Possibly, a school administrator could be invited to serve as official scorer.

STRATEGIES FOR SUCCESS IN STUDENT CONGRESS

OBJECTIVES AND KEY TERMS

After studying Chapter 16, you should be able to

1. List the personal competitive qualities that are necessary to be a successful participant in student congress, and
2. Participate in an actual floor debate as part of a session of student congress.

After reading this chapter, you should understand the following terms:

clash

interpersonal relationships

political "games"

refutation

If you study and prepare well for your participation in a student congress, you will fuel your aspirations to succeed in the activity. Yet, while thorough preparation is a major determinant of success, it is only the first step. Your actual conduct and attitude during the student congress are the variables that make participation in the event such a challenge. We have interviewed many successful participants about their impressions of the attitudes and actions most likely to contribute to effectiveness in student congress. Based on their experiences, we offer some suggestions that may be useful to future student congress members. This advice, however, is not meant to constitute a money-back guarantee for election to Outstanding congressmember. Your own personality as well as the past relationships that you have had while competing with other congressmembers will affect how well a particular strategy will work for you.

ATTITUDE

Legislative debate is a challenging and rewarding experience for a forensic student. The person who approaches student congress as if it were a step down from debate insults not only the activity but the other participants as well. Such an attitude is usually apparent and will result in immediate and far-reaching negative attitudes from others. If you want to be a successful congressmember, you must treat student congress as an event important and respected in its own right. You should demonstrate by actions and words that you care about the activity, that you are prepared to work, and that you see value in the event, regardless of outcome.

The most successful student congressmember also approaches student congress as an enjoyable event and works to *make* it that kind of experience. Such attitudes are evidenced in many ways during the sessions of congress. Promptness in reporting to committee sessions and paying close attention to the task of the committee can indicate the importance that you attach to the activity. Listening carefully to other members during house debate shows enthusiasm and support for those who have the floor and allows you to participate in cross-examination to contribute to the debate progression. A positive and concerned attitude should be evidenced at all times by all participants.

INTERPERSONAL SKILLS

Closely related to the attitude you display as a participant is your ability to relate to and work with others. In no other area of forensic competition does the success of the event directly depend on how well the competitors work together. Consequently, your ability to work with others and to construct good relationships with them is very important. No one would be naive enough to suggest that the members of a student congress gather together just for the purpose of being nice to one another. It is understood that this is a competitive activity. However, you need to understand that the competition is achieved through skillful debate on bills and resolutions, not through attacks on the participants' personalities.

Because developing positive interpersonal relationships is important to the success of the student congress, you should begin early to make contacts. If you are the only representative from your school, then you will especially need to form acquaintances with others, beginning as early as registration. Often, particularly at the NFL District Student Congress, you will be among others with whom you have competed during the year in other events. There may be an understandable residue of hostility or at least reserve among the group. Efforts should be made to set those attitudes aside and begin fresh with the student congress. One thing to avoid in the early period of the student congress is the tendency to stay among participants from your own school or region. It is important for you to circulate, learn names, and begin to build relationships.

One student who was named Most Outstanding congressmember at the National Forensic League National Student Congress believed that high visibility as soon as possible is important, especially at the national level, where very few students know one another. This visibility is necessary for building interpersonal relationships, and it can be achieved in a variety of ways. Being direct and gregarious early in the session, learning the names of others by introducing yourself, asking questions, and giving others an opportunity to respond will all give you visibility. Casual conversation during recesses and at mealtime can also promote visibility. One student congressmember observed that these times of talking about everything else except student congress probably had more to do with achieving effectiveness than any debate on the floor.

And she was probably correct in terms of building good relationships and giving students an opportunity to appraise each other's ability.

Committee work is another time to build visibility early in the session. Volunteer to chair the committee and then be efficient and pleasant in its work. You will build a nucleus of colleagues who know and respect you. In addition, you will have made a positive contribution to the success of the student congress itself.

Politics

The United States Congress is a political institution, and members of student congress are no less susceptible to playing politics than their counterparts in Washington, D.C. However, you should exercise much caution, for as national events have dramatically illustrated in recent years, the game of politics can be hazardous.

As a member of student congress, you should realize from the outset that in spite of your best efforts there will be a degree of partisanship or polarization even before debate begins. Some of these ties have already been alluded to. You may be able to mitigate them, but you will probably never be able to erase all preexisting animosities stemming from rivalries developed during the competitive season. Several personality conflicts or personal rivalries will probably exist, certainly at the district and practice level. In addition, there may be regional prejudice even at the national level, or a residue of animosity built on differences at earlier student congresses. Finally, there will be some members who arrive determined to get their pet bill passed, regardless of the consequences or the methods used to accomplish this end.

Almost every successful former student congress delegate whom the authors interviewed had one absolute word of advice about the politics that these conditions create. Their advice was simple: "Stay out of it if possible!" It was their feeling that they served their own best interests and those of the student congress simply by listening with an open mind to others' efforts to pull them into a group and then moving on without making a commitment. There may be some plots laid, even some that are somewhat underhanded, in an effort to destroy a bill or undermine the credibility of some student who supports a particular piece of legislation. Avoiding such plots and working only for the betterment of debate on the floor is a much better strategy for success.

Perhaps the best way to approach the possibility of politics in the student congress setting would be the one most of us would hope to see followed in the legislatures of our own state or nation. Align yourself with people and causes only after your careful study has determined that the cause is worthy and the people are sincere. Overall, the successful student congressmembers we interviewed believed that political power plays and behind-the-scenes plots did little in the long run to advance the cause of the persons involved. Several interviewees cited examples of promising student congressmembers who were seriously damaged by involvement in such schemes.

An additional caution: If you become frustrated by the political wheelings and dealings of your session, you become your own worst enemy. If you constantly seem to be saying, "It's just not fair" or "The system is against me," then the danger is that you will either pull back or react in anger. Instead, decide on a method of coping that will not be destructive either to yourself or to the group.

DEBATE

The strategies for success in floor debate are almost all predicated on adequate preparation and persuasiveness in presentation. It is in the actual act of standing to speak as a participant in the floor debate that you are able to get NFL points, gain greater visibility among your peers, and put yourself into a position in which you can command their respect. As a consequence, the strategies for successful debating are vital to the success you may achieve.

Perhaps the most important thing to remember is the limitations on participation. For each session, if you are fortunate, you will get to speak a maximum of five times—and for only three minutes per occasion. Frequently, you will have fewer opportunities. As a result, it is important to be aware of the speaking that is done in the context of the total event. It is also important to realize that although every speech does not have to be dazzling, the higher the quality of each speech you give, the better the possibility that you will find support for yourself and your position in the assembly. Is evidence given to support assertions and generalizations? Is the argument relevant to the point being made? Is the material structured so that it can be easily understood? Be sure to review the standards for judging speech quality that were specified for the official scorer in Chapter 14; they will help you gain an insight into successful styles for legislative debate speeches. For example, while a one-minute speech in itself is satisfactory, how do you think the scorer will judge it in comparison to other speeches?

Sometimes it is wise to try to deliver one of the first speeches for or against a bill or resolution; sometimes it is good to listen to the debate for a while before seeking recognition to speak. Listening first allows you to evaluate sides of the issue, determine which may be the prevailing side, and set up your own strategy of clashing with the opposition in the debate. Not all of the former competitors agreed about which strategy is best. In fact, most of them discovered they had used a little of each. Certainly, success breeds success. The highly competitive student congress participant might want to wait until he or she can be sure of the side that will win and then give a speech favoring that side, extending the arguments and adding clincher arguments or evidence.

On the other hand, it might be best to accept the challenge of attempting to lead the group in the formulation of opinion. This can be achieved by getting early recognition and attempting to build the bandwagon effect in the assembly. Or, after observing the tide of opinion to one side, your challenge might be to attempt to construct a speech for the losing side and make it so persuasive that it would turn the direction of opinion. Either of these strategies is based on a principle inherent in all debate: Either side has valid issues that can be supported by evidence.

Another way to add to the strength of a speech given during debate is to utilize speeches already given by referring to them and making your speech an extension and amplification of them. If, for example, the speaker has simply referred to an idea that you see as a potentially strong argument, and if you have the data by which to make it into a fully developed point, you can simply say, "Representative Green's point about the historical significance of this bill is well taken, and I would like to...." Referring to other speeches can actually make your own speech sound more substantive than you could otherwise make it in only three minutes. The practical effect is that you use their data, already introduced, as a springboard to your own position, and you gain time and impact. Overall, most scorers look for clear evidence of a spontaneous *clash*—direct response to the opposition's arguments—as opposed to a series of unrelated, memorized, pre-prepared orations.

Playing out the newly discovered role of a congressional representative and employing the inherent speaking style is a part of the strategy for floor debate. Perhaps the most difficult thing for the debater-turned-student-congressmember to do is to regain the skills of persuasive public address after a season of debating with her or his nose in a flow pad, speaking at a rate of 400 words per minute. However, if you want success in student congress, then style must be part of your delivery. The stylistic considerations that you should make involve not only the traditional use of vocal variety, gestures, intonation, and appropriate volume and pauses, but also sensitivity to the times when a little humor would be a welcome relief, especially if the humor can be used to make a valid point. Examples, analogies, similes, metaphors, paradoxes, and other rhetorical devices, when used properly, are always effective in a congress speech. Also, you should be able to sense when there is an opening for emotional as well as intellectual appeal. Further, you should be alert to moments in the debate when a carefully proposed compromise might swing two factions into agreement and bring about the passage of a particularly hard-fought piece of legislation. These are decisions that you must make on your feet—they cannot be prescribed by any other person.

SUMMARY

There are several keys to a successful student congress session. When you prepare thoroughly for the session and then participate with a positive attitude, you are doing your part to make the session go smoothly. Developing your interpersonal skills is another way you can ensure a successful session. Finally, knowing the rules governing debate and following the arguments carefully can enhance everyone's student congress experience.

In these chapters you have examined the widespread and valuable activity of student congress. You should now have a better notion of its nature and purpose and of the principles that govern it. The structure of the congress activity gives specific responsibilities to the officials and also carries obligations to the participants. You have been given here, too, a clear description of the mechanics of the student congress as well as a guide to your own preparation for competition.

The student congress member who approaches the experience with adequate preparation, with a thorough understanding of the event, and with a dedication to the value of the experience will probably find the strategies for success discussed here a natural outgrowth of her or his own attitudes toward student congress. In the authors' experiences, this event is a true blending of the best of all the forensics events. Perhaps the essence of student congress was best expressed in the March 1978 issue of the National Forensic League *Rostrum* by the late Bruno E. Jacob, Executive Secretary Emeritus of NFL. He said:

> In the student congress the students learn to think about state and national problems in terms of solutions which they can urge their colleagues to accept as necessary and practical. They learn how to influence people favorably. They acquire not only knowledge of law-making, but respect for the power of the majority and the rights of the minority —the foundations of the democratic process. This makes leaders.

QUESTIONS FOR DISCUSSION

1. Why might a congress participant be rated highly by the official scorer but do poorly in the peer voting for Outstanding Member?
2. What qualities would you choose if you were compiling the profile of an ideal congress competitor?
3. What are the dangers of playing political "games" during a student congress session?

ACTIVITIES

1. Using the general guidelines for judging the quality of student congress speeches, develop specific, written criteria that could be provided to an official scorer to judge a session of congress.
2. Arrange for a small group of students (or your entire class) to attend a state, county, or city legislative session. If necessary,

arrange for release time and transportation and contact an appropriate legislator to meet with you before or after your visit.

3. Plan an after-school practice congress, inviting students in speech or government classes from neighboring schools. Be sure to publish bills and resolutions, an apportionment plan, a proposed agenda, and rules and regulations. Invite visiting teachers to serve as official scorers, and be sure to arrange local media coverage of the event.

CHAPTER 17

PARLIAMENTARY PROCEDURE

OBJECTIVES AND KEY TERMS

After studying Chapter 17, you should be able to

1. Understand the work of committees,
2. Understand the precedence of motions,
3. List the proper ways to amend a motion,
4. Be able to properly word any motion and understand what will happen if it is passed, and
5. Understand the most frequently used motions in parliamentary procedure.

After reading this chapter, you should understand the following terms:

amendment

division of the house

germane

motions: incidental, main, privileged, subsidiary

precedence

standing committees

voice vote

Parliamentary procedure can be viewed as a necessary evil or as a great service to any organization. It *is* possible to compete in student congress without any knowledge of parliamentary procedure—just sit back and go with the flow. At the other extreme are a few students who have a great need to show off their knowledge of parliamentary procedure. The best congressperson is one who can find a happy medium between these two extremes.

Just remember that parliamentary procedure is used to expedite the business of the assembly. Any *dilatory* (delaying) motions are detrimental to the good order of the session. The agenda in National Forensic League national tournaments is set by the standing rules of the congress. In regular student congresses the agenda is set after the call to order, by one member who moves for a set order of business. Someone else seconds this motion. There may be discussion, and it could be *amended* (changed). Eventually it is voted on; if a majority agree, it is passed.

FUNDAMENTALS

There are three fundamentals of parliamentary procedure: the right of the majority to decide; the right of the minority to be heard; and the right of absentees to be protected. The purposes of parliamentary procedure are to provide an expeditious and efficient guide for all kinds of meetings and to ensure that every member of the assembly has an equal chance to introduce business, discuss or debate it, and vote on it.

COMMITTEE WORK

At the NFL and the National Catholic Forensic League national congresses, students will choose which of the three or four *standing committees* (Foreign Affairs, Domestic Affairs, Economic Affairs, Constitutional) they wish to serve upon. Each committee shall only deal with those bills and resolutions (B/R) assigned to its jurisdiction by the Presiding Officer with the advice and consent of the Chamber. The Rules Committee for each Chamber shall comprise the chairperson of each standing committee and any returning congresspersons. It will set the order of consideration of the B/R for the NCFL student congress.

The first order of committee business is the election of a chairperson. Then it selects an order of B/R that it believes will afford interesting and profitable debate by the congress. Whether a B/R should be passed by the congress is not for a committee to decide. Any discussion of the merits of the B/R is, at this time, irrelevant and should be at once ruled out of order by the Chairperson. Thus, a controversial bill is frequently better than one that might receive unanimous support. The task of the committees, then, is simply to select the best proposals containing the most interesting debate potential. This work must be completed on time.

A committee may amend or rewrite any of the B/R submitted to it, or it may combine provisions of several B/R into a new one that it drafts, provided that it does not change the original intent. Committee business proceeds informally as group discussion. The Chairperson may enter into the deliberations and should guide the discussions along constructively. Members may speak without obtaining formal recognition, provided they do not interrupt another speaker. No one should be permitted to monopolize the time. Committee meetings <u>are not scored</u>. Formal motions are not used except to achieve definite actions, such as accepting a specific amendment or recommending a certain B/R as the committee's choice. If necessary, the Chairperson may appoint subcommittees to put into proper phrasing the ideas approved by the committee.

At the time scheduled for the Rules Committee to meet, the Chairperson should appoint a Temporary Chair and leave to join the Rules Committee. The Rules Committee will arrange the B/R as it sees fit, as suggested by the three standing committees, and it *must* rotate B/R from the three or the four committees. It *must* complete its work on time, or else the Parliamentarian will step in and mandate an agenda. Should it become necessary for these committees to reconvene later during the congress, meeting time can be set at a mutually convenient hour, but it should not overlap the time scheduled for debating.

Basic Parliamentary Procedure for Student Congress

This is a summary of the ordinary rules. For more detail and to handle situations not covered here, please consult *Robert's Rules of*

Order or the Table of Most Frequently Used Parliamentary Motions provided by the NFL and shown on page 207.

Each B/R will be listed in the packet as being sponsored by a district or a diocese. Every B/R representative shall be recognized to open debate, but thereafter, they shall take their chances with the rest of the members for further speaking opportunities. They do not have any other special powers or rights, such as the right to summarize the debate.

So that debate will alternate between pro and con speakers, members shall claim the floor in debate only if they wish to oppose the views of the preceding speaker. If no one wishes to oppose the preceding speaker, the Presiding Officer may recognize a speaker upholding the same idea. Maximum time for speeches is three minutes.

Motions

Because the basic purpose of parliamentary procedure is to expedite the business of a meeting, all business is introduced by *a proposal for action by the assembly—a motion.* Here are some essential facts one needs to know in order to take part in a meeting.

Precedence means that certain motions, because of their importance, have a higher rank than other motions. A higher-ranking motion must be considered before one over which it takes precedence.

Motions have qualifications that influence their use. Ask yourself these questions: What is the purpose of the motion? Does it take a Second? Is it debatable? Can it be amended? What vote does it require? May it interrupt the speaker?

There are four types of motions. *Main motions* are used to introduce business. *Subsidiary motions* deal with action on other motions. *Incidental motions* arise out of the business at hand. *Privileged motions* deal with the rights and privileges of the members.

Amendments

Amendments must be in writing and state precisely the words to be added or stricken. They may be considered only upon a Second (by show of hands) of one-third of the members *present.* Negative one-third Seconds are never to be taken. The procedure to be used is the following: (1) The amendment is to be written out on an Amendment Form and passed to the Parliamentarian. (2) The Presiding Officer will read the amendment and will determine whether it is *germane*—relevant and appropriate. (3) The Presiding Officer will pause for motions after each speech. (4) When an amendment is proposed, the Parliamentarian will read it. (5) The Presiding Officer will ask for a one-third Second of the members present. If the amendment does not receive this Second, debate continues with the next appropriate speech. If the amendment receives the Second, the Presiding Officer shall ask for an authorship speech on the amendment. Precedence for the amendment authorship speech shall be based upon the number of speeches given (regular speaking precedence), so the writer of that amendment does not automatically have the right of authorship. Once the Chamber seconds the amendment (by one-third), it becomes the property of the Chamber. Once the first proponency speech is given, no automatic questioning period will follow; a con speech on the amendment will be in order. Debate will then alternate pro and con on the amendment until the amendment is disposed of in the proper manner. Please note: Any speech on the main motion is out of order if it does not pertain to the amendment while that amendment is on the floor.

Voting

There are many ways to conduct the voting on motions and in elections. Most items can be handled with a simple *voice vote*. The correct form is for the Presiding Officer to say, "All those in favor of the motion say 'Aye.'" After this is noted, he or she says, "all opposed say 'No.'" It is not correct to say, "All in favor same sign." The opposite of *Aye* is *No*, and any other response is confusing.

If you are the Presiding Officer and it seems obvious that a motion has strong support, you can speed the meeting by asking, "Are there any objections to this motion?" If there are none, you can conclude that the motion is passed and so state. However, if there is objection from the floor, put the motion to a vote. Another popular method is to ask members to raise their hands. When a close vote is expected and the count may be difficult, ask for members to stand so you can be sure of accuracy.

In many cases only an affirmative voice need be asked for if the assembly is overwhelmingly in favor of a motion. If the voice vote is close, ask for a *division of the house*.

Congressmembers always stand to vote on bills and resolutions and most main motions. A rule of thumb: Do the constituents back home need to know how the congressperson voted? In NFL and NCFL congresses, abstentions are not counted.

Speaking

There is a right way and a wrong way to speak in legislative session. By studying the Table of Motions and *Robert's Rules of Order*, and learning to use these motions in correct language, you will be taking a step forward in your effort to be a good congressperson and contribute to a fine congress.

The correct way to obtain the floor to offer a motion or participate in the debate is this: Immediately at the conclusion of the preceding speaker's remarks, stand and say, "Mr./Madame President" or "Mr./Madame Speaker". When offering a motion, you may also say "Motion." If the Presiding Officer recognizes you, then proceed to make your motion or discuss the pending legislation. If another member is recognized, then take your seat until he or she relinquishes the floor. When many members wish to speak, the Presiding Officer will choose those who have spoken least. Members may speak more than once on the same question. Presiding Officers should carefully record the number of times each student has spoken and use this as a guide in choosing speakers. At the start of each preliminary session, all students shall start with a clean slate (zero speeches).

Members may not yield any portion of their speaking time to another member except to answer a question. However, only a question may be asked. After authorship speeches on main motions only, the author must field all questions asked during a mandatory two-minute questioning period. After all other speeches, the speaker may decline to answer questions. The Presiding Officer may *never* yield his or her position to anyone and may not enter debate on any main motion or amendment.

Under no circumstances are you permitted to argue with the Presiding Officer or the Parliamentarian. You only have one recourse if you feel the Presiding Officer has made a serious error, but before using it, remember that *the purpose of Student Congress is to debate legislation and not show off your knowledge of procedure*. If you believe a serious error has occurred, stand up and say, "I rise to a point of parliamentary procedure." The Presiding Officer will say, "State your point." State what you believe has been done wrong and sit down. The Presiding Officer may confer with the Parliamentarian before answering. If you still believe the Presiding Officer is wrong, you can rise and say, "I appeal the decision of the Chair." This motion requires a Second. There is no debate, but the person making the motion may, in a few sentences, state why the decision should be overruled. The Presiding Officer may also state, in a few sentences, why the decision should stand. The Presiding Officer then takes the vote as follows: "Those voting to sustain the Presiding Officer.... Those voting to Overrule the Presiding Officer...." Once the vote has been taken and the results announced, the decision is irrevocable, and no further discussion is permitted in this matter.

Do not overwork the motion for the Previous Question, which forces an immediate vote. As long as anyone has something to say, give them a chance to say it. There is no limit on the length of debate required on any piece of legislation. When no one wishes to speak, the vote should be taken. Remember that calling out "Question" merely indicates that a person is ready to vote and *is not* a motion to call Previous Question. The motion of Previous Question requires two-thirds vote of the members present in the Chamber. For example, if there are twenty-one people present, fourteen is the minimum needed to invoke the Previous Question. This rule differs from *Robert's Rules of Order*.

Decisions on B/R shall be taken by *standing vote* unless a roll call is demanded by one-fifth of the members. A division of the Chamber may be demanded by any two members (Motion and Second) on any question on which a voice vote has been taken. The call for a division of the Chamber must be made before another motion has been placed before the assembly.

A motion to suspend the rules of the Chamber must be passed by a two-thirds vote of the members present. This procedure is needed when groups wish to consider a B/R that is not on the official agenda and alter the order of business. A motion to suspend the rules may not be used to alter any of the National Student Congress Rules or Regulations.

Congresspersons are reminded that the speeches they give are of primary importance in influencing the nomination process. Motions used in a proper and timely manner help further debate and are an influence in the nominating process.

Many times during a long congress session, members may stand and request a point of "personal privilege." They are asking the Presiding Officer for permission to be absent from floor debate. If permission is granted, these members need to be recognized again when they wish to re-enter the Chamber. If many students seem to be absenting themselves from the Chamber, perhaps the Chair should encourage someone to make a motion for a short recess.

SUMMARY

Although great knowledge of parliamentary procedure is not required to be successful in student congress, every student should have a good working knowledge of the basics. The committees in student congress function as a clearinghouse for bills and resolutions before they come before the entire body. In the NFL and NCFL national meets, the committees will rank the legislation sent to them. Learning the proper time to speak and how to use the motions that will help the congress expedite its business are essentials for every congressperson.

QUESTIONS FOR DISCUSSION

1. Why are bills and resolutions sent to committee?
2. What is the purpose of the Rules Committee at national meets?
3. How does one get the floor and request permission to leave the chamber?
4. What is the difference between just saying "Question" and a motion for the Previous Question?

ACTIVITIES

1. Attend a tournament and observe or compete in a student congress.
2. Discuss the steps necessary to properly add a section to a practice bill.
3. Observe the procedures of the United States Senate or House of Representatives and report on the members' use of parliamentary procedure.

APPENDIXES

COMPETING IN TOURNAMENTS

Interscholastic debate in competition has been termed by scores of ex-debaters to be the single most valuable academic experience in their school career.

This appendix is designed to help those students, teachers, moderators, and coaches who wish to be involved in interscholastic debate competition. Some of the suggestions are aimed at the student debater, while other suggestions are targeted toward those in charge of getting students into interscholastic competition. Anyone with limited tournament experience can benefit from some of the observations contained here.

STUDENT DEBATER EXPECTATIONS

Students who have completed the study of this textbook are certainly ready to try their skills in tournament competition. If your teacher or coach is preparing you for such an event, some careful planning, preparation, and practice is in order.

Planning

You should not jump immediately from classroom work into tournament competition without some special planning. *Planning* means that you have carefully considered the nature of the tournament that you plan to attend and have decided on outcomes that you hope to accomplish. Do not expect to win every debate at the very first tournament unless you know that your competitors have no more experience than you do. On the other hand, do not lower your expectations either. Be realistic. If you have worked hard, and have practiced numerous times against a variety of case positions, then you should enjoy some real success at a tournament. However, do not expect success if you have not had meaningful practice before your first event unless your opposition has had no practice either. Practice does not make your performance perfect, but practice makes its result predictable.

Goals

Establish goals for each competition. If you have been working on particular skills, then one goal should be receiving specific judge feedback on those skills. If a judge does not comment on this area, do not hesitate to ask for it if the opportunity presents itself.

Rather than making winning a goal, make accomplishment of particular skill levels a goal. Winning will come with superior debating, and superior debating will not happen unless you acquire the necessary skills. Remember that in every debate, someone will be declared the winner. Just because you win a couple of early debates does not mean that you have learned all there is to know. It just means that you are debating better than your opponents.

Assessment

Have a plan for assessment. Do not let the results of the tournament decide for you how well you performed. Only one team or entry wins a tournament, but that does not mean that everyone else is a loser. Your plan for assessment of your success needs to be more sophisticated than merely examining your win-loss record. Review your specific skill goals, consider the feedback that you receive, and do some self-assessment at each step along your path of tournament experience. Then establish new goals for the next experience.

Preparation

Preparation means acting on your plan. Take the time to do the things that you have decided are going to be important to your success. If you know that you need to do more research, then do more research. If your cases need revision, then revise them. If the evidence that you are using needs to be updated, then update it. While all of this sound simplistic, it is nonetheless critical. The fundamentals are simple, but that does not mean that they are not important. The danger lies in taking these fundamentals for granted. And when taken for granted, they are often neglected. You cannot afford to neglect preparation. Preparation takes time, so enough time to prepare must be part of your plan.

Written Rules

Your coach may establish specific requirements for your preparation. These may include expectations and activities for you as you prepare to go to a tournament (evidence requirements, case revision deadlines, practice schedules) as well as expectations at the tournament (departure and arrival times, dress, behavior). Your coach may establish written expectations for you to follow as you travel to and from the tournament (time schedules, curfews, where to be and when to be there). All of the expectations are intended to help ensure a successful tournament experience.

Written guidelines make it easy for everyone to know what is important to the tournament experience. Some of the guidelines are directed toward your work as a debater; others may be directed toward your thoughts, feelings, and actions as a person. Remember, regardless of what importance you place on tournament experience, you are an ambassador of your school and community. You represent your coach, your team, your school, your parents, your community, and most importantly yourself. Take expectations seriously, especially if the expectations are written.

Unwritten Rules

Some coaches do not provide long lists of written rules for your preparation. That does not mean that their expectations are lower; it may mean that they expect more from their students. Your coach may believe, as many do, that students who are in debate are already of a maturity level that brings with it responsible behaviors as a debater and as a person. Your coach may give you lots of freedom to prove your responsibility. Abusing that freedom will limit your success as a debater, and it may even eliminate your opportunity to continue in debate. Coaches spend lots of time deciding what kind of people their debaters seem to be. If you are a responsible and dependable person in debate (evidenced to a great extent by how seriously you approach preparation), then you will continue to be provided opportunities for more tournament experience.

Practice

The most essential ingredient to tournament success is actual debate practice. Reading, writing, and thinking about debate are important parts of preparation, but practice is the only way to simulate the tournament experience. Only if you have practiced advocating and defending your case against real attacks under timed format conditions can you have a real idea how your ideas, research, and writing will withstand attack. If your case is too long to read within format times, its actual presentation will expose that. If the arguments are too complex to extend, rebuttal practice will demonstrate that. If your reasoning is flawed, practice cross-examination will expose them.

You would not compete in a basketball tournament without having had hours of practice dribbling, passing, and shooting the ball. And you would not stop with the fundamentals; you would practice every aspect of the game. Remember, experience is one of the best teachers of debate, so you need to give yourself as much experience as possible. Practice provides important experience.

TEACHER/MODERATOR/COACH EXPECTATIONS

This section is directed to the teacher, moderator, or coach who has the responsibility of taking his or her debaters to a tournament. Experienced coaches will be well acquainted with some of this discussion, but every coach can profit from the experience of others. Taking debaters beyond the classroom into interscholastic competition gives the teacher/moderator/coach several challenges. For one, teaching debate in the classroom is different from coaching debaters for a tournament.

Coaching Tournament Debaters

Coaching tournament debaters calls for preparing students, first and foremost, for a wonderful interscholastic academic experience. Countless ex-debaters, including those with postgraduate degrees, contend without reservation that their time spent in tournament debate was their single most valuable experience from school.

Preparing students for tournament debate also requires establishing specific expectations. The debate tournament experience is not just an excursion or a field trip; it is an opportunity to engage important skills in a meaningful, hands-on interaction that tests critical thinking, persuasive communication, and effective defense of ideas. As a coach, you must stress that the experience will be demanding, energizing, and rewarding, outcomes far more meaningful than most grades from classroom assignments. Debate competition will afford growth that is not only intellectual, but also social, psychological, philosophical, and ethical. Its interscholastic nature will expose your students to thinking and values that are beyond those held in common by their academic community. The tournament experience will give your students new perspectives, new awareness, and self-actualization difficult to duplicate in any other activity.

As a teacher/moderator/coach, you must stress the importance of the various values. You help your students accomplish these values by establishing appropriate expectations.

Expectations

It is not news to any instructor that you must *expect* a great deal from your students if you hope to *get* a great deal from your students. It is very important to establish clear, demanding, but realistic expectations for your tournament debaters. Clear and demanding expectations may be easy to establish, though it may be more difficult to decide what is realistic. As observed earlier in the discussion of student debater expectations, students should not jump immediately from classroom work into tournament competition without some special planning. *Planning* means that you and your students have carefully considered the nature of the tournament that you plan to attend and have decided outcomes that you hope to accomplish. Do not expect your debaters to win every debate at the very first tournament unless you know that the students competing have no more experience than yours do. On the other hand, do not lower your expectations either. Beginning debaters often have an unrealistic view of their preparedness, so be realistic. If your students have worked hard, and have practiced numerous times against a variety of case positions, then they should enjoy some real success at a tournament. Do not expect success if they have not had meaningful practice before their first event unless their opposition has had no practice either.

Next, help your students establish goals for each competition. If they have been working on particular skills, then one of their goals should be receiving specific feedback from the judge on those skills. If a judge does not comment on those skills, encourage your debaters to ask him or her for feedback if the appropriate opportunity presents itself. Insisting upon specific judge response at the end of a debate may be inappropriate. However, perhaps between rounds, your debaters may take the opportunity to ask for more feedback. Be sure that your debaters do not seem only interested in finding out the judge's decision or challenging it. Learning about how they can improve their skills needs to be the focus of their questions.

Rather than making winning a goal, encourage your students to make accomplishment of particular levels of skill a goal. Winning will come with superior debating, and superior debating will not happen unless your students acquire the necessary skills. Remember that in every debate, someone will be declared the winner. Just because your debaters win a couple of early debates does not mean that they have learned all there is to know. It just means that they are debating better than their opponents. Remember, though, the higher your expectations of your students, the greater will be their results.

Rules

Every teacher/moderator/coach who has the responsibility of taking students to tournaments will be inclined to make some expectations into rules governing behavior during the tournament experience. You do not want your students to act irresponsibly outside of the classroom any more than you would want such behavior inside the classroom.

If rules are delivered in writing, your students will sense that these are the most important, so it is essential to avoid putting into writing those expectations that may vary by conditions. For example, you may want to declare that "observers are encouraged to attend all tournaments," but then you would have to explain that that does not apply to any travel that happens "out of town." Your debaters will simply decide that the rule was never a rule in the first place, and such a conclusion weakens the impact of the rest of the rules.

Do not establish a rule unless you plan to enforce it, and be sure that you have ready a method of enforcement. Rules can be very limiting, and thus may have a very counterproductive effect. In other words, go sparingly on the written rules. You want the tournament experience to be filled with potential, so you do not want to establish so many rules that you cannot conduct the business of tournament competition. In fact, written *expectations* may be much more effective than written *rules*.

Although written rules may seem to be more substantial, unwritten ones may be more successful. Some coaches do not distribute long lists of written rules to prepare their students. That does not mean that their expectations are lower; in fact, it may mean that their expectations are higher. As a coach, you may believe, as many of your colleagues do, that students who are in debate are already of a maturity level that brings with it responsible behaviors as a debater and as a person. You may give your debaters lots of freedom to prove their responsibility. Their abuse of that freedom will limit their success as debaters, and it may even eliminate their opportunity to continue in debate. As you know, coaches spend lots of time deciding who their debaters seem to be as people. If your students are responsible and dependable people in debate (evidenced to a great extent by how seriously they approach preparation), then you will continue to provide them with opportunities for more tournament experience. As long as you make that expectation clear to your debaters, they know what to expect; you will be left with more flexibility to meet the needs of individual debaters and specific situations; and your debaters will grow as responsible young adults.

You must decide the style of control that seems most comfortable for you. Empowering your debaters to exist responsibly as well as independently should be a goal of your rules for them. Expectations can be positively stated. Rules, written or unwritten, often exist as negatives. Keep in mind that positives are often more productive than negatives.

Once you have decided on and communicated your expectations, you have laid a foundation for strategy, tactics, and practice, all of which enhance the tournament experience.

Strategy, Tactics, and Practice

Applying all of the theory and instruction that occurs throughout this text requires time. *Strategy* means having a particular plan or approach to the tournament in general and to specific opponent teams in particular. If you are preparing debaters to compete in both your and their first tournament, then strategy is going to be very broadly based. You will try to prepare for every eventuality, but it may be difficult to predict them. Clearly, it will be important not to take anything for granted; do not make broad assumptions about what to expect. Your cases may be open to devastating attack because an opponent has discovered an obvious flaw that somehow escaped your notice. That experience is part of the overall experience of going to tournaments: to learn more by discovering the limits of what you know now. The more tournament experience recorded by you and your debaters, the more your strategy will be defined, and tactics will emerge to be practiced against particular opponents.

Stress practice throughout your program. Actual debate practice will be key to the development of your team, so schedule practice and make it an important, expected part of preparation. Make it more valuable by carefully critiquing the results of practice.

Once your debaters are prepared for tournament competition, you need be prepared to enter a tournament. Administrating your team's entry in a tournament can be as important as coaching, and as many an experienced coach will confirm, it seems to take more time!

Administrating the Tournament Entry

It has been said that every successful coach exhibits some combination of three characteristics: (1) knowledge and experience of the activity being coached; (2) good communication skills; and (3) effective administrative abilities. In fact, it has been argued that a truly successful coach only needs to be particularly qualified in two of these traits. Administration skills seem particularly important in debate, probably because debate is so highly organized and analytic in nature. There are several aspects to administrating your team's entry in tournaments. It all begins with registration.

Registration

For the purpose of discussion here, it is assumed that you have received an invitation to a tournament. If you have not received an invitation, simply contact schools that have debate programs to ask the coach for a schedule of tournaments and to request an invitation to any tournament that that school might host. Once you have the invitation, you are ready to begin the process of registration. The first steps in that process are to complete the invitation entry forms and to file them with the tournament host.

Note that the invitation will include instructions concerning entry to the tournament and usually a form that is to be completed and returned to the tournament host. Read the instructions carefully. If you have questions, contact the host. Once you have selected the entry that seems appropriate for the tournament (after considering matters such as the calendar, expenses, personnel, timetable of preparation, etc.), you are ready to submit the initial entry.

Follow the invitation instructions for submitting the initial entry. Most hosts require written submissions, so a mailed or faxed entry will be necessary. While you may phone the host to indicate your entry, be sure to follow up this contact in writing. The initial entry is your official intent to participate in the tournament, so be sure that you make every effort to meet all deadlines. Respond promptly, for there is no guarantee that a tournament will not be filled even before the deadlines.

Many tournaments require that you call to confirm your initial entry at a designated time before the tournament begins. The phone confirmation will usually include the registration of debaters' and judges' names, or their confirmation from the initial entry. Any changes in the initial entry will be registered as well. Have this information ready when you call.

An official check-in site is designated to be your first stop upon arrival at most tournaments. Here you will confirm final official registration of your entry. Often, your teams are identified by some code or label that you will be informed of at this check-in. If you have not already submitted your entry fees, have a check ready at this final registration.

Most tournaments will assess an entry fee that is indicated on the invitation to cover the expenses of the event. If you can obtain a check in advance of the tournament send it as part of the initial entry. Many tournaments will require payment in advance, and others will ask that fees be delivered at final registration. Just be sure to meet the expectations of the tournament. Neglecting fees will cause disqualification from competition.

Debate tournaments are very labor-intensive when it comes to officials. Every round of debate (two teams in policy debate or two debaters in Lincoln-Douglas debate) requires at least one judge. To meet the judging requirements of a tournament, schools entering the competition are responsible for providing one judge per two entries or fraction thereof. As a coach, you can cover one such judging obligation; if you have assistants, they can each serve as well. But if your entry requires more judges than your school can provide, you must either hire judges from outside your staff or school, or pay an additional fee to hire judges from the host school. It is very important, therefore, to assess the judge obligation that your entry demands, and that you make it your responsibility to cover that obligation.

Communication

Communication skills are an essential characteristic of good coaching. They are particularly important when taking your debaters to tournaments, because the competition is an expensive, labor-intensive, and time-consuming activity. Making sure all of the parties involved are aware of the investment is a critical element of your program's success. Be sure that your school and debate parents know the details of your competition.

Tournaments will take students away from school and home. Your school administration and faculty will be supportive of your competition if they know far in advance that it will be happening. If students will be missing classes, their teachers will need to be informed so that arrangements for advance completion of work can be made. Create a form that can be used each time such notification needs to take place. The procedures at your school will dictate distribution.

Next, create an itinerary sheet or "trip sheet" that will be the standard form you use to inform students and parents of the details concerning each debate competition outside school. The sheet should indicate the name, date(s), location, and host of the tournament; phone numbers of the tournament host and site; site and phone number of overnight lodging; departure and return times; tournament schedule; mode of transportation; food arrangements; expenses that will be the student's responsibility; and any specific information unique to preparation for the tournament. Be sure that both your students and their parents get copies of the trip sheet, and that receiving such information and being responsible for it becomes routine. It may also be a good idea that an administrator at your school has a copy on file. Each member of your staff as well as your hired judges may need to receive the same information. The trip sheet saves lots of your administrative time because it eliminates the need to keep answering the same questions about the tournament trip.

It is a valuable administrative practice to create a single-sheet form upon which you can list the room assignments for coaches, students, and judges when your team travels overnight. This sheet can be sent to the motel to inform it of your room needs, and then used at check-in to register room numbers. This sheet can be distributed to all members of the traveling squad upon arrival at the lodging site, room numbers can be announced, and then every member of the traveling squad can be expected to be responsible for the whereabouts of every other member. At the lodging site, communication about the competition schedule, preparation, and transportation is an ongoing need. Make it as easy as possible for your squad to communicate with one another and you.

Between the time that you send your initial entry to the tournament director and the time at which you make your final confirmation before departure, you should maintain communication with that director in the event of cancellation of or changes in your initial entry. A tournament director needs to know the field of entry as accurately as possible as soon as possible. Never wait until arrival at the tournament to announce major changes in your entry. The tournament director will profit from conscientious updates of entry information.

Transportation and Travel Arrangements

Competing in tournaments outside the classroom will require transportation to and from the event. Tournaments may be local, regional, or national. National tournaments may include a schedule of competition lasting several days, while a local tournament may be completed in a portion of one day. Each type of tournament will require transportation and travel arrangements to make your competition as purposeful, effective, and affordable as possible.

Getting your debaters to and from tournaments will be a major expense if your tournaments are not local. Regardless of their location, transportation is an important responsibility owing to its legal liability. Check with your local school district before taking it upon yourself to personally transport students. Your local district may be willing and able to provide transportation for your students. If the district's ability is less than your predicted expenses, you will have to tailor your travel intent, limit the numbers of students who will participate, or raise the funds from outside the district. Overestimate when predicting transportation costs. It will usually cost more than you predict.

If you travel to tournaments away from home that are more than one day in length, you will need to make overnight arrangements for lodging. Again, that means an expense and special responsibilities for you as the travel squad administrator. First, remember that the rooms will be used primarily for sleeping, and there will not be time at most tournaments for very much of that. Therefore, make arrangements that are as inexpensive as possible because your squad will have little opportunity to use any of the extras that come with more expensive lodging. Second, if possible, arrange to lodge where there is convenient access to food. The time schedules of most tournaments will make usual time for breakfast, lunch, and dinner nearly impossible. You will be starting very early and ending very late. If food is convenient to your place of lodging, then returning late at night will not mean moving everyone to someplace else to eat.

Be sure to find out whether food will be provided at the tournament site. If not, that means that you will need to arrange for transportation of your tournament debaters to a restaurant during the tournament or else arrange the transportation of food to the site. Tournament debate competition is taxing, so your debaters need to be regularly fed. While fast food is convenient, several days of it can be counterproductive to keeping your team at top performance. Meal arrangements do not require lots of planning, but they obviously cannot be neglected.

Public Relations

It has already been mentioned that communication skills and administrative skills may be critical to leading student debaters into tournament competition. An important part of that communication is by necessity inside your program. But communication and administration of tournament debate must extend beyond the coaches, students, judges, supervisors, parents, and tournaments involved. Because communication needs to extend to the school community as well, the teacher/moderator/coach of tournament debate needs to spend serious time at public relations.

Recruiting and Promoting

It has been said that recruiting and promoting are key to a coach's successful development of any competitive school program. While your students may be excited about debate and ready to go to a tournament, you cannot assume that the next class of students will be excited too. The fact that your students have worked hard and then competed successfully needs to be told to your greater school community. Debate competition is different from sports competition in several ways. For one, there is a lack of thousands of spectators and no automatic coverage by the media. People in your school need to know that your students are competing interscholastically. You need to communicate to potential debaters in your school that you have launched and/or are maintaining a competitive program, and that they can profit from participation. Tournament debate experience has been cited as one of the most valuable activities that a student can experience in school, but non-debaters do not know that. It is part of your job to recruit students and promote the values of debate.

The Regular Press Release

Because interscholastic debate does not receive automatic coverage by the media, it is important that you provide the coverage for them. Create a standard press release form (identifying school, coach, program, addresses, phone numbers, etc.) to report the schedule of tournament competition and the specific outcomes of tournaments. If you attend only one or two tournaments, school letterhead is a sufficient form. If you compete more often, then a more individualized form for press releases is valuable. Send the release wherever such communication may serve to enhance your program. Your students have worked hard to compete in tournament debate; they deserve all the recognition you can get them. Make the press release a regular routine, and recipients will come to look forward to the information.

Booster Clubs

Parents and friends of student debaters are one of your most valuable assets as a teacher/moderator/coach. While there may not be a need or time for a formally organized booster club, it is important to decide how to involve parents in the program. Parents are no less interested in the success of your debaters than you are. Their support can be integral to greater success.

Ben Davis Debate Classic

REGISTRATION FORM

ENTRIES DUE BY 9:00 p.m. WEDNESDAY, JANUARY 4

School _____

Coach _____

Home Phone_____ School Phone _____

CONGRESS
    Varsity _____
    Novice _____

LINCOLN DOUGLAS
    Varsity_____
    Novice _____

POLICY
    Varsity _____
    Sub Varsity _____
    Novice _____

We will bring one judge for every 4 debaters or fraction thereof,
for a total of _____.

This sample speech tournament registration form is reproduced here courtesy of Ben Davis High School, Indianapolis, Indiana.

Appendix B

Judging at Tournaments

As was discussed in the preceding appendix on Competing in Tournaments, a school that enters debaters in an inter-scholastic tournament has an obligation to provide judges at the tournament. This section is directed to both student debaters and teacher/moderator/coaches who find themselves filling that obligation. Student debaters who are in their senior year after three or more years in tournament debate are often invited to judge in the novice division of policy debate tournaments. In addition, student debaters who have recently graduated from a debate program are often invited to judge Lincoln-Douglas debate. Coaches are always designated as potential judges at either sort of debate tournament. If you find yourself judging or preparing others to judge, there are several important expectations to consider. Among the most important are ethical standards, knowledge of debate theory, and respect for tournament rules.

ETHICAL STANDARDS

Ethical standards are probably the most important expectation of a debate judge. Tournament debate competition centers on the belief that the competition may be one of the most valuable learning experiences that a student can have in school. However, the experience will be valuable only if everyone involved is committed to make it so. Debate involves some of the most demanding of intellectual skills: insightful analysis, sound reasoning, clear and concise organization, effective refutation, skillful use of evidence, and meaningful communication. An assigned tournament judge has the critical task of evaluating who does the best job in each skill. If judgments are made arbitrarily, capriciously, negligently, or ignorantly, then the judge's decision becomes meaningless, and tournaments serve little educational purpose. Unethically judged tournaments might still be fun to attend just because of the travel and time away from school, but such tournaments will have no justification beyond being just another school holiday, and an expensive holiday at that. And if the judges do not meet meaningful ethical standards, the tournament may actually become counterproductive and harmful in effect. Student debaters may learn that being arbitrary, capricious, negligent, and ignorant are acceptable. Dishonesty and willful wrongdoing will seem to be the norm enforced by the experience. Such learning is not only unjustifiable but dangerous.

What ethical standards need to be observed by judges?

A Judge Should Be Attentive and Respectful

Judging is a demanding process. Debaters speak, listen, and ask and answer questions at different times during the debate. A judge must consider the entire debate in making the final decision. Some debaters will be more compelling than others, and the judge's attention will be easy to attract. Other debaters will seem less able, and inattention will be tempting. In either case, the judge is responsible to consider everything to make a good decision. Regardless of the debaters' abilities, the judge needs to respect their effort being made in this valuable activity. To be inattentive or disrespectful is to be negligent. The negligent judge will make poor decisions.

A Judge Should Be Thorough and Knowledgeable

The judge who is attentive needs to keep a careful record of everything that has happened in the debate. This record has been referred to earlier as recording the "flow" of the debate, or "keeping a flow." Listening is not enough. Even in a debate that seems to be undemanding, the judge is responsible for listening carefully and making notes of the presentations. The judge who has an incomplete record of the debate will have a sketchy basis for decision.

Thoroughness also means that the judge is prepared to judge the debate, having some knowledge of the proposition and of debate theory. The ethical judge is responsible for knowing what the debate may include. Lack of thoroughness and lack of knowledge will result in an incomplete basis for decisions. Such decisions will be arbitrary.

A Judge Should Be Fair and Impartial

The most important ethical standard for judging debate may be fairness and impartiality. The judge who is biased or less than objective will make unfair decisions. Any judge may have special knowledge or opinions on the debate proposition, or special preferences when it comes to strategy, tactics, and application of debate theory. But the fair and impartial judge creates a level playing field upon which the debate occurs. The fair and impartial judge ignores the reputation of the school, individual debater, or coach. The fair and impartial judge puts bias aside to avoid decisions that are capricious by effect if not by intent. Capricious decisions become dangerous decisions because they undermine the very value of having tournaments.

APPLICATION OF DEBATE THEORY

As mentioned above, the ethical judge has an obligation to be knowledgeable about debate in general and the proposition in particular. This brings us to a specific consideration of application of debate theory. While ethical standards provide general guidelines for the judge, they do not spell out *how* to judge. There are no specific, exclusive agreed-upon rules as to how debates *must* be evaluated. Indeed, as works on debate proliferate, there continue to be several different models for evaluation that might be applied. Some people find these models of judging useful. They like to pretend that they are applying sophisticated testing tools to the debate round. Unfortunately, these models, by and large, are esoteric and of limited use. Judges using such tools may require a longer time to explain their decisions than it took the debaters to finish the debate!

Nonetheless, becoming knowledgeable of such models may still serve a judge well. Theorists of debate are sincerely interested in the activity. Their thinking about debate provides insight into argumentation generally that may be valuable both inside and outside of debate. To ignore theory is to limit knowledge of debate, which may produce ignorant decisions. The caution lies in noticing that exotic views of debate theory may impede good judgment. Unless theory becomes an unresolved issue in the debate itself, theoretical prejudices should not be imposed on the outcome of the arguments. Such an imposition becomes an ethical issue of fairness and impartiality as well as a knowledge issue. A capricious decision is worse than an ignorant one.

TOURNAMENT RULES

Every debate judge, whether student debater or teacher/moderator/ coach, has an obligation to consider the specific rules for officials that may have been established by the tournament host. Often, tournaments such as league- and association-sponsored competitions have a set of published terms and conditions to govern the conduct of the tournament. A judge at such a tournament is obligated to know these rules and to apply those that govern officials in his or her evaluation of the debates. If debaters are given specific expectations by such rules, it is the judge's job as an official to enforce such rules. A teacher/moderator/coach or student debater who ignores a tournament's specific rules may simply be disqualified from further officiating. Since each attending school has an obligation to provide judges as a part of securing entry in the tournament, disqualification of judges may result in disqualification of entry.

It is simply important to know the rules. If you are a prospective judge, and you do not approve of the tournament rules, either set aside your disapproval and follow the rules, or do not judge. Remember, you are under no ultimate obligation to be at the tournament in the first place. Committing to enter as well as committing to judge is an implicit if not explicit commitment to knowing and following the rules of the tournament.

APPENDIX **C**

HOSTING
TOURNAMENTS

This appendix is directed to the teacher/moderator/coach and debate students who are going to host an interscholastic debate tournament. Only the basic considerations will be discussed here. If you have never hosted before, contact a neighboring school that has hosted tournaments and arrange a meeting with its director of debate. Be sure to have considered the basics first: establishing the tournament, managing the tournament, and evaluating the tournament. Debate students should be aware of these basics.

ESTABLISHING THE TOURNAMENT

If you are at a school that has had tournaments in the past, you/ your team may have inherited files that will literally give you everything that you need to continue tournaments at your school. If you have not hosted before and your school does not have a tournament file, than the first decision that you will make is on the structure of the tournament.

Deciding on the Structure

There are two fundamental types of debate tournaments that you may host. The first type is the invitational, which is entirely self-generated. The other is a league or association tournament that is run by a designated group from within the league or association, but located at a particular school or university. If your school hosts an invitational, then you decide the structure. If you school hosts a league or association tournament, then you may be asked to provide the local arrangements and hospitality while the responsibility for designing and managing the tournament will usually fall to the league or association. If you are a member of the league or association's management team, then your duties may be similar to those you would face when hosting you own invitational.

The Invitational

If you inherited files on past events, they will literally give you a blueprint for the design of your tournament. If not, there are basics to any debate invitational that your design should include. Remember, these are just the basics to establishing the tournament. The details will be for you to decide. The decisions that you will need to make most fundamentally are the schools to invite; the number of entries your school will accommodate; the date(s) and length of the tournament; the number of rounds of debate; the levels or divisions of debate; whether there should be preliminary, elimination, and championship rounds; the time schedule; fees; a timetable of deadlines for yourself and the invited schools; the invitation; your management team; mailings; food, lodging, and transportation arrangements; a tabulation center with appropriate office supplies and office equipment; hired judges; awards; custodial and secretarial services; and most importantly, a budget. Keep copies of everything that your planning generates, and keep a log of everything that you do. The record of your preparation will be truly valuable to the planning of your next tournament.

League and Association Tournaments

Once it is known that you have a debate program at your school, you may be asked to host a league or association tournament. As mentioned earlier, such tournaments are usually planned outside your school, and very few of the decisions regarding tournament structure become the host's responsibility. As host you may be expected to provide local arrangements, such as room availability, custodial service, directions and maps, food service or a guide to local restaurants, a tabulation area with office supplies and equipment, a letter of information to attending schools, a hospitality area, and a budget. While most teachers/moderators/coaches of beginning programs do not think much about the possibility of hosting a league or association tournament, it is important to consider. Providing a site for a state, sectional, regional, or district tournament is an excellent way to give exposure to your program; network with established coaches, debaters, and programs; and receive insight into the establishment of tournaments. Offering to be a tournament host is a good way to put your program "on the map."

If "establishing the tournament" falls primarily to you as the host of your own tournament, there are basics to the process as well as to the structure. First, you must establish a system for registering entries.

Registration of Entries

Before schools enter interscholastic debate competition, they want to know what to expect. As host of your tournament, you have the responsibility of establishing those expectations.

The Invitation

The tournament invitation is exactly that: a letter of invitation from you and your school to everyone you would like to have attend your tournament. The letter of invitation should be simple, clear, and direct. Debate coaches receive many invitations to a wide variety of tournaments, so they select those tournaments that they believe will best meet the needs and resources of their respective programs. Information that this letter should contain includes tournament location, date(s), proposition to be debated, schedule of rounds, divisions, levels of experience, field of entry, terms and conditions or special rules, limitations upon entry, fees, judge requirements, method of determining winners, awards, forms for submitting entries, and a schedule of deadlines. Directions, maps, lodging, food, and transportation information should be included if the tournament will be receiving schools from out of town. Phone, address, fax, and e-mail information must be clear to facilitate communication. If there is to be a confirmation of entry from host, attending schools, or both, the invitation should so indicate. The invitation will be the fundamental document governing the administration of your tournament, so make sure it says everything that you think needs to be said. However, do not encumber the invitation with anything that can be omitted without sacrificing clear intentions and expectations.

The Tournament Packet

The tournament packet is a collection of materials prepared for distribution to each school upon check-in at your tournament. It should contain information valuable to those attending: a listing of the teams and schools entered; copies of the schedule of rounds (especially noting if any changes have been made to the schedule sent in the invitation); maps to rooms; announcements; a sheet verifying the individual school's respective entry (names of debaters, judges, coaches, etc.); code of entries (if the schedule will be using codes); judge assignments; and a sheet describing the history of tournament and past winners. The tournament packet serves several functions: a sort of "sports program" for your event; final confirmation of entries; and communication of information necessary to launch the tournament (telling everyone where to go, what to do, and when to be there).

The tournament packet will be one of the products of the local arrangements you have made. Many of the arrangements made to launch the tournament will happen far in advance of the event. In fact, many of the local arrangements must occur even before you write the invitation.

Local Arrangements

Whether you are hosting your own tournament or hosting for some league or association, local arrangements will determine the smooth administration of the tournament. Debate tournaments use a great deal of building space, since one debate may involve three (Lincoln-Douglas debate) to five (policy debate) individuals, including a judge. In other words, if your tournament has sixty entries, but your school can provide only ten rooms for debate, then you have a problem. Do not decide how many schools to invite or accept until you have made a realistic assessment of the number of entries your school (not to mention your community, if lodging will be required) can accommodate.

Rooms for Debates

Once you have gotten your school to agree to the specific rooms (usually classrooms) that can be used for your tournament, be sure to inform everyone who has materials there that debaters will be using those rooms during your tournament. Neither you, your school, nor the visiting teams should be held unnecessarily responsible for valuables left unsecured in the rooms. Debaters and coaches attending your tournament need to be informed of their responsibility too, to leave the rooms as they found them. But it is *your* responsibility to inform classroom teachers that their rooms will be used for the debate event so that any concerns can be addressed before the event. Arrange to have the designated debate rooms unlocked throughout the tournament. Many experienced coaches would agree that schedule delay caused by locked rooms seems almost inherent to debate tournaments. Some coaches would contend that *no* tournament has happened without this problem; work to make them wrong.

Registration, Tabulation, and Hospitality

Establish a designated place for tournament check-in and registration. Designate individuals (students will be eager to help) to administer check-in and the distribution of tournament packets. Keep yourself free from registration duties because the opening of the tournament will require troubleshooting any problems as they occur. If fees are to be collected during registration, be sure you have arranged to secure such fees. Registration can be hectic. Your management team needs to understand their responsibility for the smooth start of your tournament.

Establish a room for your team to record, tabulate, and file debate results. As the nerve center of the tournament, this room should be far enough away from the debate rooms to be quiet and out of the mainstream of traffic, yet convenient to the flow of traffic. Processing results is demanding and time-consuming work. Your management team will need to be comfortable and free from distraction, with plenty of room to work. Be sure that the tabulation room is convenient to office equipment and office supplies. Libraries or office areas are often appropriate.

Establish a hospitality area for teachers/moderators/coaches/judges and student debaters. Cafeterias make appropriate gathering areas for students; faculty lounges may be appropriate for coaches and judges. If you are providing food service, then those arrangements should be delegated to a hospitality team; parents or booster club members would be a good choice for this.

Lodging and Transportation

If your tournament requires overnight provisions or special shuttle transportation, these arrangements need to be made far in advance. Contact local motels and hotels and ask to reserve blocks of rooms until an agreed-upon deadline before the tournament. Discovering that area hotels are already booked during your intended tournament weekend is important to know *before* you send the invitation rather than when teams are trying to come to your tournament. Lodging arranged in advance often yields special rates upon request, making your tournament more attractive to those deciding to attend.

Shuttle transportation may need to be arranged if the tournament is occurring in more than one location or if you decide to offer service to and from air, bus, or train terminals. Again, the key is to make these arrangements long before your tournament.

MANAGING THE TOURNAMENT

Once the tournament is under way, a well-planned event will virtually run itself; a poorly planned tournament will self-destruct.

As tournament manager, you will not be able to do everything yourself. You will only be as effective as is your management team.

Tournament Manager

As observed earlier, as tournament manager, you need to keep yourself available to be the troubleshooter. This does not mean that you have nothing in particular to do; it simply means that every job has been identified, every job has a person or group designated to do it, and your job is to make sure that everyone with a task knows the task and is performing it.

Leading the Management Team
Do not be tempted to take on jobs as they occur; that will take you out of the mainstream of administration and will disable your ability to troubleshoot. As new jobs occur, delegate appropriate responsibility. Of course, ultimate decisions in given instances will have to be yours. But keep the tournament in the hands of your management team as much as possible. Give them the ability to do a good job. You may have the opportunity to repay their good work by being a member of *their* management team in the future.

Troubleshooting
Troubleshooting, as used here, means that as tournament manager you do not sit back and relax, even though the well-organized tournament will at times afford you that luxury. You stay mobile, you stay involved, you stay aware of every facet of your tournament organization from the beginning of the tournament to the end. You listen, you answer questions, you delegate, you decide; you carry with you or designate a location for any documents key to the administration of the tournament; a master key to the building(s) housing the tournament; and a walkie-talkie or cellular phone if the size of the tournament demands that kind of communication. As stated earlier, good administrative skills are key to successful coaching. Tournament troubleshooting will field-test those skills.

Management Team
Quite simply, the management team is composed of the individuals who will carry out the various tournament management tasks that were established during the making of local arrangements.

Registration and Hospitality

Student debaters tend to be enthusiastic members of the registration team. Registration provides them with the opportunity to meet new friends and to greet old ones. The start to the tournament depends upon the completion and accuracy of the check-in during registration, so place some of your most responsible students here.

Hospitality is an important job for both student debaters and debate parents. It is a task especially well suited to parents because it gives them tremendous hands-on involvement and interaction with the tournament without demanding debate-specific training or knowledge. Many parents will know a great deal about your program, but they may prefer to enjoy the excitement of the tournament and a chance to be a productive part of the event without becoming a part of your coaching staff. On the other hand, if you have parents that were ex-debaters, give them a choice. Put them in the tabulation room, or maybe they would even like to judge.

Schematics, Ballots, and Tabulation

Setting up the schedule of competition, assigning judges, recording ballots, and tabulating results should be placed in the hands of experienced debate professionals. Your debate students may assist in the distribution of schematics (the schedule of competition for a particular round of debate), the distribution and collection of ballots, and the filing of ballots. Some tournaments are entirely student-run inside the tabulation team, but most tabulation teams will be composed of or assisted by coaches from attending schools. Reciprocal arrangements will be made, with coaches agreeing to assist with the inside management of your tournament in exchange for your help during their tournament. The networking involved is healthy both for the management of tournaments and the development of the debate profession.

The method of scheduling the tournament and advancing winners should be decided by the tournament manager with assistance from the management team. Tournaments can be scheduled according to simple or elaborate methods. Computer programs exist to assist the scheduling of large tournaments; small tournaments may be scheduled by hand. The scheduling system should be decided and tested in advance, and made open knowledge to those attending.

A master record of results should be prepared, and a results packet should be delivered at the end of the awards ceremony to each attending school. The packet for a given school should contain its own ballots received during the tournament and a copy of the master record of results.

Recognition and Distribution of Results

As tournament manager, you may choose to announce the results and present awards in a special assembly in your school auditorium. Designating students to assist in the process is a good way to give them additional recognition. Your awards were decided, ordered, delivered, and set up in advance of the awards ceremony. Always be sure to secure delivery of awards early enough before the tournament convenes so that errors in the order can be corrected. The type of award is at your discretion and, of course, a function of your budget.

Be sure to recognize and thank your management team and all members of your tournament administration, but do not make your presentation overly long. By the end of a tournament, participants are tired, and people want to head home or on to the next round. Keep things moving. An individual packet of results prepared by the tabulation team should be delivered to each visiting school. This packet will contain a master record of results for all teams and the ballots received by the teams from the individual school.

EVALUATING THE TOURNAMENT

Because administration of a tournament is incredibly exhausting, it is tempting to follow its completion with nothing more than a huge sigh of relief. Before getting your much-needed rest, it would be wise of you as the tournament manager to conduct a postmortem on the event and a debriefing of your staff. What you learned from the just-finished tournament experience will never be fresher in everyone's mind, and the value of what you learned to make the next tournament better will never be more obvious.

Touching Base with the Management Team

As the tournament unfolds, be sure to record problems, solutions, and observations that occurred along the way. Before your management team departs, take a few minutes to assess the strengths and weaknesses of the experience. If time does not allow before the tournament ends, contact the individuals of your team during the following week for a short assessment chat. Record the observations.

Gathering and Assessing Local Feedback

Get feedback from within the school as to how things went. Did teachers find their classrooms in order? Do custodial, food service, or secretarial staff have concerns? The sheer act of asking for feedback is guaranteed to help create an understanding climate at your school for future tournaments. Should the tournament structure or process be amended based upon this feedback? Decide, and record the results.

Filing Recommendations for Improvement

Remember, you have already created a file containing copies of all tournament-related documents and a log of the tournament in process. Into this file, add the results of the postmortem and the debriefing. Create a sheet of recommendations that will be filed to assist in the management of the next tournament.

This appendix has been directed to the debate teacher/moderator/coach and students who plan to host an interscholastic debate tournament. Keep in mind that if you have a sense of the size and shape of this important experience, your conversations with your first tournament team will be comprehensive and productive, and the tournament experience that you create will provide student debaters with what has been termed the single most valuable academic experience in all of school.

SAMPLE BALLOTS AND FORMS FOR DEBATE AND STUDENT CONGRESS

NATIONAL FORENSIC LEAGUE DEBATE BALLOT

ROUND _____ DIVISION _____ DATE _____ ROOM _____ JUDGE _____

AFFIRMATIVE _____ CODE _____ | NEGATIVE _____ CODE _____

| NAME | POINTS (0-30) RANK (1-4) | NAME | POINTS (0-30) RANK (1-4) |

NAME _____ _____ ( ) NAME _____ _____ ( )

_____ _____ ( ) _____ _____ ( )

DECISION: THE WINNING TEAM IS THE_____ SIDE: TEAM CODE_____

SIGNED : _____ SCHOOL_____

SPEED BALLOT:
FILL OUT TOP WHITE SHEET WITH YOUR DECISION, POINTS AND RANKS.
THEN WRITE YOUR CRITIQUE ON MIDDLE (YELLOW) SHEET.

INSTRUCTIONS TO THE JUDGES

IN ARRIVING AT YOUR DECISION TAKE INTO CONSIDERATION THE FOLLOWING ASPECTS OF GOOD DEBATING:

ANALYSIS: GETTING TO THE HEART OF THE QUESTION
PROOF: SUPPORTING CONTENTIONS WITH SUFFICIENT AND CONVINCING EVIDENCE
ARGUMENT: SOUND REASONING; LOGICAL CONCLUSIONS
ADAPTATION: CLASHING WITH THE OPPOSITION
REFUTATION: DESTROYING OPPONENTS CONTENTIONS; REINFORCING YOUR OWN
ORGANIZATION: CLEAR, LOGICAL PRESENTATION OF MATERIAL
SPEAKING: EFFECTIVE DELIVERY; FAVORABLE IMPACT ON AUDIENCE

NATIONAL

FORENSIC

LEAGUE

TO PURCHASE NFL BALLOTS: NATIONAL FORENSIC LEAGUE P.O. BOX 38, RIPON, WI 54971, (414) 748-6206

Courtesy of the National Forensic League. (Do not copy. Carbon forms may be ordered from the NFL as noted.)

AMERICAN FORENSIC ASSOCIATION
LINCOLN-DOUGLAS DEBATE BALLOT

FORM **H**

Round _____ Room_____ Date _____ Judge_____

| | Name-Code | Points | | Name-Code | Points |

Aff. _____   _____   Neg. _____   _____

Scale: 12-15   16-19   20-23   24-27   28-30
Below Average   Average   Excellent   Outstanding   Exceptional

---

COMMENT/RECOMMENDATION (REGARDING ANALYSIS, SUPPORT, REFUTATION, DELIVERY):

AFF.

NEG.

REASONS FOR DECISION (MIGHT INCLUDE ISSUES, REASONABLENESS OF POSITION, PERSUASION):

IN MY OPINION, THE BETTER DEBATING WAS DONE BY _____ REPRESENTING _____
CODE   AFF./NEG.

_____   _____
SIGNATURE OF JUDGE   AFFILIATION

Courtesy of the American Forensic Association. (Ballots may be ordered from the American Forensic Association, Box 256, Riner Falls, WI 54022.)

Diocesan Code

N C F L

**NATIONAL CATHOLIC FORENSIC LEAGUE -- STUDENT
CONGRESS BALLOT FOR PRESIDING OFFICERS**

PRESIDING OFFICER: _____ **JUDGE:** _____

*DIRECTIONS: Rate the presiding officer 1 - 6 in each category. Feel encouraged to comment on the
back side of this ballot. In scoring, use whole numbers only -- no decimals.*

**--KNOWLEDGE OF USUAL PARLIAMENTARY
   PROCEDURE** . . . . _____

--CLARITY IN EXPLAINING RULINGS & PROCEDURES
   . . . . _____

--CONTROL OF HOUSE including willingness to rule
   dilatory motions out of order . . . . _____

**--FAIRNESS IN ORDER OF RECOGNITION AND
   RULINGS** . . . . _____

--OVERALL IMPACT & IMPRESSION

   . . . . _____ **PO**

   _____

   TOTAL . . . . _____

Courtesy of the National Catholic Forensic League. [Ballots may
be ordered from the NCFL, 21 Nancy Road, Milford, MA 01757
(Attention: Richard Gaudette).]

VOTING RECORD FOR CHAMBER: _____ #____

ELECTION FOR:_____

NOMINEE	#1	#2	#3	#4	#5	#6	#7	#8	#9
1.									
2.									
3.									
4.									
5.									
6.									
7.									
8.									
9.									
10.									
11.									
12.									

(Column group header: BALLOT & VOTES)

ELECTION WINNER:_____

PARLIAMENTARIAN:_____

SIGNATURE:_____

Student congress form courtesy of William S. Hicks. The parliamentarian of a congress may use this format to record the results of an election.

GLOSSARY

ABSOLUTE PLAN-MEETS-NEED. A plan-meets-need argument so powerful that, if carried by the negative, it demonstrates the plan to be incapable of producing any positive effects in the problem area claimed by the affirmative case. It is sufficient to win a ballot for the negative in and of itself. (See *Solvency*)

ABSOLUTE SIGNIFICANCE. The total number of units affected by the change wrought by the affirmative plan or negative disadvantage.

ADVANTAGE. A significant improvement over the status quo that can best be gained by the affirmative plan.

ADVOCATE. (v.) To support a position. (n.) One who advocates; a debater.

AFFIRMATIVE. In a debate, the side that favors (affirms) changing the status quo to conform to the debate resolution.

AGENDA. The items to be discussed. The Order of Business.

AMENDMENT. A motion to change a bill or resolution.

ANALYSIS. The process of breaking down an idea or a proposition into its elements. In debate, analysis traditionally follows a fairly standard process of seeking pro and con positions on the stock issues.

ANALOGY. Use of comparison to draw a general conclusion. The conclusion drawn is strong in relation to the number of likenesses between the things compared. Classical reasoning indicates that analogies are for clarification rather than proof; however, contemporary argumentation accepts generalizations based on strong analogies.

ARGUMENT. Two senses of this term are important to debaters. In the first sense, an argument is a message consisting of a conclusion supported by a reason documented by evidence. The emphasis is on credible proof and logical structure. In the second sense, an argument is a confrontation between two parties in disagreement over a claim. The emphasis is on refutation. Thus, a debater can *make* an argument that is tested against the standards of evidence and logic; two debaters can *have* an argument with each other that one or the other wins on the basis of his or her refutation of an opponent.

APPORTIONMENT. The study or use of argument, consisting of the dual process of *discovering* the probable truth of an issue through analysis and research and *advocating* it to an audience through appropriate logical, ethical, and persuasive techniques.

ARTISTIC VALUES. Also called aesthetic values. Values that reflect the kind and degree of pleasure one derives from the artistic aspect of persons and objects. We attach great importance to beauty, symmetry, good taste—and their opposites.

ASSERTION. An unsupported statement; a conclusion that lacks evidence for support.

ATTITUDINAL INHERENCY. The tendency of agents charged with creating or carrying out the law to avoid their responsibility. The condition exists in such features of the present system as corrupt officials, pressure groups and lobbies, conflicting laws and goals, and general apathy.

AUDIENCE. The person or persons to whom a message is directed. In academic debate the audience consists of the judge who listens to the debaters, weighs the arguments presented by each side, and then makes a decision about which team's position is the most acceptable.

AUTHORITY. One whose experience, training, position, or special study makes her or his testimony or opinion acceptable as evidence; an expert.

AUTHORSHIP SPEECH. First speech opening debate on a bill or resolution.

BALLOTS. The form used to record the outcome of a debate round or forensic event. (student congress) All ballots leave room for commentary. This extra room is used to provide reasons for the decision and suggestions for improvement.

BENEFIT. In a need-plan case, a benefit is a positive effect of the plan in addition to the solution of the major need areas.

BIAS. A prejudiced attitude on the part of the source of evidence quoted in a debate. If quoted sources are biased, their opinions are therefore questionable as credible proof. Bias exists in sources when it is shown they have some vested interest at stake in the policy being debated. There can be political or economic bias by a lobby group or political party. As a rule academic and scholarly research reports, or nonpartisan analytical "think tanks," are accepted as relatively unbiased sources in debate. Debaters should seek unbiased sources when possible.

BILL. Legislative proposal that becomes law if passed.

BLOCK. (1) A prepared set of arguments relating to a single point. (2) The second negative constructive speech and the first negative rebuttal considered as a single 12- or 15-minute *block* of time.

BRIEF. An outline of all the arguments on both sides of the debate resolution. An affirmative brief or a negative brief consists of all the arguments on the respective sides of the resolution.

BURDEN OF PROOF. The affirmative obligation to present a *prima facie* case supporting the debate resolution.

BURDEN OF PROVING. The obligation of debaters on either side to prove any argument they initiate.

BURDEN OF REBUTTAL. The obligation of the negative in any debate to meet the clash with the affirmative case.

BURDEN OF REFUTING. The obligation of either side to respond to relevant constructive arguments presented by its opponents and to advance its own arguments.

CALL TO ORDER. Presiding officer formally begins session.

CARD. A piece of evidence recorded traditionally on an index card. A card should contain only one idea or bit of information, verbatim from the source, together with complete labeling of the contents of the card and information about the source, such as the authority's name and qualifications and publication date, including the date of the source.

CASE. A debate team's basic position on the resolution, made up of all the arguments that the team presents in support of that position.

CASE SIDE ARGUMENTS. Arguments that relate to three issues: topicality, significance, and inherency.

CAUSATION. A relationship between two phenomena in which one is believed to cause the other.

CAUSE-EFFECT RELATIONSHIP. A relationship based on the assumption that in the process of interacting, there is a connecting link between one phenomenon and another. Further assumes that this connection is so strong that the relationship is predictable.

CHAIR. The presiding officer.

CLASH. The process of meeting and dealing directly with an argument of the opposition. Dealing with an argument implies denial or minimization, but not agreement with it.

CLERK OF THE CONGRESS. The person overall in charge of a congress.

COMPARATIVE ADVANTAGE. A type of affirmative case structure that shows the proposed policy of the affirmative to have significant and unique advantages over the status quo.

COMPARATIVE ADVANTAGE CASE. A kind of case in which the affirmative shows that although existing programs could possibly be modified in the present system to achieve a solution to the problem area, the affirmative proposal could do a better job. The argument focuses on the comparison between the affirmative plan and the present system. The entire case is presented in the first affirmative constructive speech.

CONCLUSION. The statement one arrives at when evidence is considered and interpreted; an inference; a claim.

CONDITIONAL COUNTERPLAN. A negative strategy of arguing the superiority of the present system over the affirmative plan; but, *on the condition* that the judge agrees with the affirmative that the present system should be changed, the negative also suggests a counterplan it is willing to defend in preference to the affirmative plan. This strategy is risky because potentially it places the negative in a self-contradictory position of claiming no need for a change, then advocating a counter-plan to change the present system.

CON SPEECH. Three minute speech in opposition to the legislation.

CONSTRUCTIVE. (adj.) A constructive argument is one offered in support of, or in opposition to, the resolution. A constructive speech is a time period in which it is permissible to present constructive arguments.

CONTENTION. A subdivision of an issue; an argument essential to support a position on an issue. Contentions may consist of either observations or indictments. The statement of a claim. In debate, a number of con-tentions make up the affirmative case. For example: The problem is significant. The problem is inherent.

CONTRADICTION. Statements or arguments within a given position that are in direct opposition to each other.

CORRELATION. A statement of a logical relationship between two phe-nomena showing that the two appear together and that they also vary together, either directly or inversely. In other words, correlation would establish a relationship less than causality.

COST-BENEFIT RATIO. An on-balance comparison of the advantages and dis-advantages of alternative proposals for change. The emphasis is on quan-tified measures of both costs and benefits, with the greatest value assigned to the most favorable ratio between costs incurred for benefits received.

COUNTERPLAN. A negative case approach admitting that the present sys-tem should be changed, but which advocates the negative team's pro-posal rather than the affirmative's. Traditionally, the counterplan is given in the first negative constructive speech; and it is demonstrated to be nontopical, competitive with the affirmative plan, superior to it in the area of analysis attacked by the affirmative, and also less disad-vantageous than the affirmative plan.

CREDIBILITY. The believability of a statement or its source.

CRITERIA-GOALS CASE. A kind of case that is an elaboration on the com-parative advantage case with greater emphasis on the policy goals of the present system. The affirmative incorporates the identification of the goal of the present system as an integral part of its analysis. Affir-mative sets up the criteria to judge the fulfillment of those particular goals. The affirmative shows its proposed plan meets the criteria better than the present system does.

CRITERION. A standard of measurement based on an underlying social value.

CRITIC JUDGE. The trained person whose duty it is to hear an academic debate, determine the winner according to the rules, and furnish sug-gestions for improvement for the student debater.

CROSS-EXAMINATION. A debate format in which debaters are permitted to ask direct questions of an opponent during specified time periods, usually immediately following the opponent's constructive speeches.

DEBATE. A contest of argumentation. In standard (policy) debate, an affirmative team presents arguments in favor of a resolution, and a negative team presents arguments against it. The contest is won by the team which presents the best arguments in the opinion of the judge.

DEDUCTION. A reasoning process that takes general statements or premises and draws a conclusion about particular or specific elements. In formal logic, deduction is contained in a chain called a "syllogism." This form of reasoning is formal, and the validity of such an argument is based on the logical relationship between premises and conclusion, not necessarily on the truth content of any premise.

DEFINITION. A formality of a debate wherein the affirmative team declares the meaning of the terms of the debate resolution. The definition of terms serves the useful function of limiting the areas encompassed by the resolution. While the affirmative team has the privilege of defining the terms, the negative team has the privilege of challenging any definition considered unacceptable. The most frequently used methods of defining terms are references to authorities, examples, or the dictionary.

DEGREE OF SIGNIFICANCE. Relative value of the advantage. Directly affects the required magnitude of the scope of the problem needed for policy action.

DESIRABILITY. A condition or state of favorability; a value judgment attached to a particular outcome of a plan, especially a benefit or an advantage. Desirability is a state lower in degree than necessity.

DILEMMA. A forced choice of one of only two possible alternatives, either of which would be undesirable.

DISADVANTAGE. An undesirable outcome of a plan, apart from considerations of workability or the desirability of the plan's justifications.

DISTORTION. A misrepresentation of a piece of evidence.

DROP. To neglect to carry on an argument, in future speeches, after the opponent's response.

DURATION OF SIGNIFICANCE. The persistence of a problem. In this sense the condition of inherency overlaps the issue of significance.

EIGHT-MINUTE RULE (or ten-minute). A tournament rule allotting to each team a cumulative total of eight minutes between speeches during the course of the debate that can be used for preparing to speak. There is no specification as to how the debaters may allocate their time.

ELIMINATION ROUNDS. The final rounds in a debate tournament. Only students who have competed successfully in the preliminary rounds advance to the elimination rounds. In debate those students with the best win-loss record advance to an octofinal or quarterfinal round.

EMPIRICAL STUDIES. Scientifically controlled experiments, usually expressed in statistical form.

ENFORCEMENT. That plank of the plan that provides for seeing that the performance or prohibition plants of the plan are carried out.

EVIDENCE. Data that form the basis for conclusions.

EXAMPLE. Single objects or events used to illustrate and show the possibility of generalized categories of similar groups of examples; a type of factual evidence. Negative examples are those used to disprove generalities.

EXPERT. An authority; one whose experience, training, or position and study makes his or her testimony acceptable as evidence.

EXTEND. To carry an argument another step forward in rebuttal; to answer the opponent's challenge and advance beyond it.

EXTENDED ANALOGY. A comparison developed at depth to demonstrate a significant similarity.

EXTRATOPICALITY. The state of nonconformity to the intent of the debate resolution. A plan is extratopical if the needs are solved or the comparative advantages are gained as a direct result of some plank of the plan that does not implement the debate resolution.

FABRICATION. The act of making up evidence.

FACT. Actual, observable objects or events in the real world; useful as evidence in debate, facts usually fall into these types: (a) examples, (b) statistics, (c) empirical studies.

FALLACY. A mistaken inference; an erroneous conclusion based on faulty reasoning.

FIAT. An assumed power to put a proposal into effect; a legal mandate binding on the parties involved, overriding their personal attitudes. Debaters are allowed to say their proposals are to be implemented "by fiat" for the sake of avoiding quibbles over whether, in the real world, such proposals could be expected to receive approval. Fiat power is limited to matters subject to law; it is not a "magic wand" to avoid substantive argument.

FLOOR. The right to speak.

FLOW SHEET (CHART). A diagram of the arguments in a debate and their relationships. Arguments are charted in parallel columns, with the affirmative case written in the left-hand column, the negative arguments in the next column, the affirmative responses in the next column, and so forth. Thus a "flow" of the arguments can be seen at a glance by tracing each argument and its responses across the flow sheet.

GENERALIZATION. Conclusions drawn from evidence or data.

GOAL. A general objective; an aim. Systems of policy are thought to exist in order to achieve goals. Affirmative cases may be developed on the premise that a laudable goal can best be met through the affirmative proposal.

GOING TO CASE SIDE. A debate expression instructing all parties that the speaker is moving to the case arguments in the debate.

GOING TO PLAN SIDE. A debate expression instructing all parties that the debater is moving to the plan arguments in the debate.

HARM. An undesirable impact resulting from the operation of a policy system. The impact may be stated in terms of deprivation or injury to parties affected by the policy. Harm exists where needs are denied or suffering or loss of life is created.

INDICTMENT. An accusatory conclusion; a charge, a contention in a debate will usually state an indictment.

INFERENCES. Conclusions based on possible relationships between known facts.

INHERENCY. The state of being an intrinsic, inseparable, necessary part of a system. The term is used to describe a feature of the status quo that exists and will continue to exist in the absence of the affirmative plan. It may also be applied to the affirmative proposal when the negative charges that disadvantages are inherent to the affirmative plan.

IN ORDER. Correct according to the rules of procedure.

ISSUE. A question concerning which the affirmative and negative teams take opposite sides; a major point of disagreement.

JUDGE. (v.) To evaluate a debate against certain standards of debating, to decide who wins and who loses. (n.) The person who fulfills the judging function.

JUSTIFICATION. To fulfill the standards of judgement. A justification argument is one in which it is charged that an affirmative case fails to "justify the resolution." As a negative strategy, the argument shows how the advantages of the affirmative case do not stem from the resolution itself but rather from other extratopical features of the plan.

LAY JUDGE. A term applied to persons who judge debates but who are neither coaches nor current debaters. Judgment of debate by such persons will probably center more on the debater's ability to communicate arguments and make them meaningful than on the technicalities of debate theory.

LINCOLN-DOUGLAS DEBATE. An academic debate format that features two speakers debating over the truth or falsity of a value proposition.

LOGIC. The system of analysis that shows the nature of relationships between statements, between facts and conclusions, causes and effects, and deductions from premises. Logic is reasoning based on rules concerning the form in which an argument is put, rather than on the nature and quality of evidence.

MAIN MOTION. To introduce business.

MAJORITY. One more than one-half of the people voting.

METHODOLOGY. The procedure by which an empirical study is conducted. An empirical study's methodology may be challenged along such lines as the size of the sample, the amount of time, the presence of a control group, etc. To challenge the methodology is to test the validity of the conclusions drawn from such a study. Debaters who quote from empirical studies should be familiar with the methodology of the studies.

MINOR REPAIR. An alteration of present policy that gains the affirmative advantage but involves substantially less change than that suggested by the resolutions.

MOTION. A proposal for action by the assembly.

NEED. An evil or harmful situation inherent in the status quo that the affirmative plan will remedy. The need is a necessary element of a traditional need-plan case.

NEED-PLAN CASE. A kind of case that develops the argument that a need for change exists. The case develops the plan and shows how the plan meets the need. The case develops the argument that the plan would be beneficial. The heart of the case is that there is a need and that the plan will meet the need.

NEGATIVE. In a debate, the side that opposes (negates) the affirmative position and therefore the resolution.

NET BENEFITS. An affirmative case construction in which the affirmative, using a systems analysis approach that change is inevitable, presents a proposal to direct that change and expects the negative to propose its own policy system.

NET BENEFITS CASE. A kind of case based on systems analysis. The case incorporates four steps: (1) Apply systems analysis to the problem area; (2) determine the components that make up the system and the rules that govern how the components are interrelated; (3) analyze and project what differences could be predicted following a change in policy governing the interrelationships; and (4) determine the most favorable ratio between the costs and the benefits of the proposed change in the system.

NONTOPICALITY. The conditions of failure to encompass the scope or intent of the resolution. A case is nontopical if it fails to justify all the terms included in the resolution.

OBJECTION. An argument against the plan.

OBSERVATION. A descriptive conclusion or assumption.

ONE-MINUTE RULE (or two-minute). A tournament rule in which each speaker is allowed one minute from the time the preceding speaker sits down in which to gather materials and approach the podium to speak. If a speaker exceeds this time, the additional time is subtracted from his or her speaking time.

OPERATIONAL DEFINITION. Practice of defining the resolution through the presentation of the affirmative plan early in the first affirmative constructive speech. Individual terms are not defined; rather, the affirmative plan constitutes the essence of the resolution.

OPINION. A statement of an attitude or belief. Opinion testimony is acceptable evidence in a debate if it is the opinion of a qualified expert.

OUT OF ORDER. Incorrect according to the rules of procedure.

PLAN. The specific program proposed by the affirmative team to implement the debate resolution. The plan is a necessary part of every affirmative case.

PLAN PLANK. Specific provisions within the affirmative plan, a set of particulars about the plan. Individual planks might specify (1) goal or intent, (2) agency of change, (3) duties or powers, (4) enforcement, or (5) financing.

POLICY. A means of achieving a goal; an action. In a narrow sense, a policy is a governmental program, such as the financing of public schools through property tax revenues. In debate a policy proposition is the proposal of some new governmental program that the affirmative team claims should be adopted.

POLITICAL VALUES. Values that reflect judgments as to what is expedient, that is, what should or should not be done for the common good. Include democracy, rights, justice, and many others.

PREDICTION. A statement of how one thinks present facts are related so that one can expect certain results in the future. Accuracy of predictions hinges on the quality of factual hinges on the quality of factual data and the quality of reasoning used in drawing relationship between known facts.

PRELIMINARY ROUND. A round of debate in which all students at the tournament participate, and a judge evaluates performances.

PREPARATION TIME. In a debate the time that elapses prior to each debater's speech, each team has a strictly regulated amount of cumulative preparation time allocated to it for the entire debate, which the team members may utilize as they wish. The amount of time and the rules governing its use are determined by the tournament director.

PRESIDING OFFICER. The person elected to "chair" a meeting or legislative session.

PRESUMPTION. Traditionally, the assumption that conditions and policies should remain as they are. The affirmative side has the burden to prove that the status quo should be changed. The present system is presumed to be adequate until the affirmative team meets its burden to prove that a change in the status quo is needed or would be advantageous. Presumption is analogous to the legal principle that the accused person is presumed to be innocent until proven guilty. Newer debate theories have altered the concept of presumption somewhat.

PRIMA FACIE. The Latin phrase may be translated as "at first look." A *prima facie* case is one that a reasonable and prudent persons would accept "at first look." In debate a *prima facie* case must include a specific plan to implement the resolution and justification for the plan—either an inherent need in the status quo, a comparative advantage of the plan over the status quo, or some other accepted justification.

PROBABILITY. (1) The relative degree of certainty with which an inference may be drawn. (2) In statistical language the level of confidence that may be placed in a conclusion expressed as a percentage.

PROBLEM AREA. The domain of issues that pertain to a topic. A problem area includes issues of long standing social concern.

PROBLEM STATEMENT. A statement narrows a general discussion area. The beginning point for analysis is a definition of the terms by which the problem is stated. Each forensic event places the problem in a different form, but each states a problem for consideration.

PROOF. That which reduces uncertainty and increases the probable truth of a claim. Evidence is transformed into proof through the use of reasoning, which demonstrates how and to what extent the claim is believable. Proof is what is given in response to the demand "Prove it!"

Proof is a relative concept, ranging from possibility through probability to certainty. The amount of proof needed to establish a claim depends on a number of variables, such as the importance of the claim, the strength of opposing claims, and the credibility of the person making the argument.

PROPOSAL. The specific affirmative plan.

PROPOSITION. A debatable statement; a statement open to interpretation; a statement about which reasonable people may accept arguments on either side. Debate theory incorporates three types of propositions: fact, value, and policy.

PROPOSITION OF FACT. A proposition that involves definition and classification in order to establish the truth or falseness of a claim. An objective statement that something exists. May be about an object or event that can be experienced directly by the senses of sight, hearing, touch, smell, and taste.

PROPOSITION OF POLICY. A proposition demanding that after establishing certain facts and values, a consideration of such things as expediency and practicality leads people to propose a certain defensible plan of action. A statement of a course of action to be considered for adoption. Includes all those problem areas deemed appropriate for government action.

PROPOSITION OF VALUE. A proposition asking that criteria be applied in order to determine the worth or value of a particular thing. Expresses judgments about the qualities of a person, place, thing, idea, or event.

PRO SPEECH. Also called the proponency speech. A speech given in favor of passing a bill or resolution.

QUORUM. The number of members present officially designated as those necessary to conduct business.

RATIONALE. (1) The philosophical framework within which a case is constructed. (2) The criteria for accepting a premise or conclusion.

REASONING. A short speech devoted to (1) rebuilding arguments that have been attacked, (2) refuting opposing arguments, and (3) summarizing the debate from the perspective of the speaker.

RECOGNIZE. The act of the chairman that allows a member to speak.

REFUTATION. The process of attacking and destroying opposing arguments.

REPAIR. A minor adjustment in present policies that would accompany part or all of what the affirmative plan is designed to accomplish.

RESEARCH. To search again. To gather information and evidence and to classify it so that it is easily retrievable for use.

RESOLUTION. A proposition stated in the form of a motion before a legislative assembly. In debate used synonymously with proposition.

RISK SIGNIFICANCE. The fractional proportion of the potential population exposed to jeopardy by the present system.

SANDBAGGING. The practice of presenting an argument initially in skeletal form, with little or no evidence so that it appears weak, and saving a bulk of evidence for second line presentation only if the argument is attacked. The strategy is to make your strongest strategy look like the weakest so that the opposition will focus the debate there.

SECOND. The support given a motion by a second member of the assembly.

SECOND LINE. Additional evidence for presentation in rebuttal or extensions.

Shift. To abandon an original position and take up a different one.

Shotgun. (1) A strategy of presenting a profusion of unrelated, scattered attacks against an opponent's case. (2) A loud, bombastic style of delivery.

Should. Usually defined as "ought to, not necessarily will." This term is always found in propositions of policy. Affirmative cases justify a proposal by showing that it will solve a need or produce a comparative advantage and *should be* adopted even if Congress won't pass the needed legislation, the Constitution forbids it, or public opinion opposes it.

Sign Reasoning. Reasoning by characteristic. Sign reasoning makes the claim that whenever a character is observed a substance must be present, or when a substance is present.

Significance. (1) The degree of importance of a conclusion. Significance may be qualitative or quantitative. Qualitative significance rests on an established value; quantitative significance rests on concrete units of measurement. (2) In statistical language the level of confidence at which a predicted conclusion may not be rejected, usually ".05 level of significance" or "95 percent probability."

Solvency. The relationship of workability between a policy and its claimed effects. Solvency is a relative concept ranging along a continuum from insolvency through degrees of partial solvency to total solvency. A plan-meet-advantage argument is an attack designed to decrease the perceived solvency of the proposal.

Statistics. Descriptive or experimental data, often used in drawing mathematical inferences.

Status Quo. The present system; the existing order, that which would be changed by adopting the affirmative plan.

Stock Issues. A series of broad questions encompassing the major debatable issues of any proposition of policy. Some stock issues are (1) Is there a need for a change? (2) Will the plan meet the need? (3) Is the plan the most desirable way to meet the need?

Straight Refutation. For every claim that the affirmative asserts is true, the negative offers a counterclaim asserting that what the affirmative says is false.

Structural Inherency. A law (or lack of a law) or barrier that prevents the present system from solving a problem.

Synthesis. The result of combining separate elements into a complete whole.

Systems Analysis. A method of analysis that assumes that everything is in a state of constant change. Its underlying principle is that ongoing decisions must be made about the kinds of changes wanted, rather than whether any change is desirable. Calls for each side to uphold a particular system for controlling the changes the present system is going through.

STUDENT CONGRESS. The legislative body that debates for and against bills and resolutions that are presented by students.

TESTIMONY. An expression of opinion; a value judgment. Testimony is acceptable evidence in debate if it is from a qualified expert.

TOPICALITY. The state of conformity to the intent of the debate resolution. A case is topical if it justifies the full intent of the resolution. A plan is topical if the needs are solved or the comparative advantages are gained as a direct result of those planks in the plan that implement the resolution.

TOURNAMENT. A competitive setting in which students practice their arguments and sharpen their thinking and speaking skills. Consists of preliminary and elimination rounds.

TURN AROUND. An argument that is the meaning of an opponent's contention is the opposite of its apparent intent so that it counts against the opponent. For example, if the negative team makes a disadvantage argument, and the affirmative rebuttalist points out that the result of that disadvantage is more positive than negative, then the argument becomes a turnaround for the affirmative team.

UNIQUENESS. In comparative advantage analysis, the condition of inherency or inseparability of the proposal and the effects that are claimed to result from it, either advantages or disadvantages.

VALUE. An underlying belief or assumption, moral or ethical, with wide enough acceptance to validate conclusions that are derived from it.

VARIABLE. A condition that may change and alter a cause-effect relationship.

WORKABILITY. A condition whereby a proposal could actually operate to solve a problem if implemented as legislation. A plan is said to be workable if it includes planks in its mechanism allowing for an agency, its powers, and administrative details.

INDEX